COLD WAR
ILLUSIONS

COLD WAR ILLUSIONS

America, Europe and Soviet Power, 1969–1989

Dana H. Allin

St. Martin's Press
New York

COLD WAR ILLUSIONS
Copyright © 1994 by Dana H. Allin

ISBN 0-312-12374-4

Book Design by Acme Art, Inc

Library of Congress Cataloging-in-Publication Data

Allin, Dana H., 1958-
    Cold War illusions : America, Europe and Soviet power, 1969-1989
/ Dana H. Allin.
        p. cm.
    Includes index.
    ISBN 0-312-12374-4
    1. United States—Foreign relations—1945-1989. 2. United States-
-Foreign relations—Soviet Union. 3. Soviet Union—Foreign
relations—United States. 4. Europe—Politics and government—1945-
5. Europe—Foreign relations—1945- 6. Cold War. I. Title.
E840.A594 1995
327.7304'09'045—dc20   94-28776
                                                                     CIP

First Edition February 1995:
10 9 8 7 6 5 4 3 2 1

To Elisabeth and John Christoph

CONTENTS

ACKNOWLEDGMENTS

Many have helped this book along its way. My first debt of gratitude is owed to David P. Calleo, a teacher, colleague and friend whose intellectual and moral enthusiasm has fundamentally shaped my scholarship. David Anderson, Philip Gordon, Frederick Fucci, and Kevin Woodfield read and commented generously on the near-final manuscript. Starting with its incarnation as a Ph.D. dissertation at the Johns Hopkins University School of Advanced International Studies (SAIS), the manuscript benefited from the criticism and suggestions of numerous scholars and journalists, including Fouad Ajami, Andrew Dennison, Adrian Lyttleton, the late Michael Harrison, Fred Holborne, Erik Jones, Patrick McCarthy, Claudia Morgenstern, Richard O'Brien, Bruce Parrot, Jeremiah Riemer, Thomas Row, Stephen Szabo, Robert W. Tucker, Thomas Waldron, Andrea Wuerth and Lanxin Xiang. Nor could the book have been written without the support of several institutions: SAIS, the Johns Hopkins Bologna Center, the Robert Bosch Foundation, Stiftung Wissenschaft und Politik, and the Aspen Institute Berlin. At Aspen Berlin, Liliana Kohls provided indispensable administrative assistance, while Matthias Brunk and Nicolas Kumanoff did some speedy research to fill some final holes.

One person took part from beginning to end. My wife, Elisabeth, gave me steady encouragement and gentle criticism and, finally, brought her scrupulous eye to the last-minute organization of an imperfectly organized manuscript. She interrupted this work, briefly, to give birth to our son, John Christoph. The book is dedicated to both of them.

Dana H. Allin
Berlin
November 1994

INTRODUCTION

In the space of a few short years, the specter that had haunted U.S. foreign policy for almost half a century vanished. An obvious question then arose: How serious was the Soviet threat in the first place?

This book argues that during the second half of the Cold War, Moscow's global power, like its power at home, was vastly overrated. By the 1970s, the Soviet Union had become a vast Potemkin village, not only in the stagnation and rot of its domestic political economy, but also in its ability to maintain its power and influence in the world at large. Such a conclusion casts startling light on the American foreign-policy debates of the 1970s and early 1980s, for it suggests that the prevailing pessimism about Soviet power fed mostly on illusions. It also has bearing on the current debate about who won the Cold War. The claims of many Reagan backers, that their man deserves the lion's share of the credit, start to look flimsy if, as I will argue, the Cold War was won before Reagan entered the White House.[1]

If Soviet power was indeed overrated, a second important question is why. A number of studies have taken up this question from the American side, arguing, for example, that an overblown enemy was needed to support the military-industrial complex or America's global economic position or to fulfill the need for a national purpose. Some of these interpretations have been implausibly conspiratorial; others have contained at least a measure of validity.

This study, however, concentrates on an important dimension that is rarely discussed: Americans' abiding pessimism about the political stability and moral resoluteness of their European allies when faced with Soviet pressure. Such doubts about Europe were critical to any broader pessimism about the global balance of power, since a plausible scenario of Soviet superiority depended first on the virtual elimination of Western Europe as an ally of any value to the United States.

Let me be clear. I am not suggesting that Soviet Communism was harmless. On the contrary, throughout most of the Cold War, the Soviet Union was a malicious antagonist, somewhat "mellowed," perhaps, but still exhibiting many of the disagreeable traits that it showed in 1946, when George F. Kennan described it as "a political force committed fanatically to the belief that with the US there can be no permanent modus vivendi." Moreover, the Soviet Union of 1980 was, in military resources, exponentially more powerful than the one of 1946, possessing a capability that Kennan at the close of World War II could have only dimly imagined—the means to effectively destroy the United States within the space of a day.

Yet this power was contained. By the 1970s, the threat of general war, or even of significant Soviet encroachment on Western interests, was small. Even after America's defeat in Vietnam, the Western Alliance held a clear advantage. With the exception of military power, which was roughly balanced, the "correlation of forces" favored the West. The West was prosperous and (notwithstanding various crises from 1968 onwards) politically stable. The Soviet Union, by contrast, faced rebellion in Poland, grumbling in the rest of its empire, economic decay and the irrevocable schism of world Communism. The nuclear "balance of terror," moreover, foreclosed any realistic option for Moscow to escape its dilemmas by resorting to general war. "Containment" had worked, much as its architects had hoped it would.

Such analysis may seem unremarkable—simple praise for the main lines of American postwar foreign policy. And yet governing American elites from 1970 to 1985 had a much darker perspective. The walls of containment were breaking down—this was explicitly the view of Reagan-era neoconservatives, but also, in a more complicated sense, implicit in the policies of Nixon/Kissinger and the Carter administration.

This judgment had some obvious sources, including the American debacle in Indochina, Soviet interventions in Angola and the Horn of Africa, the invasion of Afghanistan and a sustained build-up of Russian nuclear and conventional military forces. But the supposed breakdown of containment was based, above all, on a sophisticated intellectual construct: the impending "Finlandization" of Western Europe. This was the process by which the Soviet Union was supposed to be able to dominate Western Europe without a fight.[2] Such a Finlandized Europe might have maintained civil liberties, Western democratic institutions, and a reasonable range of political choices within national borders. But it would have been effectively cowed by Soviet military might into toeing a line set by Moscow in international affairs. In a similar fashion, Soviet interests would have determined Western Europe's economic choices. The scenario involved at least the end of significant American influence and the establishment of Soviet hegemony (however benign) over a weak and divided Western Europe.

It was in the early 1970s that the Finlandization idea started to gain currency in the American foreign policy debate. In 1973, for example, U.S. Deputy Secretary of State Kenneth Rush warned in these terms about the consequences of a substantial reduction of the U.S. military presence in Europe:

What is involved basically is this: If we brought our troops back from Europe, if we took our 6th Fleet out of the Mediterranean, we would no longer be able to convince our European allies that we are a staunch ally, that we are going to back them, that our nuclear umbrella is a shield for peace over them, that they can safely resist pressures from Russia.

The net result would be that the nations of Western Europe, which is fragmented politically still, would be competing with each other for the favor of Russia. The Russian influence would spread more and more over Western Europe. Our influence would wane more and more. And we in time, I think, would find ourselves in a very weakened and unsatisfactory position.[3]

Later in the same decade, "neoconservative" analysts pronounced a graver diagnosis: Western Europe could be lost to the West even if U.S. forces remained there. The threat from the Soviet Union was portrayed in alarming and, at the same time, subtle terms. It was conceded that nuclear deterrence was probably robust enough to deter a direct Soviet attack in Western Europe and almost certainly a nuclear attack against the United States. But alleged Soviet conventional and nuclear superiority was said to be a potent tool of intimidation in a climate of West European psychological, political and moral debility.

Power balances are, by definition, relative. The major debate in the 1970s and 1980s concerned not just Soviet power (although here too there was disagreement over CIA estimates of the Soviet economy, the "window of vulnerability," and so on) but Western weakness. It is this widespread perception of Western weakness—the heart, I argue, of a distorted strategic vision—that this book will also explore.

This study is an intellectual history concerned with the manner in which intellectual fashion can distort a nation's strategic and political debates. It examines, one might say, the power of a bad idea. As the Finlandization idea first became popular, George Kennan immediately discerned this distorting impact:

Not only is [the Finlandization scenario] sufficiently vague to leave much to the imagination (always a great advantage when it comes to arousing fears), but it makes it possible to concede at long last what experience has now amply demonstrated: that the Russian leaders are not necessarily planning to attack, seize, and occupy the remainder of Western Europe, and yet, to argue that Western Europe is no less threatened in its vital interests than if the Soviet Union were so planning. From this last it can then be argued that the need for a rigid cold war policy, based on the assumption of total and unchangeable Russian hostility, is no smaller than if the Russians were likely to attack.[4]

One consequence of writing a history of ideas is that one tends to take the ideas themselves at face value, rather than considering them as covers for more venal purposes. In researching this study, I have not looked for conspiracies to manufacture an exaggerated Soviet threat in order to support the military-industrial complex, the personal power of a politician or even America's position of global leadership. No doubt such considerations played a role in individual cases. But most of the conservative policymakers and analysts in this history were manifestly people of good will. They were inspired not by malice, but by conviction. Their convictions, however, in the matter of a growing Soviet threat, were wrong.

None of this is to deny that the Finlandization model contained elements of logic and plausibility. That military threats often can be translated into diplomatic and political power is a matter of common sense. But the critical issue in any political analysis is the degree to which an abstract model—the Finlandization model, for example—corresponds to real conditions. In this case, to what extent were America's European allies actually vulnerable to Soviet saber rattling and other forms of intimidation?

The first two sections of this book take up this question. Part I, "U.S. Foreign Policy and the Soviet Threat," traces the various postwar arguments about the stability of anti-Soviet containment and how those arguments played into the American political debate. The three chapters of this section cover the entire Cold War era, but concentrate on the years after 1970—the brief period of détente and the so-called "second Cold War" that followed it.

Part II, "Defining the Threat," analyses in detail the specific arguments advanced in the 1970s and early 1980s, about Europe's vulnerability to Soviet bullying: the Finlandization effect of military, political and economic pressures. The conclusion is that Western Europe was far less vulnerable to such pressures than the Soviet empire itself, and that containment, despite dire warnings to the contrary, remained solid. The notion of an expanding Soviet threat was largely an illusion.

Part III, "The Threat Vanishes," extends the story to the present. Chapter 7 looks to the Soviet empire's final collapse and the emerging historical controversy about the American policies that may have helped cause it. Chapter 8, an epilogue, considers the global and European power structure after Communism's collapse. In particular, it addresses Europe's current disarray. Does this disarray vindicate the earlier pessimism about Europe? Or does it merely demonstrate that successful formulas for containing a common enemy can be inadequate for coping with postimperial chaos?

An historian enjoying hindsight should exercise some humility. In arguing that certain assessments of Soviet power were exaggerated, this book does not imply those judgements were, or could have been, easy. Indeed, the flux and uncertainties of the present underscore the complexities of the past. Potential new perils are emerging in post–Cold War Europe, not least in Russia itself. It certainly would be a false reading of recent history to conclude that because Soviet power proved to be hollow, future threats can be dismissed. But that does not mean that past mistakes are irrelevant. The foreign-policy constraints imposed by America's budget deficit, for example, point to a more paradoxical conclusion: We may be unprepared for present and future dangers in some proportion to our exaggeration of past ones.

Part I

U.S. Foreign Policy and the Soviet Threat

1

Prologue:
Containment in Europe,
1945–1969

There were distant battles of Vietcong and Mujahideen and contras; but the Cold War was settled in Europe, where it began. It was over when the Berlin Wall was breached, when democratic governments took power in Central Europe, when these governments asked Soviet troops to leave, and when the Kremlin leaders agreed. It began when the convulsive ruin of World War II first brought those troops into the center of Europe.

It is a central argument of this book that Americans exaggerated the Soviet threat because of a stubborn, distorted pessimism about the vitality and moral fiber of their European allies. American leaders also tended to be preoccupied with other regions of the globe. Had they kept their focus on Europe, and understood that the balance of power there generally favored NATO, they might have maintained a more sober and hopeful assessment of the East-West strategic balance.

A European focus was certainly the basis of the original strategy for "containment" of Soviet power. The American architects of containment assumed that their plan would succeed or fail in Europe, which meant investing considerable hope in the old European powers. This came naturally to such admirers of European civilization as George F. Kennan and Dean Acheson, but it was not so natural for Americans in general. The intimate U.S.-European partnership that was built upon the rubble of World War II represented a sharp reversal of American traditions. America's pre–World War II isolationism meant, above all, isolation from Europe. It was not so in other parts of the world: Her fleet roamed unchallenged over the Pacific; Latin America feared her displeasure. But involvement in European affairs was another matter.

THE AMERICAN IDEA OF EUROPE BEFORE 1945

American isolationism always involved something more than raw prejudice. In the beginning it was simple logic.[1] The great powers of the eighteenth century were European powers. Any Great Power wars that America was to get involved in would necessarily be European wars. America's founders reasoned that the country was young and weak. If drawn into alliances, it would be only as a junior ally, easily manipulated by the Great Powers. This was the fundamental reason to avoid "entangling alliances." The fundamental opportunity stemmed from America's geographical isolation.

There were also the beginnings of a moral attitude in America's sense of isolation. Thomas Paine expressed something of that attitude when he said, "Europe is too thickly planted with kingdoms to be long at peace."[2] Thomas Jefferson imagined an American "Empire of Liberty" stretching to the Pacific, guarded and tilled by freedom-loving yeoman farmers, rich in the hardy virtues of Republican Rome.[3] Arthur Schlesinger has suggested that the American sense of moral uniqueness was partly due to the diffusion from New England of Calvinist notions about Americans as God's "elect."[4] This conceit was reinforced by geography: As geographical isolation continued during a century of continental expansion, keeping America apart from the European alliance system, Americans gradually got used to the notion that their separation was not just a matter of circumstances but one of character.

When Americans did join the European battlefield in 1917, they became part of a war that was tragically congenial to their "exceptionalist" moralism. The new scale and technology of warfare required mass national mobilizations, which meant a higher intensity of propaganda than was necessary when wars were limited affairs fought by professional armies.[5] The Americans' special sense of mission, however, added an octave or two to the pitch of allied propaganda, hence "the war to end all wars" and to "make the world safe for Democracy."

Realities, however, were quite different. The ambitiousness of Wilsonian war aims guaranteed Americans' disillusion, and the punitive peace imposed upon Germany only added to it. In revisionist interpretations of the war, it was no longer seen as a fight for democracy, but rather as a continuation of ancient, amoral European struggles. There developed a sense that Americans had been duped into participation.

In the 1930s, as it became evident that European war would resume, a strong body of American isolationist opinion argued that siding with France and Britain meant siding with the status quo powers in preserving their ill-gotten gains. While there was little American sympathy for the fascist dictatorships, there was a feeling that the status quo powers were only incidentally democracies—the struggle of democracy against fascism was not the essence of the conflict. There was also a perception, not devoid of truth, that part of the impulse to German fascism stemmed from Germany's shabby treatment by the victorious allies at Versailles. There were no principles at stake worthy of American involvement.

As it happened, the isolationist front, which looked so strong in the late 1930s, dissolved rather quickly after Hitler invaded Poland and evaporated entirely with the attack on Pearl Harbor. However, the traditional American bias against the old European powers was not something to be turned on and off like a water spigot. To begin with, there was the problem of Europe's colonial empires, which were the source of much American irritation. Many people had a premonition that there would be new areas of conflict after Hitler's defeat, but would this conflict pit America against Russia, or America against Britain? The more obvious answer was Britain. Quite late in the war, public-opinion polls suggested that the American people, for all their wartime solidarity, considered the British to be their more natural antagonists.[6] A 1942 wave of unrest in India had revived certain revolutionary memories in the United States. President Roosevelt took every opportunity to harangue Churchill over India, Hong Kong, and all the rest of British overseas possessions and protectorates. "You have 400 years of acquisitive instinct in your blood and you don't understand how a country might not want to acquire land somewhere if they can get it," Roosevelt once told Churchill.[7] At the Yalta conference, in a rather clumsy attempt at jocularity with Stalin, Roosevelt dismissed Churchill as an "imperialist." The American president had a habit of courting Stalin by disparaging the British.[8]

The British suspected, not unreasonably, that the Americans aimed to replace them on the world stage. At the very least, anticolonial idealism merged conveniently with economic self-interest. U.S. Secretary of State Cordell Hull, with little else to occupy his time during the war, devoted himself to smashing Britain's system of imperial trade preferences.[9] U.S. Treasury officials conducted a parallel campaign for a liberal financial order, which meant, in practice, against the sterling bloc. America was armed against her ally with formidable tools of leverage: Manipulation of the lend-lease tap, in particular, had the effect of reducing Britain to financial dependence. The British took note, with gathering resentment and despair, of their diminishing status.[10]

In numerous other episodes (for example, the question of maintaining occupied Italy's monarchy and Badoglio government; and the British suppression of Greek partisans)[11] the inevitable quarrels among allies were heightened by a clash of worldviews and, especially, an awareness that American aims included Britain's geopolitical demotion. Yet Roosevelt clearly admired the British people and was fond of their leader; he intended, however grudgingly, to share postwar world power with Britain.[12] Far less can be said for his attitude toward the continental European powers. Germany, of course, could expect no special magnanimity; what does seem surprising, however, is that the U.S. leadership was considerably more vengeful that the American people. Without apparent qualm, Roosevelt (and Churchill) backed Treasury Secretary Henry Morgenthau's plan to dismantle German industry and "pastoralize" its economy. Only its premature leak to the press, and a popular American reaction against it, forced the repudiation of the Morgenthau Plan. Roosevelt continued thereafter to advocate a harsh postwar German policy, partly, it has been suggested, to earn Stalin's trust. Nowhere, certainly, did he betray any inkling that it might be necessary to restore Germany as a bulwark against Soviet aggression.[13]

France fared almost as badly in the Roosevelt scheme of things. Neither the American president nor the French leader took great pains to hide the bad blood between them. De Gaulle accused Roosevelt of taking for granted the "effacement of France." Roosevelt called de Gaulle a "prima donna."[14] Personality clashes were a symptom, not the cause, of sharply diverging visions of the postwar world. De Gaulle understood as well as anyone what Roosevelt had in mind for Europe and France. Leaving aside the quasi-European powers of Britain and Russia, Roosevelt considered Europe to be finished: Its time had passed, and good riddance. France was corrupt to the core, its empire more egregious than Britain's, its moral and political decay demonstrated by its rapid collapse under Hitler's 1940 Blitzkrieg. (This last judgment was not very different from de Gaulle's own, incidentally.)

For his postwar planning, Franklin D. Roosevelt has long been accused of a fateful naïveté. The accusation got mixed up, in McCarthy times, with the "twenty-years-of-treason" thesis and various other vindictive fantasies, but it also came from more thoughtful critics, George Kennan among them. Over the years, every fresh revelation of Stalinist brutality has lent the critique of Roosevelt new weight.

Recent scholars, however, have gone some way toward rehabilitating FDR's reputation for good judgment. It is true enough, they argue, that Roosevelt invested considerable hope in Stalin's fair treatment of the Poles and other East Europeans. But hope was really all he had to go on. The Soviets were bearing the brunt of the land war. And although Roosevelt at times considered Churchill's pleas for racing the Red Army to Berlin, the collapse of Germany's eastern front made it likely that Russia alone would be in the position to "liberate" Eastern Europe. Likewise, although Roosevelt has been criticized for harboring utopian illusions, for resurrecting the League of Nations concept and imagining a "Four Policemen" directorate running the world in harmony, the Wilsonian surface covered a Bismarckian core. The four policemen—the United States, Russia, Great Britain and China—would not always work by consensus, he implied: America, Russia and China might have to gang up on Britain to force the disgorging of the colonies; America, Britain and China would constitute an ever-ready coalition against the Russians.[15] "The picture is hardly one of anticipating harmony," notes John Lewis Gaddis.[16]

In at least one respect, however, Roosevelt deserves the verdict of "unrealism." He thought he could convert a long-term secular trend—the decline of the old European powers and the rise of America, Russia and the Third World—into the ready-to-use blocks of a new international system. China would replace France on the world stage. Never mind that China had yet to emerge from warlord chaos, or that France, for all her sins and frailties, was a long-time ally who shared America's democratic vocation. Roosevelt suffered from a recognizably American blind spot, the symptom of a complex of ailments: scorn for old Europe, an overreliance on abstractions, the traditional American mystification of China. This blind spot shaped a world vision at considerable odds with the reality that would emerge.

TWO CONCEPTS OF POWER, TWO KINDS OF CONTAINMENT

Movements on the European battlefield—above all, those of the Russians in Poland—were rapidly erasing FDR's imagined postwar world. On August 1, 1944, the Red Army having reached the east bank of the Vistula, Warsaw's underground resistance launched its uprising. The Nazis moved savagely to put it down while the Red Army watched. To Churchill's cabled pleas for aid to the insurrection, Stalin responded that the "Warsaw action represents a reckless and terrible adventure" from which "the Soviet command . . . must dissociate itself."[17] The implications stunned American and British officials in Moscow.

Stalin, it seemed, found it convenient to let the Nazis complete a project he had started with the 1940 Katyn Woods massacre of Polish officers: the extermination of Poland's leadership class.[18] Five months later, Stalin, Roosevelt and Churchill met at Yalta and reached an agreement on Poland: a provisional Warsaw government, to include elements of both the exile government in London and the competing, Soviet-backed Poles in Lublin; and preparations for free elections.

If one wanted to choose a specific starting date for the Cold War, it would probably be in March 1945, some few weeks after this agreement.[19] The Soviets barred British and American observers from entering Poland and arrested on charges of "terrorism" members of the London-based government who had just arrived in Warsaw. Soviet foreign minister V. M. Molotov announced that Polish elections would be conducted "Soviet style." In the space of 32 days, Churchill fired off to Roosevelt 14 messages on Poland and Eastern Europe, their tone verging on panic. Hours after sending Churchill a brief, reassuring cable on "the general Soviet problem," Roosevelt died.[20]

Roosevelt's death may have accelerated a conscious break in U.S. policy.[21] It was generally decided to stop trusting the Soviets, to stop appealing to their good will, to stop basing policy on the hope that they could be integrated into a postwar system of cooperation, to reject what Daniel Yergin calls the "Yalta Axioms" of Roosevelt's optimism toward Russia.[22] The other aspect of the break constituted an even sharper reversal: the decision to rapidly restore European and, especially, German power.

Among the many impressive figures of postwar construction, perhaps it is George F. Kennan whom we associate most closely with that break. This is partly because of his influence in determining it, but especially because of his eloquence in defining it. There will be no effort here to add to the wealth of Kennan scholarship, but a study of Soviet-threat perceptions in any period cannot afford to leave out a brief account of Kennan's own early contribution. No other American policymaker has offered such a comprehensive analysis of the Soviet threat: an acute insight into the collective psychology of Stalin's regime coupled with an equally profound appreciation of the West's corresponding weaknesses and strengths.

As impending victory set the Allies to quarrelling over the fruits, Kennan grew increasingly frustrated with American confusion about the Russians. This confusion stemmed from a flawed understanding of the Soviet character argued Kennan (whose own "liberal education in the horrors of Stalinism," as he put it, included the Moscow show trials).[23] Soviet hostility did not result from fear of the outside world or from "misunderstandings" between great powers, but from the nature of totalitarianism. It therefore served no purpose to try to dispel

Soviet insecurities or misunderstandings. Russia would only respect and respond to American strength of purpose.[24]

Kennan worried about the liabilities of Western democracy in any intimate dealings with the Soviets. He warned that the basic good will of Americans
would be used against them. (His earliest worry about atomic weapons was that
American statesmen would rush to share the secret with Stalin.)[25] He feared
that in their enthusiasm to enlist the Soviets in various postwar agreements and
organizations, the Americans were falling into a trap: Any common declarations
about transforming occupied Germany along "democratic" lines could only
serve as a rhetorical fog to cover Stalin's patently antidemocratic intentions; and
if Stalin had any interest in the United Nations, it was only as a means of
enlisting Anglo-American support for his control of Eastern Europe.[26] Kennan
further warned that trade relations would give the Russians an inherent advantage over politically undisciplined Americans.[27]

These gloomy ruminations were conducted for the most part in relative
obscurity, an unsurprising fate for the thoughts of a midlevel foreign-service
officer whose misgivings in Moscow had little direct relevance to the larger war
effort. Then, in February 1946, the State Department asked the Moscow chargé
d'affaires to explain the belligerence of a recent Stalin speech. This was it,
Kennan recalled thinking; for months and years he had vainly tried to convey
to Washington some appreciation of the utter malevolence that reigned in
Moscow. "Now, suddenly, my opinion was being asked."[28] Kennan responded
with his famous "Long Telegram," an 8,000-word portrayal of a Russian
"political force committed fanatically to the belief that with the U.S. there can
be no permanent modus vivendi, that it is desirable and necessary that the
internal harmony of our society be disrupted, our traditional way of life be
destroyed, the international authority of our state be broken, if Soviet power is
to be secure."[29] Soviet leaders' hostility stemmed, in part, from the precarious
nature of their rule. Like the rule of their Czarist predecessors, it was "fragile
and artificial in its psychological foundation, unable to stand comparison or
contact with political systems of Western countries."[30] Thus the supposed
hostility and danger of the Western world was a necessary fiction to justify the
Soviets' savage police state. This fiction had a momentum of its own: since it
was necessary to insulate Russian society from the West, Russian leaders had
no curiosity and only distorted knowledge of the outside. The Soviet regime,
wrote Kennan, was

> seemingly inaccessible to considerations of reality. For it, the vast fund of
> objective fact about human society is not, as with us, the measure against
> which outlook is constantly being tested and reformed, but a grab bag

from which individual items are selected arbitrarily and tendentiously to
bolster an outlook already preconceived.[31]

With this dismal dissection of paranoid hostility, Kennan coupled a correspondingly alarming view of Russian political and diplomatic resources. Communist
parties in the West were almost wholly subservient to and directed by Moscow.
Official Soviet diplomacy was shrewd and single-minded in its efforts to sow
dissension among Western allies, to stir resentments among colonial peoples
and, more generally, to wreak havoc in the capitalist camp.

Later, said the author, he would look back with "horrified amusement"
at his telegraphic dispatch, which sounded "like one of those primers put out
by alarmed congressional committees or by the Daughters of the American
Revolution."[32] In fact, the Long Telegram already contained elements of a more
sober view of Soviet capabilities. It had very little to say, for example, about
Russian military power, except that the Soviets were unlikely to take "unnecessary risks." The threat Kennan described was a political threat, and compared
to the West, the Soviets were "by far the weaker force." Their own system was
"unproven" in its internal stability. Their propaganda was "basically negative"
and therefore "relatively easy to combat."[33]

However, it was the more pessimistic side of the message that resonated
with the Truman administration (as Kennan no doubt intended). It was, as the
author himself plausibly observes, a message that Washington, for its own
reasons, was ready to receive. Frustration and perplexity about the Soviets had
been growing in American policy circles since well before Yalta. Kennan's
telegram seemed to provide an elegant and reasoned explanation of what was
wrong. It enjoyed extraordinary circulation—it was studied and discussed in
the White House, the State Department, overseas embassies and the Pentagon,
where Secretary of the Navy James Forrestal "had it reproduced and evidently
made it required reading for hundreds, if not thousands" of officers.[34]

The Long Telegram made Kennan a star. Having electrified official
Washington with his definition of a Soviet threat, he was now charged with
helping produce a plan to counter it. First as director of the National War
College, then as chairman of the State Department's new Policy Planning Staff,
he spun out a series of lectures, memos and articles (one of which generated
considerable notoriety when published anonymously in *Foreign Affairs* as "The
Sources of Soviet Conduct"). And although he would deny paternity of
anything like a "Doctrine of Containment," that doctrine nonetheless remained
closely associated with his name.

" . . . [It] is clear that the main element of any United States policy toward
the Soviet Union must be that of a long-term, patient but firm and vigilant

containment of Russian expansive tendencies," wrote Kennan in one of the most quoted passages of Cold War history.[35] An important thing to notice about this prescription is its strictly defensive nature. Eventually, he predicted, after a string of frustrations, Soviet hostility could be expected to "mellow." The Russians would inevitably feel the strains of an empire they were ill-suited to manage, given their insistence on rigid ideological control. Indeed, Marxist conformity was their great vulnerability. It could not survive, for example, a Communist victory in China. (As early as 1947 Kennan predicted the Sino-Soviet split that was to bedevil Moscow.)

In the meantime, however, a defensive policy of containment would require historical patience—not one of the more conspicuous of American virtues. At times over the ensuing decades, the U.S. would seem to have a monopoly on frustration: China, Korea and Vietnam being the most dramatic examples. Right-wing bitterness about America's defensive stance produced a chronic ulcer in the American body politic, erupting in the "who-lost-China?" lament, the MacArthur-Truman confrontation, the Joseph McCarthy hysteria, Watergate (a more complicated case, it must be said), and the Iran-*contra* affairs. And yet no later administration ever really took it upon itself to alter the fundamental defensiveness of U.S. policy.

An earlier disagreement, however, was also a more subtle one, involving numerous fine distinctions about the character of Soviet power and Western defenses and pitting George Kennan, almost alone, against the Democratic foreign-policy establishment, personified best by the formidable figure of Dean Acheson. This disagreement took a while to emerge. In the first two years of Kennan's celebrity, any such philosophical discord was submerged by the immediate urgencies. These were crisis years. The European winter of 1947 was unrelievedly harsh and bracketed by summer droughts. Industry stood almost still: between Hitler and the Allied bombers, the physical destruction was staggering. What capital plant survived had little to do, given so many holes in the chain of production. The Western zones of occupied Germany had contributed, before the war, one-fifth of Europe's industrial product. Now that contribution had been cut by two-thirds. Currencies were almost worthless. Market links—between town and country, among the states of Europe, and between Europe and the outside world—were severed. Land fertility had decreased, and in any case, given the utter breakdown of economic exchange, there was little reason for farmers to produce more than they needed to feed their own families. Perversely, any reconstruction or production that *did* take place spurred insatiable demand for goods from America, thus opening a yawning "dollar gap."[36] In Germany, especially, the suffering was immense. (A young girl from Frankfurt, asked a few years later to pick the most beautiful day of her life, chose "February 17, 1947, when my brother died and I inherited his overcoat, his shoes, and his woolen jacket.")[37] In France and Italy, large Communist parties, prestige high due to Russia's and their own anti-Nazi resistance, were ready with their own solution to the crisis. In Greece, Communists and conservatives were already fighting a brutal civil war. Europe was cold, hungry and scared.

Under such circumstances, the Truman administration was easily convinced of the need for a major aid program. This Marshall Plan was manifestly more urgent than any military measures; the greater danger resided not in a Soviet attack but in Soviet opportunities for exploiting the psychological, moral and economic fragility of war-torn Europe. It should not have been difficult to see that an attack at that time would have been nothing less than insane (and it was Stalin's great paradox that, however murderously paranoid he was in running the Soviet Union, he was rarely anything but coldly rational in his foreign policies). Industrial indices were Stalin's definition of power, and Soviet industry had been demolished. The American adversary, by comparison, was richer and stronger than at any time in history.[38] There were, certainly, some war scares on the U.S. side, occasioned by the Soviet delay in removing troops from northern Iran, the 1948 Czech coup, and the 1948–49 blockade of Berlin, among other crises. The fact that the United States had largely demobilized, and the widely held (though quite erroneous) belief that Russia had *not* demobilized, added to the general nervousness. Even so, there was in Washington a certain determination not to lose one's head, to avoid the frenetic "war preparations which would bring about the very thing which we are taking steps to prevent," as Secretary of State George Marshall cautioned in May 1948.[39] The period before 1949 was a time, as Kennan later recalled, when

> the moderate Marshall Plan approach—an approach aimed at *creating* strength in the West rather than *destroying* strength in Russia—seemed to have prevailed; and I, like those others who went by the name of "Russian experts," felt that our view of the Russian problem—a view that accepted Russian-Communist attitudes and policies as a danger at the political level, but did not see either a likelihood or a necessity of war and did not regard the military plane as the one on which our response ought to be concentrated—seemed to have found general acceptance.[40]

But Kennan's intellectual exile was not long in coming. His deemphasis of the military aspects of containment was simply too far out of sync with the conventional wisdom in Washington.

Kennan's maverick analysis started with observations of the Soviet Union's unpreparedness for war in 1947, but then went deeper. The Soviet Union would rebuild, of course; its military-industrial power would grow. Yet Kennan tended to discount this later military threat. His writings are full of reflections on the limited usefulness of military power; he insisted that his prescriptions for containing Soviet influence were distorted beyond recognition by the militarization of American policy. He was opposed to the elaborate formal structure that NATO took (Kennan would have preferred a simple American guarantee to supplement the Brussels Union of Britain, France and the Benelux countries). He was opposed to NATO's "preoccupation with military affairs" and, as discussed below, he was opposed to the inclusion of West Germany in the organization.[41] And from early in the postwar era, Kennan pleaded against reliance on nuclear weapons for any purpose other than to deter their use.

The Hitler analogy occupied many minds. Yet Stalin was no Hitler. "Having inherited an immense and self-sufficient territorial empire, Stalin was not driven by Hitler's fear that his authority would collapse if he did not expand," as David Calleo has argued.[42] On the contrary, war was to be avoided, since it could cause the unravelling of Russia's empire. And if there was no plausible gain from a Soviet attack, Kennan felt justified in ruling out that attack.[43] Peace, in the meantime, however uneasy, meant a contest of systems that the West could expect to win. Western Europe's postwar economic crisis, and the prestige of its Communist parties, posed dangers, but the dangers would not last. Once restored to economic and political health, European democracies would more than hold their own against a totalitarian threat. If Soviet expansion could be stopped, the long-term processes of history would work to the West's advantage. Hence Kennan's 1948 prediction (so spectacularly confirmed in 1989) that

> . . . if economic recovery could be brought about and public confidence restored in western Europe—if western Europe, in other words, could be made the home of a vigorous, prosperous and forward-looking civilization—the Communist regime in eastern Europe . . . would never be able to stand the comparison, and the spectacle of a happier and more successful life just across the fence . . . would be bound in the end to have a disintegrating and eroding effect on the Communist world.[44]

It was a measure of his confidence in the advantages of the West that Kennan saw early possibilities for a negotiated settlement with Russia.[45] The American trump card in any such negotiations would be the threat of a rearmed

West Germany joining an anti-Soviet alliance. The Russians could be expected to pay a high price to forestall that threat; the price Kennan had in mind involved the withdrawal of Soviet (and all other foreign) troops from a reunified, neutral Germany. He believed in the long-term viability of German neutrality—given adequate negotiated guarantees, it could be maintained even in the face of Russian military power. And he believed that German neutrality was a legitimate price for the *United States* to pay, in that it would help satisfy Soviet security concerns.[46]

There were occasions, as it happened, on which the Russians showed some guarded interest in such a settlement. On March 10, 1952, Soviet Foreign Minister V. M. Molotov proposed a new four-power conference to take another stab at a peace treaty with Germany.[47] Molotov's note envisioned a reunified, rearmed and neutral Germany. After Stalin's death in 1953, the new Soviet leadership was suddenly ready to negotiate a withdrawal from Austria; the signing in May 1955 of the Austrian State Treaty must have been intended, at least in part, as a hint that similar opportunities were open to the Germans.

The Americans and their West European allies, on the other hand, evinced mainly suspicion. Among mainstream Western politicians, only Winston Churchill saw the possibility of a "profound movement of Russian feeling," arguing that it "would be a mistake to assume that nothing could be settled with Soviet Russia unless or until everything is settled."[48]

The more characteristic response, however, was Dean Acheson's, which amounted to an utter repudiation of the Kennan philosophy of international relations. "Mr. Kennan has never, in my judgement, grasped the realities of power relationships, but takes a rather mystical attitude toward them," said the former secretary of state in 1958. "To Mr. Kennan there is no Soviet military threat in Europe."[49] Disengagement from the European confrontation was a chimera, he felt, "a futile—and lethal—attempt to crawl back into the cocoon of history."[50] Negotiations on disengagement were uniquely dangerous for the West, which would raise irresistible popular hopes by entering talks and ultimately lose control of events. And "once a withdrawal begins, it will be complete . . . all forces, foreign and domestic, will combine to bring this about."[51] The Russians, not subject to the pressures of democracy, were immune to such concerns. Even if they withdrew from Central Europe, the Russian troops could return in "12 to 18 hours."[52] As for German neutrality, there was no hope for

> . . . the successful insulation of a large and vital country, situated, as Germany is, between two power systems and with ambitions and purposes of its own. Constant strain would undermine the sanctions of neutraliza-

tion. The final result would be determined by the relative strength of the pressures from the two sides. As I have already suggested, the pressure would all be from the Russian side.

Within a foreseeable time, there would have to be "an accommodation of some sort or another between an abandoned Germany and the great Power to the East." This "new Ribbentrop-Molotov agreement" would mean the "unification . . . of the Eurasian land mass."[53]

Here were two archetypal versions of the containment strategy, whose differing assumptions underlay most later arguments about the gravity of the Soviet threat. Kennan's version was distinguished by the assumption that a natural balance of power was available against the Soviets, once Western Europe recovered from the ravages of war. Containment, under this assumption, was something inherently and organically stable. To be sure, it required an original intervention of U.S. leadership, capital and (at least implicitly) military protection. Once attained, however, this balance could be expected to more or less sustain itself without an indefinite U.S. mobilization. Acheson's version was based on some far less sanguine assumptions. In his mind, the balance of power was inherently and organically unstable. The Soviet threat was something new and implacable, at the same time ideologically and militarily potent. The West European democracies were inherently weak in the face of this challenge and would remain so long after economic recovery for reasons having to do with the intrinsic natures of democratic and totalitarian societies. Only a heroic and indefinite exertion of U.S. military power could keep the dam from crumbling.

Since the preceding pages join the currently fashionable chorus of admiration for Kennan, it is important to repeat an earlier caveat: Kennan was more eloquent than influential over policy. The clarity of his observations perhaps owed something to his early retirement from the muddle of policy making. And his observations were not always right. He was prematurely optimistic in his expectation that Europe could recover and exercise complete independence. And he was overly pessimistic in his predictions about the baleful effects of America's long-term presence in Germany, which he expected the Germans to resent much more than they did.[54]

It is also fair to note that the militarization of the East-West confrontation did not, as Kennan had feared, prevent its eventual resolution. (Whether the military confrontation perpetuated Europe's division for many decades longer than necessary, however, is a matter for endless speculation.)

Yet Kennan did see, perhaps better than anyone else, the eventual path of Western victory. The superiority of Western political economies was the source of their ultimate triumph. Soviet policy, confronted with firm barriers, did "mellow." The Communist movement did fracture, with Maoist China posing an intolerable challenge to Soviet leadership. This Sino-Soviet split "was itself the greatest single measure of containment that could be conceived," Kennan wrote later.[55] Moreover, Kennan warned repeatedly against the American tendency to take on "universal" foreign commitments, and these warnings proved wise, in that disregard for them led to Vietnam, manifestly the greatest disaster of postwar American foreign policy.

Finally, Kennan discerned the underlying limits to Soviet efforts to improve their position with a military buildup. Looked at superficially, his notions about the limited value of military power seem paradoxical, given his reputation as a "realist." Such notions were attacked in the late 1970s as "fashionable" rationalizations for the decline of American power and denounced as contributing to the danger facing the West. This later neoconservative campaign to reestablish a general appreciation of the importance of military power—not just in war but also in determining peace-time political relations—is a focus of this book. And a central thesis is that Kennan, in discounting the importance of military power, proved more right than his critics.

By the middle of Truman's second term, however, Kennan had decisively lost the philosophical debate. In retrospect it can be seen that he never had a chance. It was not just the American government that rejected his proposals for a mutual disengagement from Europe; West European leaders themselves would have none of it. The British were nurturing their American "special relationship" as an antidote to imperial decline, while the French were terrified of facing a reunited Germany on their own.

The West Germans had their own version of the Kennan-Acheson debate, with the German roles played by the Socialist Kurt Schumacher and the Christian Democrat Konrad Adenauer. Schumacher conceived of a reunited, pacified Germany, neutral in the emerging Soviet-American conflict and enjoying a humane and democratic socialism distinct both from American-style "monopoly capitalism" and from Stalinist Communism. Adenauer, on the other hand, imagined a westward-looking Federal Republic, embedded in the nascent West European community and in a Western military alliance. It was, among other things, the Berlin Blockade that helped convince West German voters that Adenauer's path was safer.

The Acheson/Adenauer approach became the basis of Western policy. In 1949 the North Atlantic Treaty was signed. The following year, National Security Council Memorandum 68 codified plans for an American rearmament. When North Korean troops invaded the South, resistance to that rearmament seemed quaint at best and, at worst, dangerously naïve.

THE CURIOUS ROLE OF NUCLEAR WEAPONS

History rarely operates for the benefit of simple and schematic analysis. The militarization that Kennan feared was not carried quite so far as its logic suggested; the Truman rearmament was short-lived. Over the medium term (roughly 15 years after the war's end) Western Europe's military defense arrangements remained at least partly constrained by an appreciation of the dilemmas that Kennan had identified.

It was a matter of seeing the Soviet threat and its various components in proper perspective. NATO needed a formula for neutralizing the military threat while avoiding a costly remilitarization that would only deepen the Europeans' more perilous economic and political malaise. The answer, paradoxically, was provided by nuclear terror. American nuclear weapons provided the "reassurance" that Europe needed to undertake ambitious physical reconstruction and social renewal.[56]

This strategy of nuclear reassurance was adopted by default rather than by intent. The West Europeans never met their commitment, entered into at the 1952 Lisbon meeting of NATO governments, to increase NATO conventional forces from 25 to 96 divisions. To do so risked tearing a fragile social consensus. Nor was America prepared to provide the forces. Nuclear weapons, which were relatively cheap, filled the gap. With a determination to initiate nuclear war in retaliation for a Soviet *conventional* attack, Western Europe and the United States could forgo the expense of maintaining standing armies large enough to balance Soviet troops. Various other factors encouraged this reliance on nuclear weapons.[57] Foremost was the simple fact of overwhelming U.S. strategic superiority, which for over a decade constituted a kind of de facto nuclear monopoly. Until Sputnik, America was more or less invulnerable to Soviet nuclear retaliation.

Under these conditions of near invulnerability, the Eisenhower administration developed its doctrine of "massive retaliation." Its basic pillar was a readiness to respond to any Soviet attack against Europe with a massive nuclear strike. This posture lent itself easily to parody, and administration officials subsequently went out of their way to insist that they retained less cataclysmic options.[58] Nonetheless, the logic of massive retaliation was encouraged by economic conservatism. As a single, asymmetrical response to myriad possible provocations, massive retaliation was economical, not just in its effect on military spending, but on the whole political economy, which President Dwight D. Eisenhower feared to be fundamentally fragile.[59]

Throughout the Cold War, critics of both left and right would bemoan this debilitating "nuclear addiction,"[60] which came to be seen as NATO's original sin. In post–Cold War retrospect, however, another perspective deserves consideration: that this cheap nuclear defense—along with cheap oil supplies, a relatively open trading system, and Keynesian economic policies—helped make possible the postwar economic miracles of Western Europe, America and Japan. These economic miracles were at the same time NATO's political triumph, since the Alliance undergirded a welfare capitalism that provided an unparalleled opportunity for reconciling economic progress, individual liberty and social justice. It cannot be proved, of course, that in the absence of NATO's dependence on nuclear deterrence, higher military expenditures would have significantly impeded economic and social progress. But one can point with confidence to the clear evidence that participants in the foundation of NATO considered the expense of sufficient conventional forces to meet the perceived Soviet threat as inimical to the creation of ambitious welfare states, which confounded the Communists by combining a robust redistribution of wealth with a robust creation of wealth.[61] In this sense, nuclear terror contributed decisively to an ultimate ideological "victory" for the West.[62]

But this postwar order, however successful, was bound to be controversial, based as it was on a Faustian bargain: the demilitarization of West European societies in exchange for a permanent reliance on nuclear terror. Faustian debts eventually come due—or at least they are *expected* to come due. Eventually the Russians were bound to catch up and develop a reliable, second-strike nuclear capability against the United States. Once that point was reached, extended nuclear deterrence, with its implicit American pledge to bring down mass destruction on itself rather than see Europe overrun by Soviet forces, would be suspect.

Actually, as I will argue at length in chapter four, the balance of terror was a great deal more stable that many of its critics imagined. So was "extended deterrence"—the extension of U.S. nuclear deterrence to cover the European allies as well. The threat posed by NATO nuclear weapons was sufficient to neutralize Soviet military power (both nuclear and conventional) under the strategic circumstances prevailing in Europe throughout the Cold War. This was true even during the later decades when the Soviet nuclear arsenal was most formidable.

Nonetheless, doubts about extended deterrence fueled four decades of dispute among American and European nuclear strategists. During those 40 years, the abstract and utterly speculative nature of nuclear theology was to make possible some wildly disparate estimates of Soviet strategic power.

National strategy has been said to reflect national personality. The Kennedy team that took over the White House in 1961 was certainly self-conscious about endowing America with a new persona. They were going to "get this country moving again," to "bear any burden" in the struggle for freedom. Bold, assertive leadership was to replace Eisenhower conservatism.

This Kennedy call for a revitalized American leadership was exuberantly optimistic in tone, but rather pessimistic in content. More precisely, it was optimistic in its view of American resources[63] and capabilities while quite pessimistic in its assessment of the current global balance of power. In this sense, the liberals of 1960 presaged the neoconservatives of 1980. In both cases, an allegedly complacent conservatism of the previous decade presented a political target. Eisenhower was accused of having neglected a growing Soviet challenge in the 1950s, just as Nixon, Kissinger, Ford and Carter would be in the 1970s.

It may well be, of course, that Kennedy's alarm over the Soviet threat was largely calculated for domestic political advantage (as with allegations of a "missile gap" favoring the Russians, which were quickly forgotten after Kennedy took office). Even so, once in office the Kennedy administration launched policies and strategies—notably, the Vietnam war and a new nuclear strategy of "flexible response"—implicitly informed by the "organically unstable" view of containment. There were new and more subtle forms of Soviet pressure that massive retaliation could not deter. Even if never fired, new Soviet missiles were tools of intimidation conferring political power. During the campaign, Kennedy had pointed to (and greatly exaggerated) this increased Soviet missile power, calling it

> . . . the shield from behind which they will slowly, but surely advance—through Sputnik diplomacy, limited brushfire wars, indirect non-overt aggression, intimidation and subversion, internal revolution, increased prestige or influence, and the vicious blackmail of our allies. The periphery of the Free World will slowly be nibbled away. . . . Each such Soviet move will weaken the West; but none will seem sufficiently significant by itself to justify our initiating a nuclear war which might destroy us.[64]

The problem of Berlin figured prominently in this scenario of Western interests being "slowly nibbled away." After Stalin had lifted the city blockade in the face of a successful Western airlift, the issue had lain dormant for a few years. Clearly, however, the idea of a Western city deep in East Germany, garrisoned by American, French and British troops—a city, moreover, into which any East German could simply walk when he or she had the whim—was intolerable for the Soviets in the long run. In 1958 the Soviets delivered an ultimatum: Berlin's status had to be settled. The ultimatum spawned a four-year crisis, in the middle of which the United States changed administrations. Soviet leader Nikita Khrushchev obviously thought he could bully the new and inexperienced young president over the dispute. Because of it, the Kennedy administration considered war to be a real and imminent threat.[65]

As in 1949, the 1958–62 Berlin crisis was settled without war, but in a fashion that underscored the Cold War's ambiguous calculus of loss and gain. There were two ways to look at the Berlin Wall, which went up in August 1961. On the one hand, it revealed Moscow and its East German ally to be desperately on the defensive. To build the Berlin Wall was to grant the West a permanent propaganda victory—proof that the Communists could not organize a viable socialist society in East Germany without turning it into a virtual prison.

More pessimistic Western observers, on the other hand, could discern in the Berlin crises Soviet offensive designs going well beyond the consolidation of the East German regime. For the Western allies to relinquish their rights in any part of Berlin was a humiliation—the start of a political process whereby the United States was to be gradually forced out of Europe, and Western Europe would gradually come to acknowledge Soviet preeminence in Eurasia.[66] Critics of the Kennedy administration's essentially passive response to the Berlin Wall charged that the Soviets had been allowed to turn their desperate failure—3,000 East Germans daily fleeing west—into a diplomatic victory.[67]

Certainly the Russians had found a wedge to drive between NATO partners. The United States looked on helplessly as the Soviets and their German clients flagrantly violated four-power occupation agreements. Chancellor Adenauer, notwithstanding his alleged ambivalence about German reunification, was bitterly disappointed by U.S. passivity. His hardline strategy of negotiating German reunification only from a position of overwhelming Western strength was revealed, at least for the moment, as a failure.[68] Berlin mayor Willy Brandt wrote to Kennedy, "Inaction or merely defensive action could provoke a crisis of confidence in the Western powers."[69] Later, Brandt summarized the episode acidly: "The Soviet Union had defied the major power in the Western world and effectively humiliated it."[70]

The Americans did not deny their weakness in Berlin. In fact, they went out of their way to highlight it as part of a campaign to reorganize American nuclear strategy. On September 7, with the shock of the Wall still fresh, Assistant Defense Secretary Paul Nitze suggested that the Berlin debacle revealed the folly of relying on a threat of massive nuclear retaliation to defend Western Europe. To Nitze, such an all-or-nothing strategy looked like a transparent bluff. It implied that NATO, in order to "demonstrate its determination to have its vital interests respected," really had only one option:

nuclear war. This bluff had not been sufficient to dissuade the Soviets from erecting a wall through Berlin. And Nitze warned that it was not any more likely to prevent their next probable provocation: the closing of access routes to West Berlin.[71]

Over subsequent months, Pentagon officials hammered hard on this theme: the need for a restructured deterrence to meet more "ambiguous situations." A declared policy of attacking Soviet cities in the event of conflict, unsupported by ground forces for a significant nonnuclear defense, could not make the Russians "refrain from a series of actions designed, step by step, to erode NATO's interests," Defense Secretary Robert McNamara asserted. "[It] is simply not credible that NATO, or anyone else, would respond to a given small step—the first slice of the salami—with immediate use of nuclear weapons. Nor is it credible that a chain of small actions, no one of which is catastrophic, would evoke a response of general nuclear war." The doctrine of massive retaliation, said McNamara, "appears more likely to deter its owner from standing firm under pressure than to inhibit a potential aggressor."[72]

NATO, according to the Kennedy administration, needed a nuclear doctrine that carefully tailored the response to the provocation. The Soviets would be deterred from an attack or provocation if they understood that the West had options and plans for responding short of all-out nuclear war. The administration's solution was "flexible response," a strategy that required, first of all, a buildup of conventional forces adequate to ensure a serious and protracted fight before the escalation to nuclear battle. If the conventional battle did not convince the Russians to back down, and it was necessary to escalate to nuclear battle, escalation should be conducted in a gradual, controlled, and militarily purposeful fashion. As McNamara put it in June 1962, "The United States has come to the conclusion that, to the extent feasible, basic military strategy in a possible general nuclear war should be approached in much the same way that more conventional military operations have been regarded in the past."[73] American strategy was to be based on principles of "counterforce," the destruction of Soviet military forces, rather than "countervalue," the annihilation of Soviet civilians.

It could be, and indeed was, argued that this was a more humane way to think about nuclear war. In general, however, America's European allies were deeply unsettled by flexible response. They tended to view it as an elaborate doctrinal cover for the American effort to weasel out of its nuclear commitment to Europe. And even taking the new strategy at face value, they feared that flexible response, far from making extended deterrence more credible, would only make war more thinkable, feeding illusions on both sides that battle could be contained in central Europe. The West Germans especially feared that part of the American hope for flexible response was to prevent any war that did break out from engulfing two hemispheres. The Germans could hardly share the Americans' feelings on this score, for any modern European war would surely slaughter German civilians and destroy German cities on both sides of the Iron Curtain. Germany would be the price of American (and Russian) survival.

European resistance to flexible response reflected the logical and persistent tension between America and Western Europe over the preferable height of the nuclear threshold. Americans, it can be said, preferred the nuclear threshold to be rather high, for straightforward reasons of national survival. Western European leaders were more ready to embrace deterrence as a kind of doomsday machine that discouraged even tentative Soviet probes by threatening an almost automatic escalation to general nuclear war. If the real world lacked this kind of clarity, the French at least hoped that a sufficiently intimidating degree of uncertainty about avoiding nuclear escalation would weigh on Russian minds. They were therefore distinctly unhappy about McNamara's enthusiasm for a more predictable and more controllable battle. The doctrinal dispute took concrete political forms. McNamara criticized the French passion for independent nuclear forces, since such forces compromised his plan for centralized command and control of a conflict.[74] The French criticized flexible response for a basic lack of realism. The Americans pressed their strategy on the Alliance, and de Gaulle took France out of NATO's military command. (Flexible response, it should be noted, was just one of many stated and unstated reasons for the French withdrawal.)[75]

The West Germans, lacking nuclear weapons, lacked France's choices. They were not happy with flexible response, but had to acquiesce. However, Germany was able to fight a rear-guard defense against some of the more objectionable aspects of the U.S. proposal. This was possible mainly because the United States was not ready to provide sufficient conventional troops to make McNamara's original version of flexible response viable. The final version, adopted by the North Atlantic Council in May 1967, was a German-American compromise, which, in direct contrast to McNamara's original idea, depended on an early and deliberate use of nuclear weapons by NATO. Deterrence was to be based on convincing the Soviet leadership that its conventional attack would be met first by conventional defenses but then, after an unpredictable pause, with nuclear explosions. NATO would be determined to escalate if the war was not settled on its terms and fairly quickly. The NATO strategy was to be one of "first use": if necessary, the West remained ready to start nuclear war.[76]

THE END OF THE COLD WAR?

It could be argued, however, that by the time flexible response was adopted, the Cold War was already settled. The Berlin Wall had removed the single most dangerous ambiguity and focus of conflict from the Soviet-American relationship. It took some time for the point to sink in, but gradually it came to be understood that the Wall had clarified and settled the United States' and the Soviet Union's respective spheres of influence. A set of "rules of the road" in the U.S.-Soviet relationship had been established and accepted, making direct armed conflict unlikely.[77]

The tacit understanding over Berlin constituted one such area of agreement. The settlement of the Cuban missile crisis of October 1962 was another. What, precisely, Nikita Khrushchev was up to in the furtive emplacement of missiles in Cuba remains murky, although it may become clearer with the opening of Soviet archives. Perhaps he still sought a negotiating lever to eject the Americans from West Berlin or truly feared an attack against Cuba. Whatever his specific purposes, in a more general way he evidently wanted to turn the strategic tables on America. He failed. The Americans stood him down and his Politburo colleagues, interpreting the episode as another of Khrushchev's erratic, "hair-brained schemes," ousted him from office. His successors then attempted, with a steady buildup of intercontinental nuclear forces, to achieve gradually what Khrushchev had sought instantly: a strategic revolution favoring the Soviets.

The effort was futile. The best they could hope to achieve was a nuclear stalemate. The Soviets could start a nuclear war, if they were suicidally inclined, but they could not hope to attain any position of fundamental nuclear superiority. In this sense too, the Cold War was already over.

One man who thought so was, ironically, the American defense secretary Robert McNamara. The evolution of his views on this subject is interesting and merits some attention. McNamara's legacy to nuclear doctrine is complex. He is remembered for his lasting contribution to both of the broad and competing tendencies of U.S. strategic policy: "counterforce" and "mutual destruction." Early counterforce ideas, codified in "flexible response," were the natural product of the former Ford executive's enthusiasm for systems analysis, cost-benefit measurement and tight bureaucratic control—in short, a faith in the scope for rational management of national strategy. He installed in the Pentagon the ideas and representatives of a first generation of civilian nuclear strategists.[78] The result was a shift in thinking that involved more than nuclear strategy. It reflected, rather, a deeper shift in the American philosophy of power: a new, technocratic faith in the flexible and calibrated exertion of military force—a shift that also provided the conceptual basis for America's war in Vietnam. This technocratic faith pervaded the Kennedy White House and carried over into the Johnson administration.[79]

However, McNamara soon lost faith in this creed, insofar as it claimed to offer a way to limit the damage of nuclear war and to exploit nuclear power for political purposes. He became convinced that nuclear war, once started, would be nearly impossible to keep under control. Moreover, his views, as they developed, were more radical than this increasingly commonplace idea suggests. For McNamara also became convinced that, short of war, nuclear weapons offered virtually *no* diplomatic advantage to their possessor. This was the somewhat counterintuitive lesson that the defense secretary said he drew from the Cuban missile crisis. Despite America's overwhelming strategic superiority—a capacity to inflict much greater damage on the Soviet Union than the Soviets could inflict on the United States—President Kennedy and his advisers never considered using nuclear weapons, according to McNamara, McGeorge Bundy and other participants. Nor did the fact of that superiority enlarge the Americans' sense of maneuver space. Quite the contrary: The Americans were far more cautious than they might otherwise have been, due to an ever-present sense that nuclear war would constitute disaster and the absolute failure of their policy. It was *conventional* superiority, in the air and sea around Cuba, that allowed America to prevail in the confrontation, according to McNamara.[80]

McNamara's Pentagon experience also convinced him of the reality, and stupidity, of an arms-race ("action-reaction") spur to superpower arsenals. He recounted stories of Air Force generals glibly planning for a U.S. ICBM (intercontinental ballistic missile) force of 10,000 missiles.[81] Similar planning was doubtless going on in Soviet military circles. He was horrified at the monstrous waste and instability that such planning would engender, with the nuclear buildup accelerating out of control as each side constantly redoubled its efforts for fear of being surpassed.

Yet the simple recognition that additional nuclear weapons conferred no usable additional power allowed *either* side to unilaterally renounce the arms race. All that was necessary was a level of nuclear forces that could survive a surprise attack and still inflict "unacceptable damage" on the other side. McNamara gave "unacceptable damage" an arbitrary but plausible definition: killing 20 percent of the Soviet population and destroying 50 percent of its industry. When McNamara left the Pentagon in 1968, a full-scale U.S. attack was deemed capable of destroying half the Soviet population and almost 80 percent of its industry.[82] Under McNamara's direction, U.S. policy came to be based on a view that America already had more than enough strategic forces, including roughly 1,050 ICBMs and 650 submarine-launched missiles.

Such was the essence of "mutual assured destruction" (MAD) and "sufficiency" as guides for force planning. As can readily be seen, while McNamara had renounced faith in the rational calibration of nuclear escalation, he had by no means given up on rationality as a guide to defense planning. To the contrary, "sufficiency" appeared to him as an eminently rational concept. Later critics fixed on this concept as eminently naïve, since the Soviets were not so "reasonable" and did not subscribe to it. For his part, McNamara conceded that at the time he first propounded these ideas, the Soviets found them ludicrous.[83] But he believed that their logic would eventually prevail on both sides, especially if helped along by negotiations.[84] Such hopes were the basis of the American effort to negotiate limits on antiballistic missile (ABM) defenses. The logic of mutual vulnerability did seem to prevail when both sides signed the 1972 ABM treaty.

Arguably, then, the first stage of the Soviet-American confrontation had ended in a draw: a bearable, albeit heavily militarized modus vivendi in Europe and a strategic stalemate globally. To whose advantage was this stalemate?

Hindsight tells us that it served the West. Certainly the stand-off satisfied the conditions for "containment" as formulated by Kennan just after World War II. Western Europe was secure and democratic and undergoing an unprecedented economic miracle. With the Soviet military threat largely neutralized, the conflict became a contest of political and economic systems. As we have seen, Kennan had been rather confident, already in 1948, about who would win such a contest. Meanwhile, the Sino-Soviet schism had started to demonstrate the strategic and ideological fragility of world Communism.

After 20 years, then, might it have been possible for the West to declare victory? Instead, after a flurry of European and U.S. diplomatic efforts to negotiate a détente in tensions, a grave pessimism about the balance of power took hold of American elites. The following chapters will trace the rise and explore the causes of this pessimism, which today seems so surreal.

2

Henry Kissinger and the Decline of the West

Americans naturally found it difficult to appreciate that they might be winning the Cold War when there was a real war that they appeared to be losing. Vietnam, along with its flesh-and-blood horrors, fatefully distorted American calculations about the balance of power.

Exaggerating the importance of Vietnam, U.S. elites bore an ironic resemblance to eighteenth-century British rulers, who were convinced that losing the war against the American colonies would spell the end of British power. "It is striking," observed Barbara Tuchman, "how often the prospect of losing America inspired predictions of ruin, and how mistaken they were, for Britain was to survive the loss well enough and go on to world domination and the apogee of imperial power in the next century."[1] Like America looking at the Soviet Union, Britain had seen the Bourbon powers of France and Spain as implacable threats; no one guessed that Spain was on the road to inexorable decline and that France's ancien régime was on the verge of revolution. In both cases, moreover, there was plenty of warning that the wars were mistakes, that they were squandering rather than preserving Britain's and America's respective world positions.

In the latter case, it is not too difficult to imagine the benefits of having avoided Vietnam. It seems evident that Americans would have far better preserved the faith of their allies and their confidence in themselves. Attention might have focused far earlier on the terminal difficulties of Soviet Communism. As it was, the Vietnam war was a gift to the Kremlin. It suggested that the United States was too worried and confused to pick its fights, that a skillful enemy might "manipulate it with ruinous results," as Theodore Draper has written. "If the United States could be made to fight for eight years in Vietnam, it could be made to fight anywhere."[2]

What was missing was the confidence to walk away. A succession of U.S. presidents seemed to understand that Vietnam was precisely the wrong place to fight a war, but their pessimistic assessments of containment's stability led them tragically on. Eisenhower could not "conceive of a greater tragedy for America than to get heavily involved."[3] Yet the simplistic power of his own "falling dominoes" analogy made him refuse to sign the 1954 Geneva Accords that could have ended the conflict with an early Vietminh victory.[4] He then backed the South Vietnamese premier Ngo Dinh Diem's rejection of free elections, a policy that has justly been called America's "original sin" in Vietnam.[5] Kennedy feared that military escalation would be "like taking a drink. The effect wears off, and you have to take another."[6] But Kennedy also believed in the domino theory, thanks in part to conceptual elaboration from his advisers: a Communist victory, wrote Walt Rostow, "would generate defeatism among governments and peoples in the non-Communist world."[7] Johnson, for his part, knew that "if I left the woman I loved [his ambitious 'Great Society' domestic plans] in order to get involved in that bitch of a war on the other side of the world, then I would lose everything at home."[8] Yet along with his conviction that abandoning Vietnam "would shake the confidence" of allies "from Berlin to Thailand . . . in the value of an American commitment and in the value of America's word," Johnson feared a domestic backlash. Another "who lost China?" debate could give rise to another bout of McCarthyism. Given the growing investment of American lives, this right-wing reaction could be even more virulent and destructive of American civility than the last one.[9]

Just as Johnson had feared, Vietnam destroyed his presidency and poisoned American politics. Its next presidential victim had been an early hawk, but by the time of his election in 1968, Richard Nixon had had the benefit of eight years of involuntary detachment from politics, and he recognized the war to be a mistake. Once in office, moreover, Nixon and his foreign-policy adviser, Henry Kissinger, attempted an ambitious restructuring of U.S. foreign policy that would prevent such mistakes in the future. The "Nixon Doctrine" gave notice that Communist insurgencies in other Third World nations would have to be battled by those nations themselves. The United States might give aid, but it would not supply ground forces. In the future, Nixon announced, U.S. interests "must shape our commitments, rather than the other way around."[10]

Yet even though, according to this thinking, Vietnam was a quagmire that should never have been entered, simple withdrawal was out of the question. Though it never should have been at stake there, American "credibility" could not now be sacrificed. Nixon tried to preserve this elusive commodity by gradually handing the war over to South Vietnamese troops. Conceptually his plan was very much in keeping with the Nixon Doctrine; in practice it prolonged the American war for four excruciating years without affecting the final outcome.

The trick, as Nixon and Kissinger had hoped to make it work, was to fit disengagement from Vietnam into a broader strategy of adjustment to the relative decline in American power; in other words, devolving to a new, multipolar "structure of peace" in which the United States continued to play a leading role, but one more commensurate with its resources. Part of the strategy was, in effect, to declare the Cold War's more dangerous phase to be over. Détente would not mean an end to Soviet-American competition, but that competition could be "normalized" by enmeshing Soviet power in a restraining web of threats and inducements, the latter to include a trading relationship and recognition of Soviet legitimacy as a world superpower. The most important element of this recognition would be to acknowledge and accept Soviet nuclear parity while at the same time using McNamara-style concepts of "nuclear sufficiency" to negotiate a stabilized arms race. The most important threat, on the other hand, would be the "China card," a belated American recognition of the strategic opportunities inherent in Sino-Soviet antagonism.

The plan, in its strategic audacity and theoretical insight, was impressive. But it ran into problems, most notably, the effect of Vietnam's trauma on Nixon's brittle personality, a mix that produced the bizarre denouement of Watergate. Thus although détente, the "Nixon Doctrine" and rapprochement with China were very much team efforts, Nixon's political self-destruction left the foreign-policy stage from 1969 to 1976 largely to his national security adviser and Secretary of State, Henry Kissinger. A focus exclusively on Kissinger cannot, of course, explain all the wrinkles of U.S. policy during this period. On the level of ideas, however, it goes a long way.

Henry Kissinger poses special complications for this study. Where do we place Kissinger—and his notions about the stability of containment—in relation to Kennan and Acheson?

At first glance, Kissinger belongs closer to Kennan.[11] Both men (to quote John Lewis Gaddis on Kennan) conceived strategies "based on a pessimistic view of the international order, but a degree of measured optimism as to the possibilities for restraining rivalries within it." Both men prescribed "making use of the organic equilibrium maintained by the very tensions inherent in the system."[12]

Yet, if we consider Kissinger's pronouncements and writings both during and after his period of service for two presidents, we find a pervasive gloom that seems at odds not only with Kennan's "measured optimism" about the possibilities for international equilibrium but, indeed, with Kissinger's own strategic planning. The repeated description of Kissinger's worldview as "Spenglerian" reportedly irritated him (and may fail to capture the complexity of either thinker). Nonetheless, one cannot help but observe Kissinger's pessimistic conservatism—a sense that the Western forces of order and stability were at odds with a disintegrating tendency as fundamental as entropy. This conservative gloom became particularly conspicuous in Kissinger's dealings with Western Europe.

Kissinger's pessimism must be seen, of course, as a consequence of his position in history. Whereas Kennan warned against ignoring the limits of American power, Kissinger served at a time when those limits were painfully obvious. Whatever principles of optimism détente contained in theory, détente in practice became a defensive strategy to manage the relative decline of American power. The Sino-Soviet split was one element on the side of optimism. But stalemate in Vietnam, Russia's emergence as a military (and notably nuclear) superpower, the antimilitary mood of Congress, Western economic trouble and Watergate all contributed to the general gloom.

To someone of Kissinger's philosophical bent, détente was bound to pose dangers under the best of circumstances. Like Acheson before him, Kissinger doubted the inherent discipline of the democracies. Any lessening of East-West tensions would tend to encourage an orgy of wishful thinking. Western publics had a difficult time grasping that negotiations were part of a continued strategy of containment, in which demonstrations of will were critically important. The West Europeans in particular were likely to confuse détente with a kind of "psychotherapy" against nuclear angst.[13] The process was likely to get out of control in the United States as well (as shown early in Nixon's presidency by the Senate's near-passage of the "Mansfield Amendment," which would have cut American troop levels in Europe in half.)

Whatever its inherent problems, however, détente was hardly an optional policy. Although he imposed his own intellectual framework, it was a reality that Kissinger inherited. Its starting point was probably the Kennedy-Khrushchev atmospheric nuclear test ban treaty, negotiated in the aftermath of the Cuban missile crisis. The Johnson administration proposed Strategic Arms Limitation Talks (SALT). NATO itself, in adopting the conclusions of the 1967 Harmel report, had formally declared détente to be a central purpose of the Alliance.

But Kissinger deemed it crucial that the United States (which is to say, he himself) be able to dominate the process and restrain a European "race to Moscow."[14] There were two allies in particular, France and West Germany, whom he saw as competitors in this race.

THE GAULLIST CHALLENGE

At a Paris state dinner in 1969—one of the first official meetings between presidents Nixon and Charles de Gaulle—the French president summoned Kissinger into his presence. "Why don't you get out of Vietnam?" de Gaulle asked. Kissinger replied that "a sudden withdrawal" could damage American credibility. "Where?" de Gaulle demanded; Kissinger suggested the Middle East. "How very odd," said the French president. "It is precisely in the Middle East that I thought your enemies had the credibility problem."[15]

This conversation conveys in a nutshell the great gap between French and American assessments of the international balance. There was a certain irony in Kissinger's relation to Gaullism. Before entering the White House, Kissinger had been highly critical of U.S. resistance to Gaullist independence, insisting that the United States need not and "could not expect to perpetuate the accident of Europe's postwar exhaustion into a permanent pattern of international relations."[16] Moreover, he said, "a united Europe is likely to insist on a specifically European view of world affairs—which is another way of saying that it will challenge American hegemony in Atlantic policy."[17] At the outset of Nixon's first term, Kissinger urged an agreeable president to dissociate himself from the prevailing Kennedy/Johnson administration hostility toward the general's ideas.[18]

Yet however much he admired de Gaulle in theory, the practice of Gaullism involved a degree of resistance to U.S. leadership that the policy-making Kissinger could not accept. The final section of this chapter will show him battling against the general's successors (de Gaulle retired in April 1969) and describing their neo-Gaullist diplomacy as a grave threat to Western unity.

In fact, the American-Gaullist conflict is arguably the most enduring theme of postwar U.S.-European relations. It has certainly survived the Soviet-American antagonism. And for the latter period of the Cold War it was a principal source of American pessimism.

De Gaulle's policies can be seen to rest on two rationales: (1) the absolute necessity for France to remain master of her own house, that is, independent of American hegemony; and (2) the conviction that France could *afford* this independence—that is to say, the struggle against American hegemony would not deliver France over to Soviet hegemony, because the Soviets were, in effect, too weak. For our present purposes, of course, the second rationale is the matter of most interest. It would be highly misleading, however, to suggest that Franco-American differences were based on nothing more than differing assessments of the Soviet threat. Such a focus would hardly do justice to de Gaulle, for why not play it safe and preserve Western unity above all? But that is not how he played it, and it is necessary to explore why.

At the heart of Franco-American difficulties were very different approaches to the concept of power. It is commonplace to say that Americans have traditionally opposed "balance-of-power" diplomacy as something anachronistically and even wickedly European. But it may be more useful to argue, even at the risk of oversimplifying, that American leaders have generally lacked any notion of power as an independent entity. Power is good or bad depending on whether it is in the hands of people who are good or bad. Power in Nazi or Soviet hands was bad; power in American hands was, by definition, good.

For de Gaulle the matter was rather more complicated. The soldier-statesman was also a moral philosopher "whose entire life was a meditation on the theme of mind, power and action," as one of his admirers has written.[19] De Gaulle believed in balance of power as a moral imperative in itself, because excessive power is dangerous regardless of who wields it. The possessor of excessive power has a tendency to lose touch with reality, with the sense of limits, to become, in other words, a victim of hubris. It is worth remembering that de Gaulle was constantly accused of wanting to become a dictator. He denied such aspirations, of course, but not by dwelling on democracy's virtues (it is difficult to know from reading de Gaulle whether he had any particular affection for democracy). The dictator, he said, inevitably loses a sense of his limits, it being "the destiny of all dictators to go too far in what they undertake."[20]

The same dynamic applied to nations. America's democratic vocation did not, in de Gaulle's mind, make its imperialism less dangerous. On the contrary: it made it all the more seductive to its victims. And the American view of world politics was dangerously untempered by that touch of Machiavellian cynicism that is often more accessible to considerations of reality.

Just as he warned against overweening power, de Gaulle worried about the dynamics of excessive weakness. Deference and weakness become habits, he argued. "For a great people to have the free disposition of itself and the means to struggle to preserve it is an absolute imperative," he declared in a famous press conference. For "if one spontaneously loses, even for a while, the free disposition of oneself, there is a strong risk of never regaining it."[21] De Gaulle had seen the results of a nation's habitual weakness firsthand. As an officer, academy instructor and, briefly at the very end, a government minister of the

Third Republic, he had watched in dismay as series of quarrelsome and unstable governments failed to come to grips with the predicament of a growing German threat. That it was his own theories on tank warfare that these governments failed to embrace cannot diminish the power of his critique. For his theories derived from an elementary observation: the practice of war would be revolutionized by the internal-combustion engine. Instead of listening, French politicians deferred to reactionary generals, hid behind the Maginot Line, hoped for salvation from Britain and, when the German *Blitzkrieg* came, collapsed like a house of cards.[22]

In refusing to accept the armistice, crossing to London and broadcasting defiance (thus committing, in strictest terms, treason), de Gaulle's first priority was always the recovery of French honor. That meant repeated assertion of France's "*rang*"—rank among its allies, who accused him of devoting more worry to the struggle against them than to the one against Hitler. There was some justice to the accusation. But there was a logic to de Gaulle's struggle. He realized that the contribution of the French Resistance and Free French forces abroad to defeating Germany would be marginal anyway. Their main task was to create the myth of a French nation that had never surrendered.

Weakness was never an excuse to behave that way, because, as stated before, it could become a habit. When some of his Free French colleagues in London became embarrassed by his arrogant behavior toward their British patrons, de Gaulle cabled this dictum: "Our greatness and our weakness lies solely in our inflexibility concerning the rights of France. We will need that inflexibility until we are on the far side of the Rhine." But the principle was hardly abandoned when the Allies crossed the Rhine; after his return to power in 1958, it set the pattern for de Gaulle's behavior, and also, in large part, the behavior of his successors, vis-à-vis the same Anglo-American allies.[23]

His various irritating activities are too numerous to cover except in catalogue form. He tried to force the West Germans to choose France as a favored ally over America; when the Bundestag sought to blur that choice by attaching a pro-American preamble to the 1963 Franco-German Treaty, de Gaulle lost interest in the whole project. He vetoed Britain's application to join the European Common Market, calling the United Kingdom a stalking horse for its American patrons. He refused to join the "multilateral force," an American scheme for pooling French, British and (some) U.S. nuclear forces. He resisted the U.S. flexible-response effort to coordinate and, hopefully, restrain a possible nuclear war. He even embraced, at least in part, a French nuclear doctrine that anticipated sabotaging flexible response. He flew to Canada to praise Quebecois separatism; to South America, where he invoked Latin solidarity; and to Phnom Penh, where he denounced America's war in

Vietnam. As American efforts to pay for that war started to put the dollar under strain, de Gaulle added to the pressure by suddenly demanding gold for France's dollar balances. He even sent French planes to haul it away, rather than following the standard practice of moving it to a French account but leaving it physically at Fort Knox. He set a new course for French policy in the Middle East, courting favor with the Arabs and repudiating France's 1956 guarantee to stand by Israel if Egypt once more tried to close the Straits of Tiran. (When Israeli foreign minister Abba Eban came on the eve of the Six-Day War to remind France of its promise, de Gaulle replied haughtily that he had not been in power then, so it was not really a promise of France.) And of course, de Gaulle in 1966 withdrew France from NATO's military command, expelling American troops and bases. While reaffirming France's formal alliance with the United States, he added ominously that should war come, France would *then* decide whether to participate. On the heels of this announcement, de Gaulle flew to Moscow, met Soviet leader Leonid Brezhnev, and elaborated on his vision of a "Europe from the Atlantic to the Urals"—that is, a Europe that included Russia but not America.

Gaullism was an affront, first and foremost, to American liberalism. There were dark mutterings, from American but also British Labour politicians, that de Gaulle had an authoritarian streak verging on fascism. Certainly his disdain for party politics sounded ominously familiar. After the war, during the first part of a 12-year exile from power, the suspicions seemed confirmed by his strange political rallies, stage managed by André Malraux, with Nuremberg-style lighting and Mussolini-style thugs.[24]

The fascism charge was harder to make stick, however, after he faced down a military coup of colonial officers appalled at his decision to grant Algerian independence. Even so, at a time when the Kennedy administration was pushing anti-Communist internationalism and European federalism, de Gaulle looked every bit the reactionary nationalist (and absurdly mystical, to boot; once, during the war, as General Eisenhower's political adviser tried to discuss a point of French politics, de Gaulle interrupted him: "What you say may be true, but I've been in France for a thousand years.")[25]

The more durable charge came from both American conservatives and liberals: notwithstanding the General's Catholic antipathy toward the Communists, Gaullism was a virulent strain of European neutralism. He had, it's true, from 1958 to 1962 advocated a harder line over Berlin that the Americans were willing to contemplate, and his support for the Americans during the Cuban missile crisis was reflexive and unconditional. But thereafter, his constant harping on the threat of American hegemony, his promotion of a Yalta myth whereby the United States and the Soviet Union had divided Europe, his sorcerer's-apprentice manipulations of anti-American prejudice—how could Gaullism be seen as anything but an intentional, ideological solvent for the Western Alliance?

American anger was justified on at least one level. De Gaulle accused Americans of stressing the unity of Western power because it justified U.S. hegemony. "In politics and in strategy, as in the economy," he said, "monopoly quite naturally appears to the person who holds it to be the best possible system."[26] But his own creed of divided leadership was equally self-serving, as it justified a greater role for France. De Gaulle's ideology seemed patently opportunistic: He turned on the Anglo-Saxons only after trying to join their club, proposing to Eisenhower a three-power directorate to control the West's nuclear weapons. Moreover, it was doubly irritating to Americans that he played the game of independence while continuing to benefit from a happy fact of geography: West Germany, loaded down with U.S. troops and weapons, stood between France and the Red Army.

And yet it is impossible not to admire the man and his works. For all his supposed atavistic views, de Gaulle transformed France, modernizing her economy, replacing an unwieldy parliamentary system with a stable, presidential one and endowing the French with a reasonable sense of their place and responsibilities in the world. Certainly the French are today much closer to the Americans—in their resistance to pacifism and appreciation for the occasional necessity for military force—than are the Germans. The catalogue of de Gaulle's anti-American sins was presented above in the brutal form in which it appeared to most Americans at the time. Yet most, if not all, of his actions fit into a coherent strategy of national renewal that, arguably, made France into a better ally (that argument is too lengthy for this space, but will be elaborated upon in chapter 5.)

Furthermore, (and this brings us back to Gaullism's other basic rationale), if de Gaulle was essentially correct about the waning Soviet threat, then his neutralist posturing takes on a considerably less ominous cast. "In 1958 I considered that the world situation was very different from what it had been at the time of the creation of NATO," he would later write, recalling the year of his return to power.

> It now seemed fairly unlikely that the Soviets would set out to conquer the West, at a time when all the Western nations were back on an even keel and making steady material progress. Communism, whether it rises from within or irrupts from without, has little chance of taking root without the help of some national calamity. The Kremlin knows this very well.[27]

To impose "the totalitarian yoke" on 300 million West Europeans had to look daunting, he added, "when it was difficult enough to hold down a third as many people" in Eastern Europe. Moreover, given America's nuclear arsenal, "what madness it would be," in de Gaulle's analysis, for Moscow to launch a global war that might end in its own destruction.

"But if one does not make war, one must sooner or later make peace"— thus did de Gaulle signal his conviction that a Cold War settlement was possible and at hand.[28] He claims this insight for 1958; the claim is postdated, so we cannot be sure, but it is consistent with his general worldview. Of course, 1958 was not the beginning of a détente, but rather of a long and traumatic crisis over Berlin and the Cuban missiles. Yet the insight, whenever it came to him, was shrewd. Four years after he became president, the torments and uncertainties of Berlin were settled, in brutal fashion, via the Berlin Wall. From that moment forward, the Soviet Union became a status-quo power—such was the essence of de Gaulle's analysis. The Soviets themselves may not have appreciated this watershed; certainly they hoped to continue expanding their power in the Third World. Yet objectively analyzed, the Soviet Union became a status-quo power because important changes to the status quo were more likely to hurt Russia than the West.

De Gaulle's vision was acute because of, not in spite of, his nineteenth-century worldview. Where the more modern Americans saw ideologies, de Gaulle saw "eternal" nations and he assumed that national feeling would outlast Communism. Like Kennan, de Gaulle saw the Soviet Union as an old-style Russian empire, severely overstretched. East European nationalism would inevitably revive; the Soviets could repress it by force, as in Budapest in 1956, but that necessity would make the occupied dominions a long-term weakness rather than a strength.

Moreover, the Soviet Union faced a threat from China that was more immediate. China was linked to Moscow only by the very thin reed of ideology. Indeed, one might argue that, in the nature of conformist ideologies, shared allegiance to Communism was the most combustible fuel of their enmity. Like sixteenth-century Christians, Russians and Chinese soon began to rant at each other's alleged heresies. But as the Sino-Soviet conflict gathered in intensity, the ancient, nationalist jealousies of Asia's two major land powers took precedence.

Again, de Gaulle's stress on the primacy of nationality made him far more attuned, far earlier than the Americans, to the significance of the Sino-Soviet schism. It made nonsense of the notion of a "world Communism" that had to be fought in Vietnam. De Gaulle claimed he had warned Kennedy as early as 1961 that Vietnam would be for America as it had been for France an excruciating and pointless quagmire.[29] He certainly said so publicly in 1964.

The Americans would have done well to listen. Instead, they saw themselves to be fighting first the Chinese (a branch of world Communism) and then, when the Sino-Soviet split became too obvious to ignore, the Russians.

De Gaulle's actual détente policies were, in relation to the conceptions and rhetoric behind them, modest affairs. He took a first stab in 1944 with a somewhat comical trip to Moscow, where he tried to interest Stalin in a revival of the 1892 and 1935 Franco-Russian alliances.[30] Stalin snubbed him, and the de Gaulle of the early Cold War became a consummate Cold Warrior. In the mid-1960s, however, he returned to intensive Soviet diplomacy: An exchange of foreign ministers was followed by de Gaulle's withdrawal from NATO and, four months later, his solemn state visit to Moscow. With gathering conviction, he expressed hopes for a French-led, European détente that would dissolve the opposing blocs and bring national independence to Eastern Europe.[31] The Soviet invasion of Prague poured cold water on such hopes. Soon after, de Gaulle retired, thus leaving the world stage before he could do anything to directly annoy Dr. Kissinger. But the principles of Gaullism remained the foundation of French foreign policy.[32] The Gaullist opposition to U.S. hegemony and the idea of France as Russia's privileged Western partner would unnerve American leaders mightily throughout the ensuing decade.

OSTPOLITIK

Another European détente policy was even more worrying to the Americans, because it involved West Germany (strategically more important than France) and because it was based on a recognition of Soviet strength (rather than the Gaullist confidence in Soviet weakness). Willy Brandt's *Ostpolitik* posed a question that would reverberate throughout the German-American dialogue for 20 years: When does a recognition of reality become appeasement?

Brandt's answer was that "realities can be influenced for the better only if they are taken into account."[33] The primary reality had been dramatized by the Berlin Wall: The Soviet Union had an iron grip on Eastern Europe and a large chunk of Germany. The Adenauer-Acheson policy of "negotiation from strength" still showed no hope of dislodging the Communist occupiers.[34]

In the late 1960s the German Socialists finally got their chance to try a more flexible approach. Brandt became foreign minister of Kurt Georg Kiesinger's "grand coalition," Christian Democratic–Socialist government in December 1966. He assumed the chancellorship, in coalition with the smaller Liberal party, in 1969.

Brandt brought to office some complex baggage, both personal and ideological. A protege of Berlin mayor Ernst Reuter, and mayor himself when the Wall went up, Brandt was a leader of Social Democratic Party (SPD) reformism who embraced free markets and steered the party away from Schumacher's utopian illusions. He also believed that opposition to Stalin required unalloyed allegiance to the Americans—in the heyday of the Berlin "spy war," for example, Berlin Socialists had been enthusiastic partners of the CIA. However, Brandt and his party colleagues were also unhappy that Stalin's 1952 proposal for negotiations on reunification had not been treated more seriously. The rigidity of Adenauer's policies became one of Brandt's favorite political targets. "The German policy laid down by Konrad Adenauer made no allowance for any testing of this offer to negotiate—not even so as to counter subsequent accusations that a potential avenue had been left unexplored," Brandt later would complain. Adenauer, "with the American fear of German and European uncertainties at his back, had no wish to be delayed in his progress toward military links with Western Europe and the Atlantic Powers."[35]

For the Germans, these Cold War dilemmas were tangled up with painful burdens of national identity. Perhaps Konrad Adenauer, a conservative Rhineland Catholic, had been ideally suited to maintain a necessary balance: repudiating the Nazi past while avoiding offense to the continuing heavy patriotism of many Germans. Brandt was, in this regard, a more problematic figure. When Hitler came to power Brandt had fled Germany for Norway. During the 1960s, as a Socialist leader trying to become chancellor, he repeatedly had to battle allegations that he had fought in a Norwegian uniform against his homeland. As the first postwar chancellor to visit Poland, his spectacular gesture of falling to his knees on the site of the Warsaw ghetto stirred admiration across the world but considerable resentment at home. The single most traumatic hurdle that he helped his often unwilling countrymen to surmount was the recognition that roughly one-fourth of pre-Hitler Germany—the old East Prussia—would never be re-gained. The 1970 Polish-German treaty, recognizing the Oder-Neisse line as Germany's ultimate eastern frontier, was *Ostpolitik*'s most bitter pill. "It surrenders nothing that was not gambled away long ago," Brandt pleaded on television the night of its signing.[36] But many Germans would never forgive him.

At the same time, however, and somewhat paradoxically, Brandt made himself the spokesman of a more assertive Germany. The new leadership was secure enough in its anti-Nazi credentials that it could not be "blackmailed" with reminders of the past, said Brandt's close adviser, Egon Bahr, years later. "This chancellor considered himself to have been liberated rather than defeated at the end of the war."[37] The new perspective had some definitive consequences for *Ostpolitik*. It meant, as Brandt put it, "that, while remaining in touch with our allies and retaining their confidence, we became the advocates of our own interests vis-à-vis the governments of Eastern Europe."[38]

By 1972, Brandt's diplomacy had produced treaties with the Soviet Union, Czechoslovakia, Poland and East Germany. The four occupying powers in Berlin had signed an agreement that secured Western access to West Berlin and finally brought a degree of normality to that highly abnormal city. The Federal Republic's agreement with East Germany established a formula—two states in one nation—for reconciling their seemingly irreconcilable claims to legitimacy. The fruits of this intra-German normalization proved highly popular in West Germany. Divided families were able to visit one another—not without hassle, to be sure, but with some degree of regularity. A formalized system of bribes from the Federal Republic to the East produced a small stream of exit visas for Easterners to settle in the West.

Ostpolitik was considerably less popular in Washington. American officials could hardly oppose it, however, for the simple reason that most of the diplomatic initiatives were manifestly in the American interest. The Berlin agreement, which required the Americans' active participation and assent, was on one level an extraordinary concession by the Soviets—they were formally relinquishing an outstanding source of leverage over the West. In the other treaties between West Germany and various Eastern powers, the West Germans were signalling that they would no longer play the hardest of hardliners acting to stall America's own détente schemes.

Nonetheless, U.S. officials grumbled. At first the Americans complained that Brandt was simply moving too fast, assuming too much independence "while the Allies are on the sidelines," as Nixon put it.[39] Eventually Brandt bowed to these complaints and accepted an American-imposed "linkage": the Moscow treaty would be delayed until the Soviets made more concessions on Berlin. But Kissinger, for one, remained worried on more fundamental grounds. He could happily endorse "Brandt's wrenching decision to recognize the division of his country" as a "courageous recognition of reality." But Kissinger discerned an overall strategy—using that recognition "as a means to achieve German *unity* by building good relations with the East and turning the Federal Republic into a magnet for Eastern Europe"—and this strategy filled him with foreboding. "The question in our minds," he would later write, "was which side of the dividing line would in fact be the magnet. We feared that over time, at first imperceptibly, the Communist world would wind up in the stronger position." The other European allies were questionable enough, but Bonn's reliability was further compromised by the fact that the Soviets had control over roughly 17 million East Germans. Kissinger conceded that the Federal Republic was unlikely to leave NATO, but he did fear a "creeping dissociation" from those American and Western policies that were not directly concerned with defending the central front in Europe.[40]

Kissinger took particular exception to the description of *Ostpolitik* by Bahr, one of its principle architects. The two men had long private conversations in which Bahr frankly described *Ostpolitik* as a West German response to the end of American strategic superiority. "With Soviet strategic missiles, America was vulnerable for the first time in its history," is what Bahr has recalled saying to Kissinger.

> There [was] now a strategic balance and that meant that America would think twice before risking its own existence. Would America answer with nuclear missiles if the Russians took Hamburg? The answer [was] no. So détente was our only option.[41]

In such conversations Kissinger saw confirmed his most dire suspicions. "Europe's conventional inferiority," he would later write, "would dictate a 'political' solution—an elegant phrase for accommodation to Soviet power."[42]

It is important, conceptually, to distinguish Kissinger's worries about *Ostpolitik* from criticism directed against the morality of Bonn's policies. In his recent history of West German *Ostpolitik*, Timothy Garton Ash charges leaders of both major West German parties with an indifference to the plight of Eastern dissidents that grew in proportion to Bonn's stake in good East-West relations.[43] But that was not the concern that Kissinger expressed: He was bothered more by the West's potential for being geostrategically weakened than by the prospect of its being morally compromised.

Of course, barely 25 years after World War II, it was not only scenarios of German weakness that made people nervous. There were also dark fantasies of German nationalism erupting anew as the Germans rediscovered their eastern vocation. In Kissinger's view, *Ostpolitik* conformed to an ominous historical pattern: "From Bismarck to Rapallo it was the essence of Germany's nationalist foreign policy to maneuver freely between East and West."[44] This Rapallo analogy was a loaded one, invoking as it did memories of the many-layered Russo-German collaboration of the 1920s, which, in certain respects, had laid a practical basis for the later Hitler-Stalin Pact. The French, not surprisingly, were most sensitive to these memories. Brandt's *Ostpolitik* provoked such alarms in Paris that de Gaulle's successor, Georges Pompidou, decided it was time to reestablish an Anglo-French counterweight to German ambitions. As one consequence, the United Kingdom was finally allowed into the European Community.[45]

Rapallo analogies did not, in fact, bear up to serious analysis. Rapallo had been a marriage of desperation for Europe's two isolated powers: defeated

Germany and the Bolshevik Russia. Whatever strains NATO might suffer, it was hard to imagine the Federal Republic of Germany experiencing any comparable isolation. Likewise, comparing Brandt to Bismarck was well off the mark. Brandt's version of German unity was more cultural than political; it was pre-Bismarckian.

Yet there is no denying that Brandt represented a departure from the reassuring West Germany of Adenauer's creation. For Adenauer, the dark spirits of German history all came from or somehow involved the East. His solution was Germany's spiritual anchoring along the Rhine and the Atlantic. Brandt had every reason and, manifestly, every desire to reaffirm these Western connections. But they were not only an end in themselves; rather they offered a measure of protection and reassurance for *Ostpolitik*. From 1970 on, by increasing degree, Germany once again became a central European power, with interests and ambitions on both sides.

THE YEAR OF UNRAVELLING

Nixon's first term coincided with a sea change in the global power structure. At the same time that U.S. military superiority over the Soviets was slipping away, America's economic preeminence was also eroding. In 1971, the United States suffered its first trade deficit in one hundred years. The beneficiaries in this case were America's allies, especially the World War II losers, Germany and Japan.

The postwar recovery of Japan and Europe was as welcome as it was inevitable. But it meant a shift in relative economic power that was bound to cause strains. While this book can only gloss over these strains, one should keep in mind that they posed an extra burden on transatlantic relations during all the years of this study.

An early American response to this shift came in a series of "Nixon shocks" (so dubbed by the Japanese, whose trade-based economy was especially vulnerable to them). Nixon decided it was time to pursue American interests more explicitly—to abandon the gentlemanly rules that had heretofore governed allied economic relations. The growing conventional wisdom was that those rules had put the United States at a disadvantage. Especially onerous, in this American view, was the dollar-based international monetary system, under which a permanently overvalued dollar gave foreign-produced goods a competitive advantage. The American currency was under severe pressure anyway, partly because spending for the Vietnam war and Johnson's Great Society had never been matched by tax increases. Nixon cut the system loose from its moorings. He devalued the dollar, suspended its gold convertibility (forever, as it turned out), and, finally, let the U.S. currency float free.

The Europeans had been unhappy under the old system. To maintain dollar parity, their central banks had been obligated to buy up excess dollars. The net effect, according to one influential view, was that they expanded their monetary base and imported U.S. inflation.[46] But they did not like the new, floating-rate system any better. Despite its chronic weakness, the dollar remained the world's standard currency. Now its gyrations were to wipe out an important element of predictability, turning international trade and finance into something like a giant casino.

The closing of the gold window came in a package of measures that the Nixon administration unveiled in August 1971 under the rubric of a "new economic policy." The package included wage and price controls at home and a temporary, 10-percent surcharge on goods from abroad. The surcharge was intended as a bargaining chip as the United States sought to negotiate a new monetary system. This economic nationalism was directed and personified by Nixon's new treasury secretary, former Texas governor John Connally. Connally was decidedly not a member of the East Coast foreign-policy establishment. The Democrat turned Republican, whom Nixon evidently saw as his successor, was, in his straight-talking gruffness, well-suited to deliver the message that new rules were now in force.

He was also, at a time of economic turmoil, the only member of the Nixon administration who came close to rivalling Kissinger in the making of foreign policy. Kissinger, an acknowledged "neophyte" on these matters, turned to his own staff for economic lessons. He later reported that his first reaction to the Connally-inspired mercantilism had been "agnostic," but that he then started to worry that a lengthy economic dispute might have an "unsettling impact" on Alliance cohesion.[47] There was a risk that economic conflict would ruin his chances of getting Europe to follow the American lead on détente—a tricky business in Kissinger's view since, when the Europeans weren't flirting on the edge of appeasement, they were fretting about America selling them down the river in a kind of "super Yalta."

Vietnam imposed another burden on U.S.-European relations in this period. Vietnam was not just a burden but an obsession—no history of American diplomacy can be anything but misleading if it fails to take into account that the war was taking up the lion's share of Nixon's and Kissinger's attention. American offensives—the 1970 "incursion" into Cambodia; the 1972 Christmas bombing of Hanoi—provoked not just civil upheaval in the United States but also open criticism from Europe's leaders. Kissinger was aggrieved and Nixon furious at this criticism.[47]

In early 1973, after the Paris Agreements ended America's part in the Indochina war, Nixon and Kissinger decided it was time for renewed attention to the Atlantic Alliance. They proposed a "new Atlantic Charter" under which the allies would proclaim renewed common purposes and, hopefully, dispel some of the worrisome ambiguities that had crept into their partnership. They called it "the Year of Europe."

The "Year of Europe" turned into a fiasco. The exercise seemed silly and patronizing. Kissinger's speech unveiling the initiative offended European sensibilities by underlining the gap between America's global role and Europe's regional interests. (Kissinger insisted that European press criticisms missed the point—that he was *deploring* the situation.) Drafting of the "charter" became an occasion for more resentment. French foreign minister Michel Jobert appointed himself spokesman for the Europeans as well as a kind of guardian against suspected American designs to further U.S. hegemony. Kissinger, thoroughly exasperated by Jobert's wily tactics, decided that the Frenchman was attempting "to pursue the old Gaullist dream of building Europe on an anti-American basis."[49]

At a May meeting in Iceland, Pompidou sarcastically reminded Nixon that "for Europeans every year is the year of Europe." The French president was dying of cancer; excessive graciousness was probably too much to expect. But in 1973 Kissinger perceived that most allied leaders were showing progressively less respect for the U.S. president as the self-inflicted wound of Watergate drained more political blood. That summer Nixon found himself snubbed in his efforts to organize a summit of allied leaders to polish his foreign-policy credentials.

This, then, was the tense background to a crisis that brought U.S.-European relations to a new low. The October 1973 Arab-Israeli War proved to be a case study in the organic connection of crises, combining a Soviet-American nuclear face-off, another lurid episode in the Watergate drama, an economic revolution against the industrialized West, and a virtual shouting match among NATO allies.

Kissinger's pessimism about the alliance hit bottom at this time. He got to see neo-Gaullism in action, and he was dismayed at Western Europe's "stampede of dissociation" from American support for Israel[50] and the subsequent dissension over Kissinger's project to forge a common front against OPEC.

The October War was to strain U.S.-European relations for years to come. On the U.S. side, it was remembered as a kind of parable about the essential duplicity and cowardice of America's NATO partners. And yet if we examine this parable with any care—against the backdrop of Kissinger's Mideast diplomacy, the Arab-Israeli conflict and the October War itself—the supposed moral starts to become murky.

One ambiguous aspect is that despite Kissinger's dismay over the consequences of European "appeasement," America's position in the Middle East strengthened more or less steadily from the 1967 war onwards. It is true enough that OPEC's oil blackmail provided a nerve-wracking reminder of the West's economic dependence on sometimes hostile energy suppliers. But the economic troubles of the 1970s were only partly due to these oil shocks, and the industrialized world's demand for oil turned out to be surprisingly flexible (see chapter 6). Use of the oil weapon therefore had the ironic effect of rendering it less formidable. Meanwhile U.S. diplomacy effectively expelled Soviet power from the region. Detaching Egypt from the Soviet orbit and pulling it into America's amounted to a genuine diplomatic revolution.

Kissinger himself deserves much of the credit, for consolidating a subtle change in U.S. policy toward Israel that had started some 20 months after the 1956 Suez misadventure.[51] Suez had underscored the ambivalence of the U.S. relationship with Israel, a relationship considered by many U.S. policymakers to be a political and, perhaps, moral necessity; but, as the source of Arab radicalization and gravitation toward the Soviets, it was also considered a strategic liability. By the time of Israel's victory in the June 1967 war, however, this American attitude had changed, albeit unevenly. The old view continued to dominate the State Department, but the White House, under both Johnson and Nixon, was more inclined to see the Israeli position as an American asset.[52] The Johnson administration, at a time when the hopelessness of Vietnam had started to sink in, was quite willing "to bask"—as Conor Cruise O'Brien puts it—in the "reflected glory" of an Israeli triumph involving American weapons against Soviet-armed Arabs.[53]

The Nixon administration in its first term was preoccupied with Vietnam and tended to leave Mideast policy to the State Department, which tried—to no apparent avail—to appear "evenhanded." When Kissinger replaced William Rogers as secretary of state, however, he brought a more Machiavellian design to U.S. policy. Kissinger deemed not only Israeli power but also its intransigence to be an exploitable asset. The Arabs had to be convinced that alliance with the Soviet Union offered them no hope of regaining any of their occupied territories. Only the United States could exert a subtle enough pressure to make Israel budge.[54]

Kissinger's strategy worked. Anwar Sadat, who replaced Nasser as Egypt's president, rapidly realized that the road back to Sinai went through Washington, not Moscow.

A second ambiguity of the "parable" of the October War—again in regard to alleged European "appeasement" of the Arabs—concerns blame for the war. It is my conviction that the principal cause of the Arab-Israeli conflict has been the unremitting hostility of Arabs toward Israel's very existence. I will make no effort to justify this statement (it would require another book). However, although it began with a surprise Egyptian/Syrian attack, the October War is the one out of five wars for which *Israel* shares much of the blame.[55] I mean "blame" in the limited sense that Israel had some opportunity to avoid war, an opportunity that came in the form of an 1971 Egyptian peace offer. In fact, it is difficult to really blame the Israelis for distrusting a single peace feeler amid a continuing chorus of hate. It turns out, however, that the offer *was* genuine, and that fact must be considered when we assess the Europeans' Arab sympathies.

It is instructive to compare the October War with the Six-Day War of June 1967, in which Israel struck the first blow. That blow came after weeks of anti-Israel hysteria, hysteria that, for any historically minded Jew, must have seemed like a plausible prelude to annihilation. Syrian radio had been goading Egypt's Nasser for his cowardice, accusing him of hiding behind the UN troops that were deployed, after the Suez War, as part of the settlement separating the combatants. Nasser, in response, kicked out the UN troops, sent 80,000 of his own forces into the Sinai, and once more closed the Gulf of Aqaba to Israeli shipping, an act that Israel had always made clear would be regarded as casus belli. Yet Prime Minister Eshkol of Israel sent out repeated signals of reassurance both to Syria and to Egypt: Israel had no aggressive intentions. Israel's apparent desire to avoid war led Nasser to believe that he could threaten the Jewish state with impunity. He made clear that the challenge was to Israel's existence.[56] As O'Brien notes: "Nasser was in fact nothing like Hitler, but he managed to *sound* very much like Hitler, in his broadcast speeches. The responsive roars of the crowd sounded like Nuremberg rallies."[57] Meanwhile Israeli foreign minister Abba Eban made a tour of Paris, London and Washington—guarantee powers for the 1956 settlement—and got a collective shrug for his trouble. De Gaulle, as we have already seen, was especially dismissive. He warned Israel not to fire first.

Israel ignored this advice. Early on June 5, its planes swept in low from the sea to destroy the better part of Egypt's air force. The war was effectively won, but Jordan and Syria, misled by Cairo's surreal propaganda, joined in Egypt's "victory." The Jordanian king Hussein apparently believed that three-fourths of the *Israeli* air force had been destroyed.[58] Six days later, when a cease-fire took effect, Israel had captured the Sinai up to the Suez Canal, the Gaza Strip, East Jerusalem, the West Bank of the Jordan River and Syria's Golan Heights.

Immediately after the war, Israel's Eshkol government informed the United States that it wanted formal peace—that is, final recognition from the

Arabs—and some border modifications to ensure security, but that it was also prepared to concede the return of most captured territory. This seemed to represent a consensus within the country (although there certainly would have been trouble over the West Bank, and Jerusalem was non-negotiable).[59] It certainly accorded with the original Israeli interpretation of the United Nations Security Council's famous Resolution 242. It also seemed in line with Defense Minister Moshe Dayan's West Bank occupation regime, which left the Arab populations there under continued Jordanian control, for most civil matters.

The Arabs, on the other hand, swore publicly and solemnly to one another that they would neither recognize, nor negotiate with, nor make any kind of peace with Israel. Nasser, in early 1969, launched a war of attrition against the Israeli occupiers on the Suez Canal's east bank. The Israelis retaliated with bombing raids deep inside Egypt. In January 1970 Nasser appealed to Moscow for SAM-3 air defense missiles with Russian crews. When Brezhnev balked, Nasser threatened to resign and "hand over to a pro-American President."[60] His threat worked: The Soviets sent in missiles, missile crews, and military advisers. It was a major escalation of superpower involvement and a significant military shift against Israel.

Within a year, however, Nasser had died, and Egypt got its "pro-American President," although Anwar Sadat took some time to show these colors. Much more quickly he signalled a watershed reassessment of policy toward Israel. On February 4, 1971, Sadat announced "that if Israel withdrew her forces in Sinai to the Passes, I would be willing to reopen the Suez Canal; to have my forces cross to the East Bank . . . to make a solemn declaration of a cease-fire; to restore diplomatic relations with the United States; and to sign a peace agreement with Israel." It was, in essence, the peace treaty that Israel and Egypt were to sign seven years later. Kissinger, for one, strongly urged Israel to explore the offer in 1971. At the time, however, Israel was too suspicious and its government too divided (a perennial Israeli problem) to grasp the olive branch.

Sadat, who for his own political survival desperately needed to recover the Sinai and use of the Suez Canal, decided that only another war could jolt the Israelis out of their inertia. There have been some highly controversial suggestions that Kissinger actually encouraged Sadat's decision (whether explicitly or in code).[61] It is, at any rate, clear enough from Kissinger's memoirs that the American secretary of state viewed Sadat's war to be more or less forced upon him.

On Yom Kippur, October 6, 1973, Egyptian and Syrian troops attacked Israeli positions along the Suez Canal and Golan Heights. The attack achieved its intended surprise, as Israel had failed to mobilize and declined, or failed, to preempt the attack. Israeli leaders asked the United States to stall a Security Council cease-fire resolution for the two or three days needed to gain the

offensive and push Arab forces back to prewar lines. Kissinger readily agreed, explaining afterward that it would be a "geopolitical disaster" for the United States if Arab armies with Soviet arms regained any of their occupied territory by force. By October 9, however, it became apparent that Israeli forces were in real trouble. The Syrian army, though suffering heavy casualties, remained intact; Egypt's army was proving fierce. Israel had lost 49 planes and 500 tanks and suddenly faced the prospect of a long war of attrition that a tiny country, surrounded by massed enemies, could not hope to win.[62]

The United States started a low-key resupply to Israel and learned of a larger Soviet airlift to Syria. On October 12, after a week of war, the White House realized that Israel still had not broken the stalemate, and Nixon approved a full-scale airlift. Finally, after another perilous week, Israel was able to drive into Syria and to establish a bridgehead on the west bank of the Suez. Kissinger flew to Moscow, reached a cease-fire agreement with Brezhnev, flew from Moscow to Tel Aviv and obtained the consent of a traumatized Israeli government.

Then came the events that give this story much of its moral ambiguity. By the time the cease-fire took effect, Israeli forces had very nearly encircled the Egyptian Third Army on the east bank of the Suez. Having suffered 2,000 casualties and a vivid reminder of its national vulnerability, Israel could not resist the temptation to destroy the trapped Egyptian forces. The cease-fire disintegrated; Israeli forces cut the last supply root to Suez city and thus completely surrounded the Third Army. For Kissinger, who throughout the war had been in frequent contact with Sadat, this situation portended a kind of disaster well-known to history, arising from the immoderation of war aims. Sadat would not survive the loss of his army. And if Sadat fell, Kissinger was certain that his replacement would be more radical, more pro-Soviet, and less amenable to a long-term peace.[63]

For two days the Americans pressed Israel to stop fighting. Then a desperate Sadat appealed to the Soviet Union and to the United States to send troops to Egypt to enforce the cease-fire. Brezhnev, on the night of October 24, sent a letter warning Nixon that if the United States declined to join this peacekeeping force, the Soviets would send troops unilaterally. Intelligence reports indicated that the Soviets had stopped their airlift to Syria, implying that they were grouping planes to carry airborne troops that had been placed on alert. Eight An-22 transport planes were ready to fly from Budapest to Egypt within hours. East German troops were also to go on alert status. The Americans judged that the Warsaw Pact could fly 5,000 troops daily into Egypt.

The United States, determined to resist the reintroduction of Soviet troops into Egypt (Sadat had politely expelled most Russian advisers one year earlier), ostentatiously called its own military alert and warned Brezhnev that "we could in no event accept unilateral action," which would "produce incalculable consequences." The Americans also stopped pressing Israel to observe the cease-fire, since the White House did not want to give the impression of having caved in to Soviet blackmail.[64]

The crisis abated. By the next morning, Egypt withdrew its appeal for a joint Soviet-American force, and Soviet preparations for a troop lift appeared to wind down. Another cease-fire took hold. And after considerable American badgering, Israel allowed a truck convoy carrying food, water and medicine to resupply the trapped Third Army.

In his account of the October War, Kissinger presents himself managing the crisis by careful attention to the delicate nuance of American interests. Israel could not lose to Arab armies bearing Soviet arms, but neither could it achieve a victory that ruined Sadat. The Soviet Union had been pushed out of the Mideast under cover of détente; it could not be allowed back in under any pretext, notwithstanding that its motives for intervention, according to Kissinger, were to defend a slipping strategic position.[65] Adding to the ambiguity is Kissinger's attitude about the war's author. Not only does he admire Sadat without restraint; he praises the Egyptian president's decision to launch the war as a supreme act of statesmanship. Sadat, in his view, had gone to war not to win back territory, but to create a psychological shock that would make both Arabs and Israelis more serious about seeking peace. The Israelis needed to be shocked out of their complacent sense of military invincibility. The Egyptians needed to be liberated from their burning sense of national humiliation, a humiliation that rendered them incapable of diplomatic flexibility. It was, according to Kissinger, an extremely rare case of a statesman who fought a war "to lay the basis for moderation in its aftermath."[66]

It is hard not to share Kissinger's appreciation of Sadat, who was later to be murdered for his troubles. How, then, should we judge the attempt by European governments to distance themselves from an American-Israeli military partnership against Egypt? Their view of the matter was perhaps less nuanced than Kissinger's: They saw Arab armies fighting on what was internationally recognized to be Arab territory, trying to win it back. "Is the attempt to put one's foot back into one's own house necessarily a surprising act of aggression?" asked French foreign minister Michel Jobert on October 8.[67]

From the first day of the war, Britain and France resisted American appeals for a common Security Council position for "return to the status quo ante." Jobert, Gaullism's standard-bearer and Kissinger's special European antagonist, gave a speech to the French National Assembly blaming Israel for blocking peace and the United States and the Soviet Union for supplying the belligerents. This speech particularly riled Kissinger, in whose view Jobert had postulated "the moral equivalence of the two sides—the intellectual presupposition of European neutralism." Excepting Portugal, the Netherlands and the FRG, all NATO allies banned use of facilities on their soil or overflight of their territories by American planes airlifting supplies to Israel. And after the October 22 cease-fire disintegrated, West German officials informed Washington that they too could no longer accept the shipment of American equipment to Israel via German ports. The American alert, involving U.S. forces on European bases, worsened the Alliance tensions.[68]

These tensions deepened even further over the subsequent months of an OPEC oil embargo, production cuts and price explosions. At Sadat's behest, OPEC divided Western oil consumers into three groups. It imposed a total embargo against the United States and the Netherlands (which had criticized the Egyptian-Syrian attack). The United Kingdom and France, deemed pro-Arab, enjoyed an uninterrupted flow. Supplies to the rest of the world were to be reduced by 5 percent per month until Israel withdrew from the occupied territories. Western Europe did not respond with conspicuous unity or heroism. Instead, there was a series of bilateral negotiations with oil producers and an ostentatious diffidence about sharing supplies with the Dutch. However, the fact of the matter was that the large oil companies ignored OPEC and distributed supplies more or less evenly.[69]

The embargo was temporary, its impact largely psychological. The price hikes were another matter. On October 16, six Gulf oil producers raised their reference price for a barrel of crude oil from $3.01 to $5.12. On December 22 OPEC ministers meeting in Teheran boosted the price again to $11.65. The issue of Western support for Israel proved to be a political engine by which oil producers achieved a revolution in their terms of trade. Economists still debate the degree to which the oil shocks were responsible for a decade of economic malaise in the industrialized West. Clearly, however, this expanded share of national incomes devoted to oil purchases played some significant role in boosting the general price level and depressing demand throughout the 1970s and early 1980s.

Kissinger, conscious of these implications, in late December proposed a Washington energy conference to form a consumers' cartel against OPEC. Jobert, in opposition, pushed for a "European-Arab" dialogue. Kissinger thought he had won the battle in early February, when the Washington conference convened and Japan plus all the Europeans except France backed a U.S. plan for an International Energy Agency. The next month, however, Jobert won his compensating victory when the European Community decided on a series of European-Arab consultations to prepare for a foreign ministers meeting. Thus, in Kissinger's view, the Europeans made clear that whatever they had agreed to in Washington, they did not intend to confront the Arabs. It demonstrated the "demoralization—verging on abdication—of the democracies" and a readiness to choose "among varieties of appeasement."[70]

But this form of indictment leaves open the question of how the Europeans would have behaved if they had not already supported at least some of the Arab demands even in the absence of any blackmail. The Europeans were consistently clear in their belief that Israel should return to its 1967 borders. Kissinger admitted that this European view had some merit. But he argued that in an "emergency," allies "have an obligation to subordinate their differences to the realization that the humiliation of the ally who, for better or worse, is *most* strategically placed to affect the outcome weakens the structure of common defense and the achievement of joint purposes."[71]

Yet, what should define an "emergency" as a distinct period when willingness to acknowledge "a specifically European view of world affairs" is suspended? Any confrontation involving Soviet troops? That was only a brief part of the story, lasting a few hours on the night of October 25.

What is obvious is that in 1973 Kissinger felt deeply the crisis of American leadership. The October War coincided with one of the most dramatic moments of the Watergate affair, the so-called Saturday Night Massacre, in which Nixon's firing of Special Prosecutor Archibald Cox was followed by the resignations of Attorney General Elliot Richardson and Deputy Attorney General William Ruckelshaus. Congress had just passed the War Powers Act, restricting presidential authority to deploy troops in foreign combat. Kissinger was convinced that this was a time of maximum weakness when America's allies should have understood that it was in their interest to support rather than to undermine NATO's leadership.

My point here is not to argue that Kissinger was entirely wrong in this view. Nor am I attempting to absolve European behavior in response to oil blackmail. Nor am I endorsing the view, widespread in Europe, that Israeli policies constituted the major obstacle to peace. I am only suggesting that the indictment of European cravenness would be more persuasive if the political and moral issues surrounding this particular episode, the 1973 war, were clearer.[72] The obvious retort is that aside from a direct military threat against a NATO member, there would always be a degree of moral and political ambiguity to international confrontations. Perhaps, then, a more modest view of Alliance purposes was needed.

But such minimalist expectations of the Western Alliance would have required, once again, a rather optimistic view of the West's stability vis-à-vis its enemies. Kissinger, for all his rhetorical homage to Gaullist independence, did not appear confident that the West could really afford that independence.[73]

3

The Neoconservative Alarm

A bitterness entered American politics. It was partly an aftertaste of the 1960s: a souring of liberalism, with the assassinations, urban riots, an unpopular war, campus unrest and (for most Americans) a generally bewildering counterculture. In the 1970s, this menace of social disorder gave way to a new anxiety about America's limits and vulnerabilities in the world. The inner turmoil and outer anxiety were linked: As John Judis notes, the tarnishing of liberalism's "Social Gospel" came together with a shattering "of hopes for an American Century."[1] Global economic and military-strategic trends seemed connected in a kind of Spenglerian synergy: the heretofore unknown trade deficits, the collapse of the dollar's gold link and OPEC price explosions, together with a buildup of Moscow's nuclear and conventional forces and a new series of Soviet forays into the Third World.

With the debacle in Indochina, the American political establishment turned against itself. Kissinger felt betrayed by attacks from the liberal elite—many of them former colleagues from Harvard and the Council on Foreign Relations—who, as Kissinger saw it, had started the war in the first place. Nixon, even more bitter, lumped his opponents into a club that was trying to ruin both his presidency and American foreign policy. (His opponents probably did pursue the president with some extra zeal, inspired by their memories of Nixon's own behavior during the McCarthy era.) The Watergate conspiracy grew out of this bitter climate.

Nixon resigned on August 9, 1974. Three months later liberal Democratic majorities were elected to both houses of Congress, and another five months later, Saigon fell to the Communists. This short interval between Nixon's fall and Saigon's surrender could only add to the recriminations that were no doubt inevitable after America's first defeat in war. Norman Podhoretz, for example, would later charge that the congressional investigations into Watergate and CIA abuses were really part of a concerted liberal attack on the principles of containment. These investigations may not have been "explicitly" directed against containment, Podhoretz conceded. "Yet it is hard to believe that liberals would have mounted an offensive against the 'imperial presidency' or the CIA at a time when they were still enthusiastic about countering—to quote John F. Kennedy's words again—'indirect non-overt aggression, intimidation and subversion, internal revolution.'"[2]

There were the makings here of an American *Dolchstoßlegende*. (The German stab-in-the-back legend had found political scapegoats for the military defeat in World War I.) Kissinger's contribution, though relatively mild, made him sound unaccountably naïve. He said that he negotiated the Paris Peace Accords with an understanding of the "obvious fact that the peace settlement was not self-enforcing." Kissinger "never believed that Hanoi would reconcile itself" to the results of the Paris agreements; thus, "American air power was . . . always seen as an essential deterrent to the resumption of all-out war."[3] But this view failed to account for the great disparity of will, between Hanoi and Washington, for continuing the fight. As it happened, Hanoi broke its Paris pledges at a time when the American presidency had been thoroughly discredited by Watergate, and a Congress infused with the country's antimilitary exhaustion was unwilling to accept the reassertion of presidential authority for another Indochina intervention. Now, as Kissinger saw it, his job was to salvage what he could of an ambitious foreign policy whose foundation in actual American power was crumbling. Détente with the Soviets, which had been the centerpiece of more ambitious Nixon/Kissinger designs in the world, was now reduced to a defensive holding action to stabilize a status quo that the American body politic, under "McGovernite" control, would not back up with real power.

That was only the beginning of Kissinger's problems. He was also under attack from the right; anti-Communists under the leadership of Democratic senator Henry M. Jackson were reconstituting themselves as a political force. Kissinger would later charge that in this intensely ideological atmosphere, an almost rabid American moralism had displaced any attempt either to understand

U.S. interests in the world or to put up the resources to defend them.[4] He saw himself trapped "between a liberal idealism unrelated to a concept of power and the liturgical anti-Communism of the Right."[5]

DÉTENTE AND THE NEOCONSERVATIVES

These strange bedfellows soon produced ideological offspring. Narrowly defined, neoconservatives were (and are) former liberal Democrats (many of whom remained Democrats) and, in a few cases, Marxist leftists who recoiled against the tendencies of their earlier philosophies. Their own conversion gave way to a bitter critique of liberal political culture. Thus such former liberals as Jeane Kirkpatrick and Max Kampelman, Minnesota associates of Hubert Humphrey, became angered and disgusted by the trends they associated with Humphrey's defeat in the 1968 presidential election: the anarchic student counterculture and the rise of McGovernite isolationism in their own party. Many of these converted liberals were Jews, often refugees or children of refugees from Europe, who detected on the campuses echoes of a Weimar societal collapse. They saw at Democratic party conventions echoes of the British interwar failure of nerve. They were concerned with the fate of Israel and therefore particularly angered by the American and European left-wing embrace of a romantic Third Worldism when Third World governments denounced Zionism as "racism." (It seemed in fact, that many American Jewish liberals arrived during the 1970s at a grudging logical conclusion: Their former rejection of belligerent anti-Communism was no longer consistent with support for Israel.)[6]

Beyond this rejection of antiwar liberalism, neoconservativism drew much of its spirit from a more dramatic renunciation of left ideology by former Marxists and members of the New Left. Irving Kristol and Norman Podhoretz are famous examples. Sidney Blumenthal argues that some of the harshness of neoconservativism derives from the continued effects of Marxist training. Where Communists once denounced Social Democracy as "social fascism," neoconservatives now accused liberals of assuming a "moral equivalence" between the United States and the Soviet Union and thereby "objectively" aiding the Soviets.[7] Whatever the justice of Blumenthal's comparison, it does seem clear that neoconservatives' emotional scorn for the political left has much to do with the fact that they once participated in it. Hence Norman Podhoretz, who as late as 1971 still fiercely opposed the Vietnam war, was nine years later attacking antiwar critics for cultivating a post-Vietnam "culture of appeasement."[8] He was particularly scornful of former literary colleagues, comparing them to the British literary figures of interwar years whose revulsion against the carnage of World War I allegedly undermined Britain's moral resistance to Hitler.

A "true" neoconservative, then, had once been a liberal or even a Communist. But this narrow definition should not obscure the fact that neoconservatism, especially in the area of foreign policy, provided much of the intellectual and ideological vigor of the rightward movement of American politics that helped carry Ronald Reagan into the presidency. As such, it is reasonable to apply the term to a large number of Republicans and Democrats, including Reagan himself. Neoconservatism was a distinct world view, in particular, a pronounced pessimism about the Soviet threat.

Coral Bell, in a penetrating analysis of the Reagan administration, insists on a special litmus test: The essential difference between neoconservatives and more "traditional conservatives," a difference that stood out starkly in Ronald Reagan's 1976 bid to unseat Gerald Ford as the Republican presidential candidate, was the neoconservatives' "far more pessimistic 'bottom line'" assessment of the East-West balance of power. This assessment was the basis for attacks on détente, an essentially conservative project whose architects have included Nixon and Kissinger along with "such unimpeachably conservative nationalists as Churchill and de Gaulle." To such conservatives, the Soviet threat was dangerous, but manageable. "The neo-conservative approach" wrote Bell, "is not so historically relativist: It implies instead that the Soviet challenge is unique and irreconcilable."[9]

This philosophical divide was no less bitter for being an argument largely between varieties of conservatives. The early debate over détente was highly charged in another way as well, for it took place on a peculiar, not to say bizarre stage: Washington, D.C. in the throes of Watergate. Early in Nixon's second term, his presidency started unravelling in an unending string of revelations. The supposedly "third-rate burglary" of the Democratic National Committee's Watergate offices turned out to be part of a much larger, albeit highly amateurish, operation of investigations and "dirty tricks," directed from the White House against opponents of Nixon and the Vietnam war. Even more damaging was the emerging evidence of a criminal conspiracy—leading into the Oval Office itself—to obstruct Watergate investigations and pay out "hush money" in order to hide the original White House connection.

For Kissinger, who was briefly affected by controversy about the wiretapping of his staff, but left largely untarnished, the steady hemorrhaging of presidential authority was a foreign-policy nightmare. A media feeding frenzy, Senate investigations and, finally, House impeachment proceedings produced a climate of unremitting obsession that made a rational discussion of American policy toward the Soviets impossible. With the president weakened, his détente policies presented an easy target, as "conservatives who hated Communists and liberals who hated Nixon came together in a rare convergence, like an eclipse of the sun."[10] Senator Henry Jackson, flanked by aide Richard Perle, led the attack—the spearhead of a decade-long neoconservative reaction. The central elements of Soviet-American détente, trade relations and nuclear arms–control treaties, both required congressional approval, which Jackson endeavored to deny.

The trade side had started out with a special embarrassment. In May 1972, as the United States intensified the bombing of North Vietnam and placed mines in Hanoi's harbor, White House officials worried about the Soviet reaction: Would Moscow, for instance, cancel the summit meeting between Nixon and Brezhnev planned for later in the month? Soviet officials acted surprised, however, that anyone would imagine such a drastic reaction. One reason for this Soviet equanimity soon became apparent. Over the subsequent summer, Soviet purchasers fanned out across the American farm belt, making quiet grain purchases, which the U.S. grain companies, for their own commercial reasons, hid from each other. In fact, the Soviets bought almost a quarter of the American harvest and at fixed contracts 80 cents below the $2.43 per bushel that world prices hit once the extent of the "great grain robbery" became known in September. It also emerged only belatedly that the Soviet Union was suffering another dismal harvest—one that might have led to food riots but for the purchases from the United States.[11]

The general view was that America had been taken. "The episode," wrote a leading American Soviet expert, "epitomizes the Soviets' ability, displayed on so many occasions . . . to compensate by superior negotiating skills for the inherent weaknesses of their system."[12] Of course, the episode was also a boon for U.S. farmers. The enthusiasm of some cabinet officials for such deals lent unintended ammunition to the administration's critics. Commerce Secretary Peter G. Peterson spoke of an effort "to build in both countries a vested economic interest in the maintenance of a harmonious and enduring relationship."[13] This, the critics noted, was precisely the ideology of commerce that held sway in Europe right up to August 1914.

Kissinger maintains that it was not *his* ideology. "We did not believe—as was later alleged—that trade by itself could moderate Soviet conduct," he insisted in his memoirs. The administration's "basic reliance" continued to be a strategy of containment based on a "global balance" of military forces. "We believed, however, that Soviet restraint would be more solidly based if reinforced by positive inducements, including East-West trade."[14]

Here was the famous and rather simple concept of "linkage." The political benefits from trade would not occur spontaneously; they would have to be cultivated through a conscious project of quid pro quo.[15] But Kissinger's more subtle view of the operation of that linkage did not impress his critics in Congress. Jackson wreaked havoc by turning linkage on its head. Whereas Nixon and Kissinger conceived it as a tool of leverage over Soviet foreign policy, the Jackson forces applied it to Soviet domestic policy, "a much more problematical and sensitive area," in Kissinger's view.[16]

Notwithstanding his skepticism about meddling in Soviet domestic affairs, Kissinger recounted that initially he was not entirely displeased. To establish serious export opportunities in the United States, the Soviets needed Congress to grant most-favored-nation (MFN) trade status. Senator Jackson's first endeavor was to deny them this favor unless they rescinded a newly imposed exit tax on Jewish emigrants. Although Kissinger was convinced that the Soviets had already allowed a major increase in Jewish emigration precisely in order to soften America's ideological resistance to trade, Jackson's legislative undertaking allowed Kissinger to push the Soviets for more in a kind of good-cop/bad-cop routine. It worked. In April 1973 the Soviets agreed to suspend the exit tax. But Jackson had no intention of accepting this victory. He now pushed his trade-bill amendment (sponsored in the House of Representatives by Representative Charles Vanik) denying MFN status to any Communist country that maintained any restrictions whatsoever on emigration. This, needless to say, was a demand that the Soviets fundamentally change their political system.

It is not surprising that the Jackson forces failed to respect a distinction in the linkage strategy between international and domestic behavior. Their basic concept was that domestic and international behavior were inseparable: Soviet foreign policy flowed from the totalitarian nature of its domestic system. No concept of limits or divisions made any sense, because totalitarians by definition could not accept such divisions. Kissinger became convinced that Jackson embraced linkage to kill it—an intentional reductio ad absurdum.[17]

In the area of arms control, the Nixon administration and the Soviet leadership commenced in November 1969 the "Strategic Arms Limitations Talks" (SALT) that had been proposed by President Johnson three years earlier. In 1972, Nixon and Brezhnev signed the SALT I treaty, the most significant element of which was the agreement limiting each side to two ABM sites (the United States only built one and eventually scrapped it; the Russians maintained a single system for Moscow). There was also an interim agreement on offensive weapons, freezing each side's number of strategic missiles for five years at their 1972 levels.

Like the Soviet grain purchases of the same summer, this interim agreement did nothing to enhance détente's reputation. Freezing the number of missiles meant conceding a Soviet numerical advantage: The pact allowed the Soviet Union 1,409 land-based, intercontinental missiles (ICBMs) and 950 submarine-launched missiles (SLBMs), against American totals of 1,054 ICBMs and 656 SLBMs. The treaty passed the U.S. Senate, but not before Jackson was able to tack on an amendment directing the president to seek an agreement during the next round of negotiations "that, *inter alia,* would not limit the United States to levels of intercontinental strategic forces inferior to the limits provided for the Soviet Union."[18]

The implied rebuke was, to Kissinger's mind, both strategically and politically illiterate. In strategic terms, he argued, Jackson failed to note the trade-off of superior U.S. technology, and the fact that the treaty made no mention of long-range bombers, in which the United States held a vast lead. Politically, Kissinger maintained, the Jackson criticism ignored the current Congressional mood, the fact that no U.S. programs, actual or potential, were affected by the limit. The next planned weapons—the B-1 long-range bomber and the Trident sub-launched missile—would be ready for deployment only after the interim agreement expired in 1977. Under these circumstances, Kissinger thought he had done well to curb the ongoing Soviet deployments.

For the next round, SALT II, confusion reigned on the American side about what its purpose should be. The idea of "equal aggregates," as embodied in the Jackson amendment, maintained the appeal of simplicity. But the superpowers' actual strategic forces were anything but simple: They had been constructed differently according to different preferences and constraints. The Soviets had invested much more in heavy, land-based missiles, initially because they lacked the knack for miniaturization. The United States had invested more in bombers, high-quality submarines, and advanced technology—especially low-flying cruise missiles and the trick of placing multiple warheads (MIRVs) on a single missile. (On the other hand, the Russians caught up in MIRV technology faster than anyone expected.)

The only practical basis for a long-term deal, argued Kissinger, was to balance some of these asymmetrical advantages. The United States should go in with the goal of reducing the threat that Russian heavy missiles, once "MIRVed," would pose to America's own land-based force. It should be willing, under the circumstances, to accept higher Soviet aggregates in exchange for specific limitations on the number of ICBMs they could equip with multiple warheads.[19]

But any such formula was bound to be complex and controversial, especially insofar as Nixon now faced the suspicion that he would settle for any deal, no matter how bad, in order to win the mantle of peacemaker and perhaps save his presidency. In the final weeks of Watergate, Nixon could not even hold his own administration in line. In an act verging on insubordination, Defense Secretary James Schlesinger wrote a letter to Jackson publicly endorsing the latter's insistence on equal aggregates.[20] And in early June 1974, on the eve of Nixon's final summit in Moscow, Paul Nitze, the chief Pentagon negotiator, resigned with a withering broadside against the president: "Until the office of the presidency has been restored to its principal function of upholding the Constitution and taking care of the fair execution of the laws, and thus be able to function effectively at home and abroad, I see no real prospect for reversing certain unfortunate trends in the evolving situation." Watergate was thus the proximate cause of Nitze's departure, but this was coupled with his little overall faith in Nixon and Kissinger's vigilance against the Russian threat.[21]

Alongside Kennan, Paul Nitze will loom in this book as its chief intellectual figure. A patrician millionaire, a man of fierce integrity and absolute confidence in his own judgment, Nitze's career as a public servant started before and continued until the end of the Cold War. Neither the man nor the career lends itself to easy ideological classification. For much of his life a Democrat, his views about the East-West conflict would be among the central ideological pillars supporting the 1980 Reagan campaign. To be sure, he came into conflict with hardliners in both the Reagan and Bush administrations because of his pragmatic conviction that *some* arms deals with the Soviets were both negotiable and in the American interest. Nonetheless, Nitze devoted most of his career to pushing America away from what he deemed a woolly-headed impulse toward superpower accommodation. In the Truman administration he had replaced Kennan as the State Department's chief of policy planning; there, as the primary author of NSC-68, he scripted America's radical departure from Kennan's more measured and modest version of containment. Three decades later, Nitze would make no effort to hide his irritation at Kennan's elevation to the status of an American icon; Kennan's ideas had inspired American weakness, Nitze said. And his disdain for Kissinger, an icon of the celebrity age, was even stronger. In large measure their conflict was personal, but there was also a very large gap in worldviews: Nitze's central idea was an utter scorn for the McNamara orthodoxy that nuclear superiority was unusable and therefore meaningless.[22]

Kissinger found himself in a political and ideological maelstrom that continued after Nitze's resignation. Three weeks before Nixon's own resignation—in a Moscow press conference infused with the drama, bitterness and intrigue of an administration's dying days—Kissinger let out a famous *cri de coeur*, demanding of his critics: "What in the name of God is strategic superiority? What is the significance of it, politically, militarily, operationally, at these levels of numbers? What do you do with it?"[23]

THE COMMITTEE ON THE PRESENT DANGER

These questions became the stuff of a much larger and very bitter ideological struggle. Neoconservatives charged that U.S. nuclear policies—adopted under McNamara and Johnson, continued under Nixon, Ford and Carter—reflected a spiritual and moral failure of the first order. Put simply, the United States had succumbed to the evasions and alibis of appeasement. This appeasement was embodied in an intellectual and moral error—the concept of nuclear "sufficiency." To claim that peace rested on the assured destruction of both superpowers in a nuclear war, that America's present nuclear force was sufficient for the task, and that any weapons beyond this number were at best useless and at worst dangerous, was to hand the West's fate over to its determined enemy.

A big part of the problem, according to one neoconservative critique, was the influence and leftist bias of American science. Nuclear physicists had invented atomic weapons during what was, for them, a rare period of ideological clarity: a world war against fascism. But when faced with the threat from Soviet Communism, about which they were either complacent or ambivalent, the scientists were overcome by their customary pacifist angst. They felt guilty for inventing the nuclear bomb, and due to a peculiar confluence of economic and political circumstances, they had an unprecedented opportunity to saddle the world's greatest economic and military power with their guilt complex. They did so, according to such critics as historian Richard Pipes, first by creating out of thin air, and then by using their scientific credentials to popularize, the concept of a "nuclear revolution," by which science had abolished warfare. War was finally too destructive to be fought. "This conclusion," Pipes charged, was reached without consulting the military experts or even considering any "traditional principles of warfare." It was nothing more than "an act of faith on the part of an intellectual community which held strong pacifist convictions and felt deep guilt at having participated in the creation of a weapon of such destructive power."[24]

The natural scientist's pacifism was injected into U.S. policy with the help of the economist's preoccupation with cost, according to Pipes. McNamara's background was in finance and accounting; in the Pentagon he surrounded himself with civilian economists and proceeded to procure weapons "on the basis of cost effectiveness" rather than military effectiveness. The notion of nuclear "sufficiency" was an inevitable product of the Pentagon's new "accounting" mindset, with its aversion to paying for diminishing marginal return. "Current U.S. strategic policy was thus born of a marriage between the scientist and the accountant," wrote Pipes. "The professional soldier was jilted."[25]

While American society denigrated military values, it indulged a kind of mystical horror of nuclear war. Scientists acted as a priesthood for this mysticism, intimating that nuclear weapons were, in and of themselves, uniquely evil. Wellsprings of religious "doomsday" imagery were tapped in an emotional campaign to attack all things nuclear. In this manner an "anxiety that has its origins in religious beliefs" combined with modern agnosticism to produce "an overpowering sense of helplessness that the unscrupulous exploit for their political ends." Thus, according to Pipes, American strategic culture had generated so much general fear of nuclear war that it pushed society at large toward a readiness to appease its enemies. Hysteria about nuclear weapons simply encouraged "those in the Soviet Union who want to use them to terrorize and blackmail foreign powers and their citizens."[26]

Fred Charles Iklé, in his own contribution to this critique, argued that scientists and other antiwar strategists not only propagated this hysteria directly; they also embraced a strategic doctrine, mutual assured destruction (MAD), that inevitably generated even more hysteria. The Soviets enjoyed a critical advantage in any competition based on the balance of terror, an advantage derived from the essentially terrorist nature of totalitarian regimes. MAD simply played to their advantage, as it was bound to cause the West's profound demoralization long before it bothered the Leninists in Moscow.[27]

An early target for these attacks was, as we have already seen, the Nixon administration. Despite Nixon's near paranoia about his liberal "enemies," the neoconservatives considered Nixon-Ford foreign policy to be fatally under the sway of liberal concepts and orthodoxies. In the mid-1970s, this indictment was handed down in the famous "Team B" critique of the CIA's Soviet analyses. For a number of years conservatives had charged that the CIA consistently understated Soviet strategic capabilities and intentions. There were allegations that both Nixon and Kissinger, out of commitment to détente, had intervened to make sure that the yearly intelligence estimates avoided speculations about Soviet aggressive aims and concentrated solely on hardware accounting. More broadly, conservative critics charged that CIA analysts had a penchant for "neutral" interpretations, which, in effect, meant a benign view of Soviet military planning. This was, Richard Pipes argued, because the CIA's "analytic staff, filled with American PhD's in the natural and social sciences along with engineers, inevitably share[d] the outlook of U.S. academe, with its penchant for philosophical positivism, cultural agnosticism, and political liberalism."[28] Specifically, these analysts were accused of sharing the American science community's devotion to the strategic concepts of MAD and "sufficiency." Through a pernicious process of "mirror-imaging"—assuming that the Soviets shared the same devotions—the intelligence analysts blinded themselves to the significance of an ongoing Soviet military buildup.

Nixon and his CIA director, William Colby, resisted the suggestion that an independent board look into the CIA estimating process. But in 1975 Colby's job went to George Bush, who was more receptive to the idea. "Team B" was set up under the direction of Richard Pipes, a Harvard professor of Russian history. Its members, including Paul Nitze, issued a scathing report that, in essence, backed the charge of a liberal bias to CIA analysis. This bias led to the false conclusion that the Soviet nuclear arsenal was designed for the purpose of defensive retaliation. And this conclusion, argued Team B's chairman, just "happened to favor détente and to place the main burden for its success on the United States, to the extent that Soviet deviations from MAD were ascribed to Russian paranoia that America alone could assuage." Agency analysts had simply ignored both technical and political evidence that, according to Pipes, "indicated beyond reasonable doubt that the Soviet leadership did not subscribe to MAD but regarded nuclear weapons as tools of war whose proper employment, in offensive as well as defensive modes, promised victory."[29]

Team B's report was, in a sense, the intellectual seed of an organized effort to alert the broader public to this Soviet "grand strategy." In March 1976 a number of disaffected foreign policy figures—including Nitze, former undersecretary of state Eugene Rostow and the recently resigned defense secretary, James Schlesinger—met to organize a committee for that purpose. To avoid charges of partisanship, they delayed going public with the "Committee on the Present Danger" until just after Jimmy Carter's November 1976 election to the presidency. Their executive committee included three members of Team B—Nitze, Pipes, and William R. Van Cleave. Over the next four years the Committee devoted most of its efforts to a successful campaign to block the SALT II Treaty.[30]

The Committee's critique covered the whole spectrum of East-West and military issues. But running through it were two broad arguments. First, Soviet grand strategy was based on isolating and dominating Western Europe. Once this primary goal was achieved, China and Japan would realize that a new balance favored the Soviets, and they would submit to this reality. The United States would be effectively isolated.[31] Second, the Soviets had a multitude of military, political and economic means by which it could dominate Europe. The most important was a strategy and, by sometime in the 1980s, a capability to fight and win a nuclear war against Europe's protector, the United States.

"The nuclear balance is, of course, only one element in the overall balance of power," said Paul Nitze in 1978. "But in the Soviet view, it is the fulcrum upon which all other levers of influence—military, economic, or political—rest. Can we be confident that there is not at least a measure of validity to that viewpoint?"[32]

The answer from Nitze and his Committee colleagues was this: Only through blind and really perverse faith in MAD doctrine could Americans dismiss the implications of Russia's growing arsenal. Once MAD was questioned, the growth in Soviet missile power took on a far more ominous light.

Between 1972 (when the SALT I Interim Agreement was signed) and 1978, the Soviets had deployed three new MIRVed ICBMs: the SS-17, the SS-18 and the SS-19. The U.S. advantage in MIRV technology had proven transient—the Soviets would be in a position, by 1983, to nearly double their ICBM throw-weight (from between 6.7 and 9 million pounds to between 11 and 13 million pounds) and thus vastly increase their number of deliverable ICBM warheads (from 1,600 to between 6,500 and 9,200). They were accomplishing this strategic revolution while observing SALT I limits on ICBM silos.[33] "The United States, in contrast," noted the Committee, "will, by the early 1980s have deployed no additional ICBM throw-weight since 1972" (when it wielded an ICBM throw-weight of 2.9 million pounds, or 2,154 ICBM warheads).[34]

The new, heavy, land-based missiles in the Soviet arsenal were the consummate first-strike weapons, the Committee claimed. By the mid-1980s, the Russians would have sufficient numbers of accurate MIRVed warheads to take out most of America's land-based ICBM arsenal. With multiple warheads, it was claimed, the Russians needed to expend only one-fifth to one-third of their ICBMs to destroy virtually the entire U.S. force.[35] The U.S. strategic arsenal, of course, had been designed and built as a redundant "triad" of land- and sea-based missiles and manned bombers, a vast redundancy the purpose of which was to ensure the preservation of an annihilating retaliatory capability. Even after a nightmarish Soviet attack, the United States would still retain its submarine-based (SLBM) force and whatever long-range bombers were airborne or could take off before the Soviet warheads struck. But this was not enough, according to the Committee. The bombers would be vulnerable to Soviet air defenses, while the sea-launched missiles lacked the accuracy for precise counterforce missions.[36] The option of controlled nuclear attacks on Russian military assets would no longer exist.

The Committee asked Americans to imagine a U.S. president who confronted this fait accompli: his more accurate ICBMs destroyed in their silos and a surrender ultimatum from the Soviets. Would it not require a madman to launch submarine-based missiles against millions of innocent Russian civilians, knowing it would lead only to a comparable slaughter of many million Americans? Would not surrender be the only available course of sanity and humanity?

MAD's liberal defenders called this "window-of-vulnerability" thesis fantastical. First of all, they claimed, the Soviet leadership would have to be confident that their rocket forces could execute the most powerful and complex attack in human history without failure and without any realistic rehearsal. And even if they possessed such confidence, the Soviets knew that the Americans always had the option of launching their own ICBMs "on warning" of the Soviet attack—that is, in the first minutes after U.S. satellites detected the Soviet missiles leaving their silos.[37] Finally, even if the Soviets knew they could destroy every single U.S. land-based ICBM, how could they be sure that the American president would then choose the "saner" course of surrender? "The President, in response, might be paralysed with fear and horror, or stirred into a ferocious retaliation," noted Laurence Freedman in the early 1980s.[38] No rule of human nature suggests that the former response would be more plausible than the latter. There would remain enough uncertainty to deter all but the most insane of adversaries.

But all of this was beside the point, argued Nitze's circle. To be nervous about the Soviet heavy missiles, one did not have to believe that the Russians would use them in a cold, calculated and unprovoked surprise attack. The fundamental issues were how these calculations would affect the dynamics of a crisis, and, of most immediate concern, how even a merely theoretical and partial Soviet first-strike capability would degrade the credibility of America's alliance commitments.

In a crisis, perhaps convinced that nuclear war was inevitable, the Russians would have a great incentive to launch their own ICBM attack first, hoping to destroy the most effective leg of America's retaliatory force in the fashion described above. The incentive was all the greater because multiple warheads gave the attacker a favorable cost-exchange ratio—that is, it could hope to destroy more of the U.S. force than it would expend in its attack.[39]

However, the Committee focused less on the problem of crisis instability and more on their premise that " . . . the state of the U.S.-Soviet military balance [is] basic to the evolution of political and psychological relations in the significant areas of the world."[40] The main threat, in other words, was Soviet nuclear blackmail. Moreover, Russia's ability to exploit a favorable strategic balance for the purposes of blackmail was immune to any ultimate judgment about whether its leaders were really reckless enough to launch a first strike. "We do not have to assume that the Soviet Union will actually attack U.S. strategic forces," the Committee argued. Just the theoretical possibility that the Soviets would improve their numerical missile-advantage through a counter-force first strike would have a psychological impact. Under such conditions the United States would

> . . . lose the "battle of perceived capabilities." The horrors of nuclear war may continue to deter its actual occurrence. But the political effects of

such a shift, and its effects on the feasibility of conventional or proxy war, are very great.[41]

The men who forged a new consensus against MAD, such as Paul Nitze and James Schlesinger, came in large part from the community of defense specialists who had generated the counterforce concepts described in chapter 1. As chief of the State Department's Policy Planning Staff in 1950, Nitze had been prime author of NSC-68; nine years later, as McNamara's Pentagon deputy, he was a key promoter of the "flexible-response" revival of those ideas. Schlesinger, who helped push U.S. policy partly away from MAD after he was appointed defense secretary in 1973,[42] came from the group of civilian strategists at the RAND Corporation whose theories had been shaped by McNamara's Defense Department into counterforce plans.

From the perspective of these counterforce advocates, of course, it had been Robert McNamara who committed heresy by shifting from flexible response to MAD. After all, the critique put forward by Nitze and Schlesinger against mutual assured destruction was little different from the arguments they and their colleagues had advanced in the 1950s against massive retaliation. In 1959, for example, RAND's Albert Wohlstetter had challenged the notion of a stable balance of terror. "At critical junctures in the 1960s, we may not have the power to deter attack," he wrote, a warning that he repeated 15 years later in an influential attack on MAD.[43] In 1960 Wohlstetter's RAND colleague Herman Kahn had warned that accepting the "balance of terror" principle would have a demoralizing effect on NATO. Even though such terror might suffice to deter a Soviet first strike against the United States, it would also put the United States in a position where it could never afford to attack the Soviets, "no matter what the provocation." For the Americans to allow themselves to be put into that position, Kahn insisted, "would be equivalent to disowning our alliance obligations by signing what would amount to a non-aggression treaty with the Soviets—a non-aggression treaty with almost 200 million American hostages to guarantee performance."[44]

Perhaps the most important concept that the early RAND strategists handed down to the 1970s debate was that of "escalation dominance." The term was coined by Kahn in a 1965 book, in which he imagined a 44-rung "escalation ladder." Kahn defined escalation dominance as "the net effect of the competing capabilities on the rung being occupied, the estimate by each side of what would happen if the confrontation moved to other rungs, and the means each side has to shift the confrontation to other rungs."[45]

This was the critical concept from which McNamara had turned when he embraced MAD. McNamara never denied the desirability of having nuclear options other than that of an all-out attack on Soviet cities. But he did deny the usefulness of possessing escalation dominance on higher (nuclear) rungs of the ladder. He rejected this implicitly in his later years as defense secretary, and explicitly thereafter.[46]

However, for McNamara's critics throughout the 1970s and early 1980s, it was precisely this concept of escalation dominance that meant that nuclear weapons retained political utility. In effect, they argued that the reality of this concept invalidated the claims of a "nuclear revolution" that had changed the nature of international relations. Nuclear war might be horrible for both sides, but it would be significantly less so for the side that enjoyed escalation dominance. In a war or severe crisis, at a given rung on the ladder, the side with military superiority should be able to win a game of "chicken," because its threat to escalate was credible and its opponent's was not. Moreover, well before any crisis became acute, the side enjoying *overall* escalation dominance should be able to pressure its opponent into a gradual but steady series of bad bargains, since both sides would appreciate that the inferior nuclear power could not afford a confrontation. In 1979 Paul Nitze wrote:

> It is a copybook principle in strategy that, in actual war, advantage tends to go to the side in a better position to raise the stakes by expanding the scope, duration or destructive intensity of the conflict. By the same token, at junctures of high contention short of war, the side better able to cope with the potential consequences of raising the stakes has the advantage. The other side is the one under greater pressure to scramble for a peaceful way out. To have the advantage at the utmost level of violence helps at every lesser level.[47]

Such "nuclear blackmail" by the side possessing escalation dominance would be exponentially more effective when applied against third countries who looked to the inferior power for protection. Everyone—blackmailer, protector and pro-tectorate—would be calculating who could best afford a confrontation. Over the long run, these calculations would inevitably determine political relations.[48]

JIMMY CARTER'S MISFORTUNES

It was the Republican party's singular luck that these strategic theories were "proven" during Jimmy Carter's ill-starred administration: a 4-year Democratic parenthesis inside 20 years of Republican presidents. The Carter years, 1977 to 1980, coincided with a conspicuous expansion of Moscow's presence in the Third World. It started in 1975 with the fall of Saigon and then Phnom Penh.

That same year Moscow moved decisively to support one of the three rebel factions in Portugal's African colony of Angola. Soviet planes airlifted Cuban troops into the country while the U.S. Congress, under the slogan of "no more Vietnams," cut off aid to rival guerrillas. The Soviet-backed faction prevailed, and Angola became a base for rebel attacks on the South African protectorate of Namibia, while a Marxist regime took over in Mozambique. On the horn of Africa, in alarming proximity to Persian Gulf oil, the Soviets racked up more success: A 1977 coup brought Ethiopia into the Soviet camp; the same occurred the following year in South Yemen. Another military coup in 1978 brought a Marxist government into Afghanistan. Meanwhile, after two decades of futile efforts by Castro's Cuba to export its revolution to the rest of Latin America, the Caribbean basin started to heat up. In Nicaragua the middle class finally recoiled against the ostentatious greed of dictator Anastasio Somoza; a popular revolution, condoned, if not supported, by the United States, drove him from the presidential palace in 1979. Thereafter the Marxist members of the coalition gradually gathered effective power among themselves and started to funnel aid from Cuba to the rebels in neighboring El Salvador.

In Central Asia, meanwhile, the Soviets found that their clients could not always be counted on to keep things under control; the Islamic, anti-Communist resistance in Afghanistan was growing bolder, while the government looked ever more ineffectual. In December 1979 the Soviets sponsored the assassination of President Hafizullah Amin, replaced him with the more reliable Babrak Karmal, and invaded the country.

Already in the winter of 1980, there were voices suggesting that the Soviets were embarrassingly overextended and that Afghanistan would turn out to be Russia's Vietnam.[49] It was argued, moreover, that pro-Soviet governments from Vietnam to Nicaragua would have little geostrategic effect except to make costly demands on Russian aid and prove how quickly a Marxist regime could ruin an economy.

To the luminaries of the Committee on the Present Danger, however, the Third World adventures fit into a Soviet plan that was clear enough to anyone who cared to see it. Had not Brezhnev himself promised in 1973 that the "correlation of forces" was shifting in favor of Moscow, which would soon reap the geopolitical rewards? Third World expansion, a strategic nuclear buildup, and mounting military and political pressure on Western Europe were all elements of a Soviet grand strategy in which Europe was the penultimate prize, as Eugene Rostow argued in 1978:

> the centerpiece of the Soviet strategic view of world politics has always been that if Russia could control Western Europe and bring it under

dominion, and the areas upon which Western Europe is dependent in the Middle East and Africa, that it would thereby control the world. There can be no question that Soviet reduction of Western Europe or equally of China, but more emphatically Western Europe, either envelopment or through direct attack, or through coercion and political influence, would be read in Japan and in China and in many other parts of the world as a clear political signal that the balance of power had shifted disastrously against the United States, that American guarantees were no longer effective or credible and that China and Japan would correspondingly make the best deal they could with the Soviet Union.[50]

Richard Pipes, on the same theme, said that the Russians intended to achieve control of Western Europe

with a variety of means of which perhaps an across-the-frontier invasion is the least likely. The most effective form which this threat takes is first, an enormous military build-up on the European frontier, which has the psychological effect of intimidating European public opinion and creating a sense of helplessness; and, secondly, through a flanking movement, via the Middle East and Africa, which endangers European oil supplies and a large proportion of European mineral supplies from South Africa. These measures can bring Europe to its knees without any shots necessarily being fired.[51]

This notion that Soviet adventures in Africa and the Middle East were part of a "flanking" movement, to cut Europe off from oil and other supplies, was one of the Committee's oft-repeated arguments. It suggested a method to almost all Soviet activities of the 1970s: support for the Arab side against Israel, encouragement of OPEC's oil embargo and price fixing, the Angola intervention and the backing of radical Marxist regimes in Ethiopia and Yemen. This pattern looked even more ominous as the decade ended. The Iranian upheaval (with alleged Soviet involvement) and the invasion of Afghanistan suggested a pincer movement, from Africa and now Central Asia, closing in on the Persian Gulf. In a 1980 article, Nitze again tied all these events to a Soviet grand strategy that had control of Western Europe as its principal aim.[52] Nitze linked a Russian threat to Persian Gulf oil supplies to an argument that the Soviets would soon be able to dominate Europe economically.[53] This economic dimension of the "Finlandization" argument will be discussed at length in chapter 6. For now it should be noted that the Committee saw the Russian threat to Europe as part of a seamless web of strategy that included economic, political, and military dimensions—and that the military-nuclear dimension was seen as most important.

Here was a coherent and rhetorically satisfying explanation of geopolitical trends. President Carter, by contrast, seemed confused. He started his term with a promise to rid American foreign policy of its "inordinate fear of communism." That promise was most clearly vindicated when the Carter administration helped nudge Somoza out of office, aware that the Sandinista coalition replacing him had its share of Castro-style Marxists. No longer would the specter of Soviet expansion drive Washington to embrace the usual right-wing, bloody-minded dictators. In the dichotomy of this book, this policy put Carter squarely in the Kennanesque, "containment is stable" school of thought.

Unfortunately, however, it seemed as though there *was* a significant Soviet expansion underway, and it was generating considerable fear in Washington. It strengthened the case of Zbigniew Brzezinski, Carter's hardline, anti-Soviet national security adviser, against the more conciliatory Secretary of State Cyrus Vance. Brzezinski's advice led to one particularly grotesque irony: America's tighter alignment with China and, by extension, its Khmer Rouge allies against Moscow-backed Vietnam's invasion of Cambodia. That invasion, however much it offended against the geostrategic order, had the practical effect of ending one of history's most heinous genocides. But Brzezinski, ardently solicitous of a tacit Sino-American alliance against Moscow, battled against the State Department to be sure that the United States responded to China's retaliatory incursion into Vietnam in the mildest possible terms, providing a "partial diplomatic umbrella for the Chinese action without associating the United States with it," in Brzezinski's own words.[54] (The Chinese were, astonishingly, humiliated by Hanoi's troops, an event that only added to the idea of a pro-Soviet tilt in the correlation of forces.)[55]

The Soviet invasion of Afghanistan fully opened the president's eyes, Carter declared with unfortunate candor.[56] The president's critics seized gleefully on the implication of previous naïveté. Carter launched a military buildup, shelved the already signed but not yet ratified SALT-II treaty, and declared a "Carter Doctrine," under which a Soviet move into the Persian Gulf would be considered casus belli.[57] It was, in political terms, too late. The ordeal of Americans taken hostage in the Tehran embassy painfully dramatized Carter's general image of fecklessness.

As argued above, the Carter presidency constituted a Republican stroke of luck, diverting the Republicans from their own political fratricide. After all, the neoconservative alarm had been sounded against the détente policies of Republican presidents; the bloodletting of Ronald Reagan's 1976 bid for the GOP nomination, along with the continued effects of Watergate, had helped to fatally weaken President Ford's election bid. But now there was a Democratic president to help the Republicans forget their own quarrels. In September 1979, the Republican establishment's leading foreign-policy figure served notice that a new Republican consensus had been forged. Henry Kissinger, the object of so much neoconservative scorn, more or less recanted in public.

In a much-publicized speech in Brussels, Kissinger embraced the Committee on the Present Danger's critique of U.S. nuclear strategy. He coupled a gloomy assessment of the strategic balance with an accusation that NATO had fallen back on MAD as an "alibi" for inaction. With this speech, Kissinger seemed to have come full circle. In the 1950s he had been a leading academic critic of massive retaliation and a proponent of counterforce.[58] In the Nixon administration he had encouraged a "conscious policy of stabilizing the arms race"; he advised Nixon to accept the loss of strategic superiority and settle instead for "sufficiency."[59] Now, along with his own critics from the Committee on the Present Danger, Kissinger called MAD "the script for selective nuclear blackmail" of America's European allies.[60]

Such shifts, writes Lawrence Freedman, show Kissinger "as a weather-vane for changes in the intellectual climate, reflecting the dominant ideas of any period yet able to anticipate movements in fashion."[61] The Brussels speech, delivered just a year before Ronald Reagan's election, may have shocked some Europeans into recognizing just how far the prevailing winds of an American strategic debate had shifted.[62] Heretofore, Europeans had been able to discount (albeit with a sometimes troubled conscience) all the warnings—about the end of American superiority, windows of vulnerability, the untenable nature of extended deterrence—as something like sour grapes from right-wing figures rejected by American voters in 1964 and again in 1976. But here now was the central figure of American foreign policy for the past decade taking up and endorsing many of their themes. Here, for example, was Kissinger adopting the Iklé line about the West's moral disabilities in a struggle based on nuclear terrorism. "One cannot," said Kissinger, "ask a nation to design forces that have no military significance, whose primary purpose is the extermination of civilians, and expect that these factors will not affect a nation's resoluteness in a crisis."

The situation as described by Kissinger was every bit as grim as the Committee on the Present Danger had been claiming. By sometime in the 1980s the United States would be in a position where "many of our strategic forces, including all of our land-based ICBMs, will be vulnerable, and such an insignificant percentage of Soviet strategic forces will be vulnerable as not to represent a meaningful strategic attack option for the United States." In fact, said Kissinger, under such circumstances the United States would probably find that attacking Soviet ICBMs made no military sense, "because it may represent a marginal expenditure of our own strategic striking force that does not help greatly to ensure the safety of our forces." NATO officials and other MAD apologists (here Kissinger acknowledged his earlier incarnation as a "sufficiency" standard-bearer) had generated some bizarre rationalizations for this problem: "There is nothing to worry about so long as the capacity exists to kill 100 million people"; as well as "the historically amazing theory that vulnerability contributed to peace and invulnerability contributed to the risks of war." What these rationalizations could not get around, however, was the awkward problem of America's commitment to Europe, a commitment to use nuclear weapons first. The strategic impact, said Kissinger, "that is produced by our limited vulnerability is more fundamental for the United States than even total vulnerability would be for the Soviet Union because our strategic doctrine has relied extraordinarily, perhaps exclusively, on superior strategic power."

These depressing ruminations, coming from Kissinger, were disquieting enough to America's allies. But what made the Brussels speech particularly troubling was the explicit admission of something many Europeans had attempted not to perceive: that Secretary of State Kissinger had been virtually lying when he affirmed America's unwavering nuclear commitment to Europe—and that his successors were most probably lying as well. The Europeans, said Kissinger, should stop "asking us to multiply strategic reassurances that we cannot possibly mean or if we do mean, we should not want to execute because if we execute, we risk the destruction of civilization."[63]

REAGAN AND NUCLEAR WAR

One might imagine, given the rhetoric of various neoconservatives and now Kissinger, that U.S. strategic policy in the late 1970s was based on a single, massive and apocalyptic attack on Soviet cities. But this was not so. Strategy for the European battlefield continued to anticipate the graduated escalation of "flexible response." At the strategic level, even during McNamara's later years as defense secretary, U.S. targeting plans contained a mix of "countervalue" (cities and other civilian hostages) and "counterforce" (military) targets. Throughout the 1970s, U.S. strategic policy reached for more and more counterforce options, moving in fits and starts away from an explicit threat to attack cities. President Nixon had promoted a rather vague concept of "sufficiency," for which he gave two definitions: (1) a narrow military capability to deter attack; and (2) a broader political meaning of sufficient forces "to prevent us and our allies from being coerced."[64] His second defense secretary, James Schlesinger, publicly announced a change in doctrine toward greater counterforce targeting, which he justified based on the second of those definitions, specifically, the necessity of maintaining the credibility of extended deterrence for Europe.[65] President Carter and his defense secretary, Harold Brown, both expressed skepticism about the possibility of controlled counterforce exchanges leading to anything but catastrophe.[66] Nonetheless, there was a further elaboration of counterforce targeting options under Brown, with focus on political and economic targets as well as strictly military ones.[67] The Carter administration also sought to remedy the alleged vulnerability of U.S. land-based missiles. Carter approved development of the new MX intercontinental missile, which was to be housed either in superhardened silos or hidden from the Soviets in tunnels linking a large number of silos, the idea being to prevent the Soviets from knowing—through satellite surveillance—which silos were loaded and which were dummies.[68]

What *was* true was that throughout the 1970s, these efforts to prepare for a counterforce exchange of nuclear warheads seemed half-hearted, at best. Even when the Carter administration spoke of "countervailing" capabilities to match the Soviets, U.S. policy never fully embraced the goal of escalation dominance. As Robert W. Tucker has noted, it continued to rely on a "pervasive uncertainty" as to "whether any meaningful limits" could be expected in a nuclear war.[69] After leaving office, Carter continued to insist that "mutual assured *vulnerability*" (which he conceded was only rhetorically different from MAD) remained the only sensible premise for nuclear strategy. "Any sort of *radical* departure from this premise is an extremely disturbing factor," he said.[70]

Carter was obviously referring to the Reagan administration, which seemed geared up for just such a departure. The new administration's strategic principles, at least on a rhetorical level, were those drafted in detail by the Committee on the Present Danger in the four years prior to Reagan's taking office. Sixty Committee board members, including Reagan himself, served in the new administration. Many of them worked in the Pentagon, which drew up a new doctrine of "prevailing" in a "protracted" nuclear war. Should deterrence fail, "United States nuclear capabilities must prevail even under the conditions of a prolonged war," stated a "Fiscal Year 1984–1988 Defense Guidance" document (which was circulated secretly in 1982 but almost immediately leaked to the *New York Times*).[71] This "prevailing" was defined elsewhere in the document as the ability "to achieve political objectives and secure early war termination on terms favorable to the United States and its allies." After the document was publicized, Defense Secretary Caspar Weinberger went to great lengths in denying that U.S. officials believed "victory" to be possible in a general nuclear war.[72] The distinction appeared obfuscatory. Pentagon plans showed that, at a minimum, leading administration officials believed that the concept of escalation dominance made sense even near the highest level of escalation: all-out, intercontinental nuclear war. That did not mean that the new administration was a militarist monster that wanted war or thought one was necessary. In fact, at the level of operational detail, the Reagan administration's "prevailing" was not obviously different from the Carter administration's "countervailing." But even so, the writings and statements of Reagan officials both before and after taking office suggested strongly that the new administration had self-consciously adopted a new deterrence philosophy.

A second element in this departure—perhaps the most striking one—was Reagan's Strategic Defense Initiative (SDI). Reagan apparently got the idea in private conversations with his mentor, the physicist Edward Teller, and launched the scheme with little discussion within the administration. Reagan's vision of an impermeable, space-based shield to guard the United States from ballistic missiles—rendering nuclear weapons "obsolete"—was, it seemed, sincerely held. It was also almost universally derided by scientists, who noted that it rested on an historically preposterous assumption: That defensive technology would somehow achieve a permanent and decisive advantage over offensive technology. For many of Reagan's neoconservative backers and aides, however, SDI held out a tantalizing, real-world promise. Even an imperfect, "leaky" shield would move the terms of the strategic competition away from mutual vulnerability. While U.S. cities might be protected only haphazardly, U.S. strategic forces could be guarded much more effectively. And if the United States could maintain an edge in SDI technology, a plausible prospect, then it could arguably recover a measure of counterforce superiority. Perhaps not forever, but long enough, it was argued, to bankrupt the Soviet Union with a new arms race. An added bonus, in neoconservative eyes, was the fact that SDI (notwithstanding the various sophisticated disclaimers) would require renunciation of the ABM treaty, that hated document which actually codified the principle of mutual vulnerability.[73]

A final element of the Reagan departure was really no departure at all: a series of comments about the feasibility of limited nuclear war. "I could see where you could have the exchange of tactical weapons against troops in the field without it bringing either one of the major powers to pushing the button," said Reagan in a much-cited "gaffe" to a group of newspaper editors.[74] This, of course, is what flexible response had always been about. But in conjunction with all the other signs of an administration determined to shatter the cozy rules that had heretofore governed East-West competition (and that the administration viewed as a cover for Soviet expansion), these statements could only add to European unease. For a "limited nuclear war is a war limited to Europe," as Theodore Draper observed. "That circumstance has always made a limited war more attractive to Americans than to Europeans."[75]

The Europeans remained committed to a concept of nuclear deterrence that they regarded as pure—MAD in American parlance. In direct opposition to the then-current American concepts, they were diffident about any effort to demonstrate NATO resolve by preparing to fight nuclear war, as war has been defined and understood historically. Nuclear deterrence, in their view, rested not on the threat to fight, but on the threat to initiate general destruction. This position had separate, indigenous European roots in French military literature and in the plight of West Germans who saw modern warfare leading to total destruction of their homeland very quickly in any event. The only significant defections from this Euro-strategic culture came from people who were either nuclear pacifists or were ambivalent about the low nuclear threshold and thus proponents of stronger conventional forces. The European right shared the strategic principles of the American center-left. West German "Gaullists"—that is, right-wing members of the CDU/CSU—were also "Gaullist" in their philosophy of nuclear deterrence.[76] Even though many European elites shared the American neoconservative worries about NATO irresolution, the detailed strategic principles that animated the Committee on the Present Danger found few significant proponents in Western Europe.

A stark divergence in strategic cultures opened up. American officials saw McNamara-style strategic and moral errors repeated and writ large in Western Europe. European officials saw Americans ready to abandon the common, long-accepted principles of deterrence. Meanwhile, a conflict over some missiles in Europe—the subject of the next chapter—was turning these philosophic differences into a full-scale transatlantic crisis.

REAGAN AND THE SOVIET THREAT

Ronald Reagan's election constituted the political triumph of what Sidney Blumenthal has called the "counter-establishment."[77] Blumenthal was referring to American conservatives' conviction, expressed already in the earliest writings of William F. Buckley, Jr., that a "liberal establishment" had controlled American politics since the FDR administration. Conservatives thus consciously set out to create a counterestablishment of foundations, journals and academics—in effect, a revolutionary intellectual infrastructure. Arguably, the Committee on the Present Danger was the counterestablishment's most effective institution.

The idea of a counterestablishment is useful, as it expresses how many of its members viewed themselves and what inspired their more strident rhetoric. They saw themselves defending a Reagan revolution and tearing down the remaining idols of the deposed liberal establishment. The counterestablishment included several distinguishable traditions: Goldwater-style conservatism of the American West; the religious New Right, mainly of the south; and neoconservativism, with its strong northeastern and Jewish flavoring. In foreign-policy terms, neoconservativism dominated.

For the Reagan administration itself, however, a difficult question arises. How much real foreign-policy content did the neoconservative sound and fury signify? Notwithstanding Reagan's taunts to the Soviet "evil empire," and near hysteria on the European and American left about the threat of nuclear war, the first Reagan term was a time of considerable stability in the superpower relationship. "True crises . . . must be defined as episodes in which the superpowers approach the brink of hostilities with each other, not episodes in which they are merely exchanging insults at rather above the standard rate," as Coral Bell has sensibly observed. "By that criterion, there was not even an approximation of a true superpower crisis in the years concerned."[78]

The United States and the Soviet Union did exchange insults at an accelerated clip. The Soviets intensified their usual stream of anti-American blather—crude propaganda and subtler disinformation. Reagan, abandoning the putative civility of international dialogue, denounced the Soviet Union as "the focus of evil in the modern world." The tensest moment came when a Soviet fighter shot down and killed passengers and crew of Korean Airlines Flight 007 as it strayed over Soviet airspace on September 1, 1983. Still, it was not a crisis by the Bell definition.[79]

Reagan administration policies were more measured. The United States invaded the tiny Marxist *redoute* of Grenada and conducted a proxy war against the Sandinista government of Nicaragua. But both actions were probably more disturbing to American liberals than a genuine bother for Moscow. American aid to the resistance forces in Afghanistan surely *was* a problem for Moscow. But it was hardly a Reagan initiative; the Carter administration had started funnelling aid soon after the Soviet invasion.[80] Reagan policies in the area of arms control were moderate. He did move, with SDI, to stretch the ABM treaty past the breaking point. On the advice of his military joint chiefs, however, Reagan observed the provisions of the unratified SALT II treaty that he had denounced in his campaign against Carter. And early in his second term, guided by his (almost) unerring instinct for the political moment, Reagan embraced Gorbachev as a genuine reformer, while the neoconservative ideologues surrounding him warned of an elaborate trick. By mid-1985 many neoconservatives looked at Reagan and cried betrayal.[81]

A more dispassionate judgment comes from Coral Bell, who emphasizes the distinction between "declaratory policy" and "operational policy." In the Reagan administration this gap was very large, according to Bell. Declaratory policy came from ideologues such as Richard Perle. Operational policy was in the hands of such traditional conservatives as Alexander Haig and George Shultz. (Of course, there is *always* such a gap, as Bell herself concedes, quoting a French proverb that "the soup is never eaten as hot as it is cooked." Bureaucratic conservatism and dictates of political consensus make for a certain stability in any foreign policy.)

Bell's measured history is a useful reminder that the Reagan administration was an ideologically diverse and sometimes quite pragmatic institution. But it would be wrong to conclude that neoconservative ideology was essentially irrelevant to Reagan policies. The ideological center of gravity shifted unmistakably to the right during the Reagan administration, and the resulting unbalanced assessments of the Soviet threat brought disequilibrium to America's constitutional harmony, political morality and national economy.

Some former Reagan officials have tried to suggest that they knew all along that the Soviet Union was a paper tiger and that Reagan administration policies were cleverly designed to hasten its collapse. It was really "the liberals" who tended to exaggerate Soviet power, said former Pentagon official Richard Perle in a 1993 interview.[82] At the time, however, Perle and his colleagues were hardly describing that power as inconsequential. On the contrary, they portrayed a global threat of a subtlety, sophistication and ubiquity that was literally incompatible with the hollow shell that ultimately emerged.

While the gravest point of Western weakness was supposed to be Western Europe, Reagan officials did not limit their alarm geographically. William P. Clark, Reagan's first national security adviser, was apparently serious in suggesting that unless America resolutely battled Communism in Central America, "can we not expect El Salvador to join Nicaragua in targeting other recruits for the Soviet brand of Communism? When, some ask, will Mexico and the United Sta become the immediate rather than the ultimate targets?"[83] Clark's NSC successor, Robert McFarlane, explained in 1984 how the Soviets had succeeded in rendering containment "obsolete" now that they were "militarily strong and adventurous enough to leapfrog the buffer states and jump anywhere in the world that suits their own strategies."[84]

This new orthodoxy caused bitter bureaucratic conflict between the CIA's new leadership, under Director William Casey and Deputy Director Robert Gates, and the intelligence agency's Soviet analysts, whose "liberal" tendencies

Team B had criticized a decade earlier. In 1982 Gates rejected assessments from the CIA's Office of Soviet Analysis that asserted that, after the gains of the 1970s, Soviet expansionism in the Third World had reached its limits, that "the costs of an expanding empire could not be sustained," and that there were already hard intelligence data indicating a retrenchment. In 1985, over the strenuous skepticism of the same Soviet analysts, CIA senior management issued a Special National Intelligence Estimate highlighting the prospects of Soviet political penetration into revolutionary Iran (In the course of actual events, revolutionary Iran was considerably more successful in penetrating the Soviet Union).[85] As late as November 1986, Gates warned of a Soviet offensive against four targets: Mideast oil, southern African mineral wealth, the Panama isthmus and canal, and the ultimate target, the Western Alliance itself, which could be divided by using Soviet Third World successes " . . . to recreate the internal divisions caused by Vietnam." Gates continued: "It is imperative that, at long last, Americans recognize the strategic significance of the Soviet offensive—that it is in reality a war, a war waged between nations and against Western influence and presence, against economic development, and against the growth of democratic values."[86]

There was a climate of obsession in Reagan's Washington that should not be forgotten. Only by reference to the gravest and most immediate danger could Reagan officials justify the bizarre liberties that they took with the Constitution in order to provide aid to the Nicaraguan contras. The clique around Reagan that was responsible for the Iran-contra disaster included military officers who had fought in Vietnam and burned with a conviction that politicians and media elites had betrayed the cause for which their comrades had died. They operated on the assumption that the present danger was so acute as to justify flouting the Constitution, defying the mandate of Congress in the patriotic tradition (or so some argued) of Franklin Roosevelt and Abraham Lincoln.[87] But Lincoln and Roosevelt had faced real emergencies. "The first question that must be asked in the circumstances of a Franklin D. Roosevelt or Abraham Lincoln is: How serious, even desperate, is the situation?" Draper wrote. "Very few situations can compare with theirs."[88] Certainly not the Communist threat of 1986.

American foreign policy also lost its moral balance, supporting thugs, murderers and right-wing dictators as aggressive antibodies to the Communist virus. This was the pattern for most administrations throughout the Cold War, but the Reagan administration certainly did not improve matters. In late 1993 there were new revelations, for example, of the administration's refusal to acknowledge clear evidence of massacres committed by army units and right-wing death squads in El Salvador.[89]

One should not oversimplify a morally complicated situation, and much foreign policy consists of such situations. An easy resort to moral righteousness is rarely appropriate. The Reagan administration supported no colonel or dictator who was more evil than Stalin, and the U.S. alliance with Stalin has to be judged a necessary, one could even say "moral," expedient to fight Nazi Germany. But this justification derives entirely from the gravity of the Nazi menace. Was the gravity of the Soviet threat such to justify America's alignment, even indirectly, with Salvadoran death squads? People of good will could judge the Soviet threat differently. But the judgment, however difficult, ultimately has moral implications. American actions in El Salvador were "immoral" in some proportion to the degree that estimates of the Communist threat were exaggerated.

A final source of disequilibrium—to the national economy—is still with us in the form of a national debt that tripled during the Reagan years. This Reagan legacy has had a deleterious effect not only on the American domestic political economy, but also or even especially on its foreign policy. After the Cold War, America found itself, in practical terms, broke: saddled with a federal budget deficit that soaked up an absurd share of world savings and rendered the United States incapable of contributing adequately to the economic stabilization of Eastern Europe and the former Soviet Union.[90]

Not all of this debt can be blamed on military spending. As a matter of first principles, one can argue whether it resulted from overspending or undertaxing. But the fact remains that of $896.6 billion in new expenditures under Reagan, $434.2 billion—or 48 percent—was the bill for a massive military buildup.[91]

So there were constitutional, moral and financial costs to the Reagan administration's interpretation of and measures against the Soviet threat. As retroactive justification for this bill, it helps to promote a particular historiography: The price was steep, but winning the Cold War was worth it. The historical assumption here is that the Cold War, as late as 1980, still hung in the balance, to be tipped by Reagan's tougher foreign policies and marginal increases in defense spending. The next four chapters argue in detail why this assumption is false.

Part II

Defining the Threat

4

The Military Threat: Nuclear Blackmail

That containment had failed was something like an article of faith for members of the Reagan administration. They saw, or thought they saw, the sorry results of that failure around the globe, from Vietnam to Afghanistan to Angola to Nicaragua.

But the central argument of this book bears repeating: The fantasy of impending Soviet global preeminence depended above all on the virtual elimination of Western Europe as an ally of any value. "The centerpiece of the Soviet strategic view of world politics has always been that if Russia could control Western Europe . . . it would thereby control the world," said Eugene Rostow, a Committee on the Present Danger founder and leading spokesman in 1978.[1] The three chapters in this section describe in some detail how American pessimists imagined that this control—or "Finlandization"—would be achieved.

The most obvious way was through direct military threats. It was generally assumed that only a credible U.S. nuclear guarantee could shield the Europeans from such threats. This meant, in practice, that the United States had to convince both its allies and its potential enemy that it was prepared to start a nuclear war if the Russians attacked Western Europe. Deterring Soviet nuclear aggression was not enough.

The historical roots of this "first-use" strategy were discussed in chapter 1. One can easily imagine the problems such a posture caused. Why was it not abandoned?

A main reason was the durable assumption of almost unmatchable Soviet superiority in nonnuclear forces. This assumption appears debatable, to say the least. A tual troop levels on the two sides were not so radically different. In 1985 on the central front (Denmark, the Benelux countries, Germany, Poland and Czechoslovakia), the Warsaw Pact fielded roughly 975,000 troops against NATO's 814,300—a 1.2 to 1 ratio. Overall in Europe, the ratio was about the same, while globally the two alliances had roughly an equal number under arms as well. The Soviets *did* have a large advantage in main battle tanks (16,620 to NATO's 8,050). NATO had a qualitative superiority in airpower, while the numbers were roughly balanced.[2]

Raw numbers can be misleading of course. Critical questions of training, technology and morale come into play. The largest question marks seemed to hang over the Warsaw Pact. How would East German, Czech, Hungarian and especially Polish troops have acted in a war against the West? There can be little doubt that the vast majority of Polish people would have favored NATO. Were their soldiers so very different? Finally, one should recall that even at the time most analysts gave NATO the edge in training and equipment. Subsequent revelations have only tended to confirm this judgment.

Yet there is no denying that NATO suffered from some inherent obstacles to a credible conventional defense. Most glaring was the fact that the Alliance depended for its operational reserves on five American divisions that were stationed in the United States. Notwithstanding the horrific state of Soviet and East European transportation networks, it was presumably easier to move troops over central European plains than across an ocean. A common scenario saw NATO holding its own for a couple of weeks, but then being overrun by Soviet reserves brought up from Russia before the bulk of U.S. troops could be transported across the Atlantic.[3]

A second fundamental problem was the absence of France from NATO's military command. A detached analyst might reasonably assume that France would fight on its allies' side against any Soviet invasion. But France's withdrawal from the NATO command made it impossible for the planners to plan on it. The most egregious result was the unavailability of French territory as a staging and resupply zone, which left forward-based NATO troops dependent on north German, Dutch and Belgian ports, which were between 25 and 145 miles from East Germany and thus vulnerable to attack. France's absence also deprived the Alliance, at least for planning purposes, of an obvious source of reserves.[4]

The most serious problem, perhaps, concerned the strategic shackles introduced by Bonn's insistence on "forward defense," a commitment not to cede any West German territory for tactical purposes. Numerous military analysts argued that a mobile "defense in depth" offered better odds of defeating a Soviet invasion, but German officials countered that the likely cost in an era of high-tech weaponry would be the effective destruction of Germany. Because of its operational disadvantages, forward defense came to be seen as a West German lever to ensure that nuclear deterrence remained the bedrock of NATO strategy.

If the first use of nuclear weapons was an essential element of NATO's defense, it followed logically that any political or diplomatic pressures for "denuclearization" would play into Soviet hands. "If nuclear weapons were now disinvented," warned military analyst Edward Luttwak in 1982, "if all the hopes of the nuclear disarmers were fully realized, the Soviet Union would automatically emerge as the dominant power on the continent, fully capable of invading and conquering Western Europe if its political domination were resisted."[5] The conventional defense of Western Europe was an utter illusion, Luttwak asserted, even though NATO had the capacity to field more men than the Warsaw Pact, even though it was rich enough to overcome the Warsaw Pact's advantage in tanks and other armaments, and even though the Soviet Union suffered such obvious handicaps as restive, unreliable satellite states and a huge, bitter Chinese enemy. NATO, according to Luttwak, had two fundamental strategic disadvantages that dwarfed all the Soviet problems. First was the fact that NATO was a defensive alliance. It had to defend a 600-kilometer border, while the Soviet high command could concentrate its forces for a breakthrough. The second disadvantage came from the offensive power of tank forces, which enabled the Russians to probe for openings in the opposite defensive line, find and exploit them for a breakthrough, and overwhelmingly disrupt the defensive structure in NATO's rear.[6]

In theory NATO might counteract these disadvantages, according to Luttwak, but in practice it would not. It lacked "the political will, the training, and the organization to strike first in the face of massing Soviet forces" so as to ensure that the Russians "could not safely form up in deep columns for the attack and would instead have to dilute their strength to form a defensive array of their own."[7] It was, in Luttwak's view,

> . . . impossible to imagine that so many diverse governments would agree to let their national forces engage in a preemptive attack to anticipate a Soviet invasion before the outbreak of war. More likely, in the face of a Soviet mobilization and a build-up of divisions opposite NATO, there would be demands for negotiations to settle the crisis by what would no doubt be called "political means," i.e., eager concessions.[8]

This pessimistic analysis of NATO's conventional forces ended on a surprisingly optimistic note: Western Europe could be defended so long as

NATO leaders remained committed to "the architecture of nuclear deterrence
. . . [then] in place."[9] But such faith in extended nuclear deterrence had to
contend with growing doubts about the credibility of America's nuclear commitment. Numerous skeptics pointed out that a deterrence based on mutual
assured destruction hardly seemed consistent with the U.S. threat to launch
nuclear strikes against an invading Red Army. A new term of art—strategic
"decoupling"—came into vogue. This meant the process whereby the credibility of America's nuclear guarantee to Western Europe would become so
devalued by the realities of increasing American vulnerability to Soviet nuclear
attack that the West Europeans would feel helpless in the face of Soviet
intimidation and behave accordingly. Since hardly anyone imagined the Soviets
starting a war if they could achieve their goals without one, "decoupling" and
"Finlandization" were often used as different codes for the same fear.[10] In
response to shifting strategic realities, including the appearance of a new
generation of Soviet intermediate-range nuclear missiles, the West Europeans
were ready for (and according to the harsher critics already engaged in) a
wholesale submission of their interests and values to Soviet wishes.

"Decoupling" was more than just a figment of the neoconservative
imagination. It was supremely logical and widely anticipated from almost the
start of the nuclear age that the Europeans would feel less secure about American
protection once the Russians were able to deliver a massive nuclear blow to the
American homeland. So the coming of strategic parity obviously "decoupled"
Europe from America in a certain sense. What remained to be argued was the
seriousness of the break—to what extent did it require new arrangements for
defending Europe? For those, like McNamara, who considered the nuclear
balance of terror to be reasonably stable, this measure of nuclear decoupling was
regrettable but unavoidable. It was, moreover, a one-shot affair, a sea change,
to which NATO could adjust with strong conventional forces and improved
political cohesion.

However critics such as Paul Nitze, who worried that Moscow was already
tipping the balance of terror, held a very different view of the inner workings
of nuclear decoupling. In this view, decoupling was not a sea change but a
process of erosion that would continue for as long as the Russians improved on
their impending position of strategic nuclear superiority. This was an argument,
as Lawrence Freedman notes, that "further, and politically more radical, accommodation [to Soviet demands] might result from changes in *relative* strategic
power."[11] The Russians, according to this view, knew that military power,
whether conventional or nuclear, mattered. The Russians knew what to do with
nuclear superiority; fashionable American ideas about the "uselessness" of
nuclear weapons gave them no pause.

THE SS-20

In late 1977, some new Soviet missiles appeared along the Chinese border. Soon 240 of these SS-20s were deployed and aimed at Western Europe.[12] A two-stage version of the problem-ridden SS-16 ICBM, the SS-20 had a range of 4,400 to 5,000 kilometers, allow: coverage of all Western European targets from launch sites in western Russia. It was mobile and solid-fueled, which meant a low degree of vulnerability and a high state of readiness. Launchers could be reloaded and refired in the space of about an hour. The missile could carry three, independently targetable warheads. And it was accurate: Each warhead had a "circular error probable" (CEP) of 0.2 kilometer. This allowed for lower-yield warheads—an estimated 150 kilotons. Together, this greater accuracy and lower yield meant less collateral damage.[13]

It was frequently argued over the ensuing years of Euromissile debate that these technical features just dazzled the military technicians without adding appreciably to the Russian capability for destroying key NATO targets. From the neoconservative perspective, however, these new missiles demonstrated quite vividly the political utility of nuclear weapons. The SS-20s would erase any ambiguity about the superpowers' new strategic relationship and its inevitable political consequences for Europe.

The purpose of the SS-20 was thus "to serve as the ultimate engine of the process of nuclear blackmail," Eugene Rostow, serving as President Reagan's Arms Control and Disarmament Agency chief, told a Congressional committee in early 1982. It was, Rostow continued, "the most dramatic example we have witnessed since . . . the Cuban missile crisis of the stunning political impact of the existence—not the use, but the existence—of nuclear weapons."[14] Reagan himself declared:

> The Soviets' fundamental foreign policy aim is to break the link that binds us to our NATO allies. Their growing nuclear threat to Europe, especially since the mid-seventies, has a political as well as a military purpose—the deliberate fostering of a sense of insecurity among the peoples of Western Europe, and pressure for accommodation to Soviet power. The ultimate Soviet goal in Europe is to force the nations to accommodate themselves to Soviet interests on Soviet terms.[15]

This idea that political power accrued from the mere existence of additional nuclear forces was already quite familiar from the theories of the Committee on the Present Danger. But in discussions of the SS-20 there was often stated, and almost always implied, a special twist on this argument. It was suggested that the special characteristics of the SS-20 gave it a unique, *theater* role as an instrument of intimidation. Precisely because it could not reach the United States, but could strike anywhere in Western Europe, the missile supposedly underscored the separation of fates between Western Europe and the United States. The new Soviet missile's "range and mobility was designed to exploit the new strategic relationship between the U.S. and the USSR," Richard Burt, head of the State Department's Bureau of Politico-Military Affairs, told a House subcommittee.[16] The SS-20 thus might be the critical, final tool to decouple Europe from the United States, convince the Europeans of the unchallengeable sway of Soviet regional power, and establish a form of Russian hegemony.

This logic was vehemently rejected by that group of defense experts who remained the American standard-bearers for the notion of nuclear sufficiency. The most prominent of these were the so-called gang of four—McNamara himself, George Kennan, McGeorge Bundy, and former U.S. SALT negotiator Gerard Smith—who came together in the midst of the Euromissile crisis to argue that NATO would do a lot better to renounce the first use of nuclear weapons.

The whole idea of a theater nuclear imbalance was both pernicious and senseless, they charged. It was pernicious because, to the extent that it gained acceptance, it fostered the very anxiety and vulnerability to intimidation that it prophesied. And they viewed as utter nonsense the proposition that the SS-20 should be especially intimidating to the Europeans because it could hit them but not the Americans. Soviet ICBMs could hit both. The SS-20 enjoyed special decoupling properties only in an imaginary nuclear world where a European theater, and the possibility of theater nuclear war, existed apart and independent from the strategic level. The Europeans could find the SS-20 more threatening than the Soviets' already more than ample ICBMs and IRBMs only by going to literally absurd lengths.[17]

This seems a powerful argument. It would have been even more persuasive if it were just an abstract debate between the gang of four and the Committee on the Present Danger about the logical perceptions and behavior of the Europeans. However, the fact is that many European leaders *were* anxious about the theater balance, and not just those few who shared the strategic perspectives of the Committee on the Present Danger.

The most celebrated case was that of West German chancellor Helmut Schmidt, whose October 1977 speech to the International Institute for Strategic Studies in London is often cited as the seminal European appeal for new American missiles to redress Europe's theater imbalance.[18] The speech was largely devoted to economic issues. He mentioned briefly the dangers of Soviet conventional and tactical nuclear superiority in Europe and made only oblique reference to the new Soviet intermediate-range missiles. But his speech did suggest a context for understanding why the SS-20s might appear particularly ominous to the Europeans. Their range placed them just outside SALT constraints. Thus SALT itself might be viewed as a covenant that somehow legitimized an unrestrained nuclear threat against the Europeans. In this context, the SS-20 stood as a symbol of what *Le Monde* foreign editor Michel Tatu called Russia's "regional vocation," that is, its determination to dominate the continent.[19] Or, to put it more simply, the SS-20 was a tangible and permanent threat. That threat seemed to enjoy deepening seriousness with the simultaneous rise of a general political sense that America was increasingly uncertain about its commitment to Europe. European complaints about the Carter administration's vacillations were perhaps overstated, but deeply felt nonetheless. European leaders worried that American urgency to achieve a SALT II agreement would result in a sellout of European security interests. They were particularly worried that the Americans would trade away the option of deploying cruise missiles, which were considered to be exceptionally useful instruments of European deterrence. Meanwhile, stories appeared in the U.S. press that the Carter administration was reconsidering the American commitment to forward defense.[20]

A strained transatlantic mood was made worse by controversy over deployment of the so-called neutron bomb. This enhanced radiation warhead (ERW) promised a significant improvement in NATO's ability to defeat a Soviet armored attack. It was designed as a low-yield bomb for short-range Lance missiles and artillery. Its blast and long-term fallout would be minimal; most of its energy would be released in a stream of neutrons to kill Warsaw Pact infantry and especially tank crews. Because its collateral damage to the surrounding German population and countryside would be limited, the ERW seemed like a more usable nuclear weapon. But because it was, ultimately, a nuclear weapon, the risk of further escalation appeared great. For both these reasons it was said to enhance deterrence. It was both effective militarily and a bridge psychologically between conventional and nuclear war.

Of course, any such qualitative advance in nuclear weaponry was bound to provoke an emotional and political furor. The ERW was easily pilloried by European and American antinuclear activists and by Soviet propaganda as a "capitalist bomb" designed to kill people and leave property standing. More sober critics challenged the idea that a more usable nuclear weapon would improve deterrence rather than cause its breakdown.

The Carter administration managed to make the worst out of an already bad situation. Carter aides pressed the Schmidt government, which had grave political difficulties from within its own party in even accepting such a weapon, to ask the United States for its deployment in the Federal Republic. Schmidt reluctantly did so, whereupon Carter—beset by moral doubts of his own—decided to delay the program indefinitely. It was generally agreed that the whole affair dealt a damaging blow to the credibility of American leadership.[21]

Aside from SALT, and aside from the neutron bomb embarrassment, there was the decoupling logic, which said that by extending nuclear deterrence to Europe, America was tolerating risks that were essentially intolerable. A future American president might be more or less reliable than Carter, more or less committed to Western Europe's independence, but this logic would inevitably press him to avoid the risks.

NATO'S "EUROMISSILE" SOLUTION

European unease and American chagrin helped inspire the Carter administration's proposal, accepted by NATO ministers in December 1979, for the United States to deploy 572 new long-range nuclear missiles in West Germany, the United Kingdom, Italy, Belgium and the Netherlands. These were to comprise 108 Pershing II ballistic missiles in the Federal Republic and 464 ground-launched cruise missiles (GLCMs) scattered among the five countries. This so-called Intermediate Nuclear Forces (INF) program, once implemented, would give the United States a capability that the Kennedy administration had deliberately renounced: to send nuclear missiles from bases in Europe into Soviet territory. Over the following eight years, this program, and the struggle to see it completed, was the object of constant philosophical tinkering to make it serve the rather disparate purposes and ideologies of several European governments and two American administrations. As a result, the rationales for the INF deployments were multiple and, quite often, contradictory. Since these contradictions contributed much to the transatlantic bitterness of the early 1980s, a brief summary of the various rationales seems in order:

Countering the SS-20

A cursory glance at this history leads to the most straightforward explanation. In its so-called two-track decision, NATO tied the deployment announcement to a promise of negotiations to restore the theater balance upset by SS-20s. When the Russians were finally persuaded to remove the latter, the former would no longer be necessary, hence the historically elegant solution of the "zero option," ratified in the December 1987 INF Treaty.

Symbolic Recoupling

According to this rationale, the Europeans required new evidence, in the form of military hardware, of American reliability. In this sense the exact function of the new U.S. missiles might be less important than their visibility. Hence the argument for land-basing as opposed to sea-basing.[22] From this requirement flowed also the seemingly arbitrary decision on the number of new missiles: NATO wanted enough to serve as a credible symbol of U.S. commitment, but not so many as to suggest the intention to fight a nuclear war limited to the European theater.[23]

A Nuclear "Trigger"

Some supporters of the NATO deployments argued that the Pershing IIs in particular enjoyed special characteristics that were needed to establish a distinct bridge between the European battlefield and American strategic nuclear forces, or, to put it somewhat differently, a nearly automatic "trigger" for those strategic forces. To understand this argument, one must go back to the early debates over flexible response.[24] It will be recalled that a doctrine of early first use won out, despite the Americans' strong misgivings. Although massive retaliation was abandoned, NATO continued to depend on the explicit threat to use nuclear weapons against a Soviet conventional attack.

But the American misgivings remained, and they intensified as the Soviets built up their intercontinental forces. Not only did it appear less and less likely that an American president would order the escalation to nuclear war, but what was worse, the need to do so seemed to many like the antithesis of what was required to fortify political courage and unity among democracies in a gathering crisis.

The new NATO Euromissiles, and especially the Pershing IIs, were seized upon as a logical solution to this dilemma. From launchers in West Germany, they could hit important military targets in the western Soviet Union. With a new generation of guided warheads, they were considered phenomenally accurate. They had all the damage-limiting characteristics of the SS-20, and if the Russians believed that their use was therefore more likely, then they had every reason to fear them.[25] At the same time, despite their mobile launchers, forward deployment on German soil made them vulnerable to capture or destruction. This was the root of the famous "use it or lose it" pressure that would supposedly involve America in nuclear war against targets deep inside Russia well before the Red Army could establish control over West German territory. America would be unable to stand aloof from a European war. The Soviets would be convinced of this, and the West Europeans would be reassured and reinforced in their resistance to blackmail.

This reasoning had its critics, who argued that a U.S. president was no more likely to order the firing of Pershing IIs from West Germany than the launch of ICBMs from Kansas. They were both American missiles; the Russians knew it and could be counted on to retaliate accordingly. So the risks and inhibitions for America's leadership were unchanged.[26]

But it was nonetheless difficult to argue that the situation was unchanged from a Soviet perspective. The Russians could hardly plan a European war as if the Pershing IIs did not exist. The threat posed by the missiles was so great that they compelled the Russians to plan on preempting their use early in a war. And it was argued that the Russians could be confident about preempting only by nuclear means. Hence the Pershing II deployments solved NATO's first-use dilemma. The Russians would be forced to make any attack on Western Europe a nuclear attack. Given the possible reaction, this was a far more daunting prospect for them to contemplate.[27] The Euromissile deployments thus lowered the threshold of nuclear war, reshaping the deterrence mechanism into something more closely resembling a doomsday machine.

A Test of European Resolve

At some point in this history, a critical shift took place: Where at first the intermediate-range missiles were desired by European governments as a token of American commitment, they came to be interpreted by the Reagan administration as a test of European resolve. If the Europeans refused to go ahead with the deployments, it would be seen as caving in to Soviet blackmail. Circumstances were complicated by the fact that the idea outlined above, of the Pershing IIs as a kind of doomsday trigger, was fundamentally at odds with the neoconservative opposition to mutual assured destruction. So while the Reagan administration interpreted the deployment commitment as a political test, it never was very clear what it was testing.

THE EUROMISSILE CRISIS AND ITS INTERPRETATIONS

In the half-decade following the decision to deploy new U.S. Pershings and GLCMs in Europe, NATO was consumed by a struggle to implement it. The scale of this crisis came as something of a surprise. In most of Europe, the antinuclear movement had been rather quiet for over a decade. Such antinuclear activism as there was seemed largely ecological in focus, directed against nuclear power plants. In West Germany, the neutron-bomb controversy had aroused only limited public interest, despite the controversy it stirred within the government and the SPD. In Britain, 'ban the bomb' forces had been withering since the early 1960s. The same year as the neutron-bomb controversy, 1977, Britain accepted with hardly a stir another 90 American F-111s, effectively doubling the number of U.S. nuclear-capable fighter-bombers based there.

But in June 1980, 20,000 Britons massed in Hyde Park to protest the NATO INF deployment decision. Over the next three years hundreds of thousands marched in London, Rome, Milan, the Hague, Brussels, Amsterdam, Berlin and Bonn. In the fall of 1983, just before the scheduled start of deployments, Western Europe was engulfed in a virtual wave of demonstrations. Most dramatically, an estimated million West Germans came out for the largest street protests in the Federal Republic's history.[28]

In Britain and West Germany, at the level of political leadership, the consensus on defense appeared shattered, as the Labour Party and parts of the SPD embraced nuclear pacifism. West German polls showed a majority of voters opposed to the NATO deployments. But the overriding Western mood seemed not so much a principled and informed opposition to NATO or its policies as a general fear of nuclear war and belief in its imminence. The fear spread to both sides of the Atlantic, with a public focus on books, articles and films on the details and horror of a hypothetical nuclear war. In both Europe and America, the movement to forestall this war became a moral cause célèbre, taken up by writers, scientists, politicians and theologians.

In the midst of these developments, Soviet propaganda kept up a steady barrage of threats, distortions and lies about the deployments. The Russians seemed hopeful of manipulating the issue to split the Alliance, and many observers thought they might succeed. After all, Henry Kissinger complained, the "clamor for peace in much of the West [was] in most respects addressed to the wrong governments" and was "unmatched . . . by comparable agitation in the East." The result, he warned, was a "psychological imbalance" that would "tend inevitably toward a unilateral psychological, and even physical, disarmament."[29]

Clearly the Alliance suffered politically as the result of the nuclear issue. But if the Reagan administration wanted to alleviate the suffering it seems to have hit upon the wrong diagnosis. The general idea seemed to be that the Europeans were behaving fearfully because they knew that the MAD doctrine and the balance of nuclear forces favored the Soviets. Thus, as we have seen, the administration responded with repeated affirmations of its adherence to the neoconservative concepts of nuclear competition, with an emphasis on matching Soviet "war-fighting" forces, a belief in the efficacy of nuclear superiority and the possibility of "prevailing" in nuclear war. "You show me a Secretary of

Defense who's not planning to prevail, and I'll show you a Secretary of Defense who ought to be impeached," declared Defense Secretary Casper Weinberger in 1983.[30] Predictably, this "cure" had about as much healing benefit as an eighteenth-century physician's bloodletting. As Weinberger's predecessor, Harold Brown, observed, the crisis was only "exacerbated by European concern that the U.S. Government, or important officials in it, [took] the horrors of nuclear war too lightly."[31]

At about this time, George Kennan, Robert McNamara, McGeorge Bundy and Gerard Smith came up with an alternative prescription. They argued that NATO's doctrine of first use was very dangerous in its own right and causing the Alliance to unravel. The four senior statesmen—who caused something of a furor when they published their "no first use" proposal in the spring of 1982—were not really laying out a new position.[32] In his promotion of flexible-response strategy in the early 1960s, McNamara campaigned publicly for a policy of no *early* first use. He later revealed that in "long private conversations" with presidents Kennedy and Johnson he had "recommended, without qualification, that they never initiate, under any circumstances, the use of nuclear weapons."[33] Kennan, for his part, had expressed his no-first-use convictions soon after the beginning of the nuclear age.[34]

However, the ongoing Euromissile crisis apparently galvanized the four into an intellectual alliance and allowed them to revive their old arguments in conjunction with the currently fashionable fear of Europe's Finlandization. In effect, they turned the neoconservative argument on its head. The threat of a Finlandized Europe came not from a dearth of nuclear capabilities and plans, they argued, but from an excess. The political uproar over the Euromissile deployments demonstrated that first use was a divisive strategy with serious costs to the "political coherence" of NATO.[35]

NATO had decided to deploy the Pershing IIs and GLCMs based on the idea that a credible first-use guarantee was the best (and, in fact, only) way to reassure the allies and recouple the two continents. But the subsequent political storm showed that it was impossible to instill the U.S. nuclear guarantee with credibility without frightening Western European publics.[36] This was not because the European people lacked the sophistication to appreciate the paradox of nuclear deterrence. Quite the contrary: The no-first-use advocates had a view of crisis dynamics similar to the one held instinctively by European publics. European publics recognized intuitively that the large number of nuclear warheads deployed on the central front made their use likely in the event of war and that such a nuclear war would be very difficult to contain. Their political leaders recognized this also, but considered this danger the best possible guarantee against the Soviets' provoking or taking advantage of a crisis. But such confidence was based on a complacent extrapolation of current conditions and psychologies.

> The balance of terror, and the caution of both sides, appear strong enough today to prevent . . . a catastrophe, at least in the absence of some deeply destabilizing political change which might lead to panic or adventurism on either side. But the present unbalanced reliance on nuclear weapons, if long continued, might produce exactly such a political change. The events of the last year have shown that differing perceptions of the role of nuclear weapons can lead to destructive recriminations, and when these differences are compounded by understandable disagreements on other matters such as Poland and the Middle East, the possibilities for trouble among Allies are evident.[37]

The political problems posed by first use doctrine fed back into reduced military effectiveness. While there was "little risk" that NATO would fail to observe Warsaw Pact preparations for an invasion, there was "significant risk" that NATO, "out of fear of alarming the Soviet Union and provoking an attack, would fail to authorize prudent actions in response." This was partly because the "commingling" of NATO's nuclear and conventional forces would make any mobilization more threatening to the Soviets. As a result, Western leaders would likely hold back, and such "delays in NATO mobilization and reinforcement could significantly shift the conventional balance in favor of the Warsaw Pact and would present the worst possible conventional scenario."[38]

In a crisis the Soviets might have been tempted by the thought that they "could achieve some quick and limited gain that would be accepted because no defense or reply could be concerted."[39] Then, of course, the Soviets might be victorious, or a nuclear war might come despite their calculations—a war that these no-first-use advocates expected to escalate almost inevitably. Put differently, Europe's distress over nuclear weapons was not only predictable; it was quite logical as well.

The diagnosis of NATO problems offered by the no-first-use advocates made a lot more sense than that of the Reagan administration.[40] Their prescription, however, amounted to radical surgery. European governments had no interest in it. They just hoped to get through their current ordeal, and the way to do that, they thought, was to prove to their publics that they sincerely desired a negotiated end to the East-West confrontation. Thus the negotiating track of the "two-track" decision was critical. They repeatedly urged the Americans to show comparable sincerity in the INF negotiations.

But these appeals simply reinforced Reagan administration pessimism about Western Europe's capacity to maintain its freedom and values. Neoconservatives considered this faith in the "atmospherics" of negotiating to be another manifestation of the "détente ideology"—a lever for Moscow to manipulate the inherent Western yearning to accommodate.

The Reagan administration's most outstanding exponent of this critique was Richard Perle, who had attained early neoconservative prominence as an aide to Senator Henry Jackson, scripting Jackson's attacks on SALT and Kissingerian diplomacy. In the Reagan administration, as assistant secretary of defense for international security policy, Perle led an effort to shatter what he and his colleagues regarded as the détente mindset. In testimony for congressional hearings on the INF talks, Perle warned against a fixation on negotiations and arms control:

> [If] we harbor illusions about our adversary and build policies of disarmament upon those illusions, if we sign treaties that create the impression but not the reality that our adversaries have joined us in a search for restraint and accommodation, we will set in motion the trends of history that weapons procurement and budget levels may prove powerless to arrest.[41]

These dark "trends of history" were, in Perle's view, driven by the same psychological dynamic that had led Britain and France to sacrifice Czechoslovakia to Hitler. Quoting at length from a British participant in the 1938 Munich negotiations, Perle warned against a commitment to negotiations for their own sake.[42] Twelve years of strategic arms talks with the Soviets had done real harm, according to Perle, because they had generated a myth of superpower cooperation and helped to create an American commitment to accommodation, while at the same time, the Soviets were tirelessly and successfully pursuing superiority. The same process now threatened to repeat itself in the INF negotiations.[43]

Perle reportedly viewed the whole Pershing/GLCM initiative as another Carter administration mistake; the deployments would be militarily marginal, while the negotiating track would only cause trouble for NATO.[44] It was nonetheless a commitment that NATO had to fulfill.

Some of Perle's administration colleagues, who did not necessarily share his general hostility toward negotiations, were nonetheless unhappy about the opportunities that the INF talks presented to the Soviets. By promising to negotiate before deploying, the allies seemed to be extending to the Russians an effective veto over NATO policy.[45] It would be difficult politically for NATO to deploy while talks were still going on, and it would be relatively easy for the Soviets to prolong the talks indefinitely without ever negotiating in good faith.

Furthermore, there was a danger that the Soviets could use NATO's eagerness for an agreement to get codified certain weapons counts that would have the effect of establishing, in principle, a Russian right to military preeminence in Europe. This was how the Americans interpreted the whole series of Russian INF proposals. One pernicious Soviet technique was to play on the image of a besieged and encircled Russia that therefore needed to match not just American nuclear weapons, but also French, British and, logically, even Chinese forces. "In essence," said Eugene Rostow, "we are being asked to accept and perpetuate an overwhelming Soviet nuclear advantage based on the rationale that the Soviet Union has more enemies than the United States and thus has a 'right' to more offensive systems."[46]

Another Soviet stratagem was the way they tried to define the subject of the negotiations. They seemed to exclude "literally thousands of Soviet aircraft with nuclear capabilities comparable to those of the American aircraft they do include," as Rostow put it. The Soviets preferred to focus on American "forward-based" systems: land- or sea-based aircraft in Europe with a sufficient range to reach the Soviet Union. They argued that their own equivalent aircraft were qualitatively different because they could not reach the continental United States. It was, said Rostow, "a most significant argument, which throws a clear light on the Soviet Union's major interest in these negotiations so far—to drive a wedge between the United States and its allies." It was "a shorthand way of saying that the United States has no business being in Europe . . . a bare-faced claim not to equality but to hegemony."[47]

Reagan officials were worried that Bonn, committed as it was to *Ostpolitik*, was eager for a compromise even if it embodied such insidious Soviet concepts. This worry gave rise to the shift in American thinking that was mentioned earlier: The INF deployment battle was converted in the American mind from a token of U.S. commitment to a test of West European resolve.

The shift began, ironically, in the same Carter administration whose vacillations had contributed to the European yearning for a renewed token of America's nuclear commitment. Once having decided to bestow that token—in the form of 572 Euromissiles—the administration was determined that it be accepted. The administration was also predisposed, partly due to the sharp personal rancor between Carter and German chancellor Helmut Schmidt, to assign the worst possible interpretation to German behavior.[48] As it happened, Schmidt came under immediate pressure from his own party to encourage some Soviet-American settlement that would forestall the deployments. He had earlier tried to set himself up as an intermediary between Carter and Brezhnev, an offer rejected by the Americans.[49] Now, six months after NATO's December 1979 deployment decision, Schmidt suggested "it would serve peace if both sides did not deploy for the next three years, and instead negotiated soon on mutual reductions."[50] Schmidt's aides immediately insisted that the chancellor meant this three-year moratorium to be consistent with the NATO two-track decision, since the first actual American deployments were planned for late 1983. But the Carter administration interpreted the proposal as a sign of German wavering that would "further undercut Western European support for the nuclear initiative."[51] Carter, at the urging of National Security Adviser Zbigniew Brzezinski, sent Schmidt a stern warning not to offer any new proposals on his upcoming trip to Moscow (a journey that the Americans had unsuccessfully opposed). Schmidt, furious, replied publicly, in English, "You can rest assured that you can depend on the bloody Germans!"[52]

The Reagan administration's distrust of the Germans was even deeper, a recurrent theme in administration deliberations over how to handle the INF negotiations. Most of the work of these deliberations fell to middle-level White House officials, among whom Richard Perle was especially contemptuous of West German reliability.[53] "During the INF negotiations the Germans were a source of constant pressure," he complained several years later. "At NATO meetings you couldn't get past the '*Guten Morgen*'before they would urge the abandonment of one NATO position or another."[54] In this bitter recounting of his INF experience, Perle described "the collapse of the traditional German security policy— culminating nearly a decade of deepening neutralist, anti-defense sentiment." West Germany's old policy had given way to a new one that was "shaped by an abject failure of nerve" and by a "neo-romantic abandon that appeals to many Germans much as neo-isolationism appeals to many Americans."[55]

Perle's distrust was evident in 1982 in his insistence that the United States stand firm behind its "zero-option" proposal for banning all medium-range missiles. The zero option (derived by the Reagan administration from Schmidt's "Null Lösung" proposal) initially won praise from the Europeans as a visionary scheme, but was later dismissed as a propaganda ploy—patently and intentionally nonnegotiable so as to spare the Americans the necessity of serious bargaining.[56] However, this criteria of "negotiability" struck Perle as symptomatic of precisely the same mindset that had turned détente into a one-sided American rush to concessions. Now it was the Germans whose desire for an agreement at any cost would ensnare the United States in its old game of crafting its proposals according to how they would play in Moscow, rather than to how they served NATO interests. The impulse toward this kind of conciliation was so strong among the Europeans that any wavering from the zero option would set off an avalanche of concessions—such was the gist of Perle's analysis.

On the basis of this analysis, Perle opposed the most significant move toward a Soviet-American compromise during the first round of INF negotiations.[57] On July 16, 1982, U.S. chief negotiator Paul Nitze took a famous walk in the woods with Yuli Kvitsinsky, his Soviet counterpart. In the forested Jura Mountains near the Swiss-French border, the two men put together a tentative package agreement that would leave the Americans 75 Tomahawk cruise missile launchers (with four missiles each) against 75 SS-20s on the Soviet side (a two-thirds reduction). The Americans would drop plans for deploying the Pershing IIs. The balance of intermediate-range warheads would be 300 for the Americans and 225 for the Soviets, since each American launcher carried four missiles, while each Soviet missile carried three warheads.

The scheme was designed as a joint proposal for each negotiator to float with his respective government. In truth, the impetus for and the main lines of the proposal came from Nitze. The plan's most radical feature was Nitze's willingness to forgo the Pershing IIs. This would leave the Soviets with a monopoly on intermediate-range ballistic missiles in Europe (and allow them to pretend they had been compensated for French and British ballistic missiles).

In essence, Nitze had become convinced that the Pershing IIs were more trouble than they were worth. They were to replace the Pershing IAs, which had a much shorter range (800 kilometers). But that meant that NATO would have to change its targets—the closer targets would now go uncovered or would have to be covered by other means. Why not instead replace the IA with a modernized missile of the same range, the IB, and cover the deeper targets inside the Soviet Union with Tomahawk GLCMs and U.S. ICBMs? The plan had the added bonus, in Nitze's eyes, of completely banning Soviet ground-launched cruise missiles with a range over 600 kilometers, thus ridding NATO of a potential military and arms-control headache. At the same time, while cutting Soviet missiles massively, the plan envisioned a significant U.S. deployment of cruise missiles, thus preserving a visible presence of ground-launched missiles that could reach the Soviet Union from bases in Europe. These cruise missiles would remain as an explicit bridge between the U.S. theater and strategic arsenals, a bridge that many NATO strategists deemed necessary regardless of what happened to the SS-20. True, the cruise missiles would be based much farther from the central front and thus would not enjoy the characteristics of vulnerability and automatic triggering that some strategists also favored. But Nitze, hostile to MAD, was not inclined to the paradoxical logic whereby vulnerability should be welcomed.

When Nitze returned to pitch his plan in Washington, he initially encountered wary interest, but the reception soon turned hostile. Perle organized and led the opposition.[58] Richard Burt, head of the State Department's Bureau of Politico-Military Affairs, was also opposed; these two men influenced their Pentagon and State Department chiefs, and ultimately President

Reagan became convinced that it was a bad plan. The opposition centered around three broad arguments. First, Nitze was faulted on procedural grounds; he had "wandered off the reservation" in a sharp departure from the official U.S. position without adequately consulting his Washington superiors.[59] Second, on military grounds, there was disquiet at the prospect of balancing Soviet ballistic missile with U.S. cruise missiles only; Reagan himself reportedly became fixated on the inequity of trading "fast flying" weapons for "slow flying" weapons.[60] Finally, there was the deep distrust of America's allies stressed above. The Pershing IIs were deemed symbolically important not only as the military centerpiece of the program but also as the only missile Germany was scheduled to receive in the early years of the program; Tomahawks were to be set up in Britain and Italy at the same time, but not in Germany until 1986. A delay in missiles for Germany was seen as psychologically debilitating. "If we let the Germans off the hook, we can wave goodbye to everyone else as they run for cover," Burt reportedly said, in reference to the British and Italians.[61] In a similar vein, Perle worried aloud that the Soviets would violate their secrecy agreement and leak news of the Nitze plan. This would give the West Germans an excuse to back out, since Nitze had conceded in principle that the Pershing IIs might not be critical for NATO's defense.[62] Thus, in the American mind, a commitment to deploy some specific military hardware was like taking the pledge: One single lapse, and the alcoholic's sickness would inevitably regain control.

It is not my intention to suggest that this third factor was the critical one that killed the proposal. Nitze himself said years later that he remained convinced that if the Soviets had responded favorably, U.S. opposition would have melted away.[63] What I am trying to show is that the American government's pessimism about its allies was a recurrent and influential factor in all its deliberations. (This pessimism emerged again in 1989 in a Bush administration unwilling to enter negotiations on short-range missiles because it feared an uncontrollable German antinuclear impulse.)

Analyzing the role of Europessimism in the walk-in-the-woods episode is complicated for another reason. One basis on which Perle and Burt attacked Nitze's initiative was that the initiative itself grew out of excessive gloominess. Nitze was desperate for an agreement because he doubted that the Germans would stick to their deployment commitment. Nitze freely admitted the charge. "Yeah, particularly Rick Burt," he said years later, "was full of condemnation of me for being too anxious to get an agreement because I thought the German political scene wouldn't take the strains if we deployed, with the Soviets walking out [and] making all kinds of threats. . . . I thought that would be disastrous, yes. I was wrong. We got through it all right."[64]

A FARCICAL POSTSCRIPT

Finally, the NATO supporters of a bolstered nuclear deterrence based on first use won a clear, albeit costly, victory. Labour and the SPD were repudiated at the polls. The Italian Communists did not even dare to make a major issue of the deployments. The French were treated to the rare spectacle of their left-wing president standing before the Bundestag and urging the West Germans to strengthen their nuclear ties to America. The missile deployments began, and the Russians stormed out of arms control talks.

Then, with this victory in sight, Ronald Reagan seemed to run away from it. This, at any rate, was the verdict of many of his neoconservative backers, along with much of the West European defense establishment. When the newly installed Kremlin chief, Mikhail Gorbachev, realizing that he could not get a better deal on INF than the U.S. zero option, decided to make a virtue of necessity by proposing a three-stage abolition of all nuclear weapons by the end of this century, Reagan responded favorably. He did so despite the conventional wisdom that a "denuclearized Europe" was the Soviet Union's long-cherished goal and one that NATO had always resisted. Reagan met Gorbachev at a hastily called summit meeting in Reykjavik and, by most accounts, came very close to agreeing to the complete abolition of nuclear weapons. American officials spent much of the succeeding weeks promising bewildered West European governments that the United States had no intention of repudiating NATO's hard-won commitment to nuclear deterrence.

But Reagan's utopian rhetoric was starting to make everyone uneasy. The 1987 Soviet-American INF treaty was in fact a fairly modest agreement to dismantle the SS-20s and American Euromissiles; it had only a marginal impact on the superpowers' nuclear firepower. But the sudden revelation of the American president as an antinuclear idealist caused many to view it as an element of Europe's new "denuclearization dynamic." And it was assumed, for all the reasons discussed above, that a denuclearized Europe would be easy prey to Soviet domination.[65]

"I don't think Ronald Reagan has ever been comfortable with nuclear weapons," Richard Perle complained several years later to a television interviewer. "And this idea of a nuclear-free world, which I think is rubbish, and dangerous rubbish, has always been present in his thinking. But it wasn't always obvious to his supporters."[66] Perle's lament constitutes a rather extraordinary comment on the neoconservative movement. The structure of extended nuclear deterrence was layered with contradictions that were causing strains by the 1970s. American neoconservatives sought to cut through these contradictions by achieving a moral and psychological liberation from the paralysis of nuclear angst. Their vehicle was a charismatic president who, while not notoriously clear-thinking himself, did represent in American political life a set of clear and appealing ideas. He was a populist whose people responded to his appeals for a renewal of national confidence. They responded with somewhat less enthusiasm to his call for a crusade against Communism. But they would not steel themselves for the neoconservatives' unflinching bluff in the face of nuclear holocaust. So Reagan responded to *their* nuclear angst. SDI, with no apparent basis in scientific reality, was Reagan's nearly religious vision of a protective shield against nuclear harm. Neoconservatives embraced this vision because they had little choice and because an achievable, imperfect ballistic-missile defense might have restored U.S. counterforce superiority. But Reagan never shifted his rhetoric to reflect their more prosaic intentions, and the damage was done—a further blow to the ideological legitimacy of nuclear deterrence.[67]

Meanwhile, the Reagan administration had proceeded with its costly buildup of conventional and nuclear forces. Yet the supposedly overriding strategic threat—the alleged vulnerability of U.S. land-based missiles—was effectively ignored.[68]

It would be a mistake, in retrospect, to be very critical of Reagan's reversals and inconsistencies on nuclear matters. After all, a winning politician is expected to adjust his campaign program to the realities of governing—and from 1985 those realities included an extraordinary transformation of the Soviet adversary. Yet it is astonishing that after these eight years of American tergiversations, U.S. officials were nonetheless ready to lambaste their European allies for the latter's allegedly insufficient devotion to nuclear deterrence. Nonetheless, this is what happened. In 1989, the early months of the Bush administration, after all but the most stubborn Cold Warriors understood that the Cold War had ended, the Euromissile history repeated itself as farce. Another bitter intra-NATO dispute was caused almost entirely by the distorting effects of the Finlandization idea on Americans' geopolitical imagination.

The United States, strongly backed by the government of British prime minister Margaret Thatcher, was resolved to deploy a new generation of short-range nuclear weapons in Western Europe (primarily West Germany). The army would replace its two-decade-old Lance missile with a new model with a range four times greater (450 kilometers, just under the 500-kilometer limit set by the INF treaty). It would also get new nuclear artillery shells. The air force would deploy a new air-launched missile with a range also just under the 500-kilometer limit.[69]

It was clear that such a program would run into heavy resistance in West Germany. The country's CDU/CSU leadership still felt shaken by the INF ordeal and, in some cases, almost betrayed by the haste with which America had negotiated the final INF accord. Its popularity was waning, with its chances for surviving the 1990 elections looking increasingly dim. The SPD was growing correspondingly more confident. Disquiet about nuclear weapons remained a salient feature of German politics, and while SPD leaders had recently nudged some of their security positions back toward the center, they threatened to make the government pay dearly if it acceded to the American program. There was also something particularly galling to German sensibilities about the particular weapons in question. While the air-launched missiles might threaten the same targets in western Soviet territory at which the Pershing IIs had aimed, the Lance replacement could reach only western Poland or, more likely, East Germany.[70] Talk of new SNF (short-range nuclear forces) deployments thus underscored the singular status of both Germanys as the most likely nuclear battlefield. West German strategists started repeating a grim slogan: "The shorter the range, the deader the German."[71]

The NATO dispute flared up after Gorbachev's December 1988 promise, in a speech before the United Nations General Assembly, to withdraw six tank divisions from Eastern Europe. Most Western military experts agreed that after a string of propagandistic and otherwise spurious "unilateral" arms cuts, these Gorbachev cuts would significantly dent the Warsaw Pact's edge in a conventional war.[72] Among Western statesmen, FRG foreign minister Hans-Dietrich Genscher was probably Gorbachev's most enthusiastic booster. After Gorbachev's UN speech, Genscher sharpened his opposition to any new nuclear initiative by NATO. Genscher not only had the weight of West German public opinion behind him, but the fact that his small Free Democratic Party was, at the time, a necessary coalition partner for any West German government. More important, there was no great difference in view between Genscher and the CDU, or for that matter, the SPD. No major German political leader was going to associate himself with a new nuclear-weapons program.[73] Chancellor Helmut Kohl tried for a while to evade the issue, but in February 1989 he announced that he saw no need for a decision on new deployments before 1991.[74] Two months later he infuriated the Americans by sending Genscher and Defense Minister Gerhard Stoltenberg on a surprise mission to Washington to plead for early U.S.-Soviet negotiations on reducing short-range and battlefield nuclear weapons. Washington rejected the plea. Neither side looked willing to back down, and the dispute threatened to darken NATO's 40th anniversary at the very moment when the Alliance should have been celebrating a historical success.[75]

With the West German government in such obvious political distress, why did the Bush administration insist on an early replay of the INF trauma?

Military arguments for the new deployments were fuzzy. This was partly because the NATO military establishment insisted on labelling the program a "modernization," which was sheer euphemism. If, as some NATO officials said, the problem was an aging Lance that would deteriorate to uselessness by the mid-1990s, it would seem logical to replace it with a new version of comparable range. (Such a move would appear less likely to disturb the Germans; Egon Bahr, a senior leader of the SPD disarmament lobby, said he would accept "modernization" along these lines.)[76] A number of NATO military commanders came closer to avowing a more likely purpose of the program: to compensate in part for the Pershing and cruise missiles renounced under the INF treaty. General Bernard Rogers, during his final days as NATO's military chief, had openly grumbled about the treaty, warning that it would reopen a "gap in the spectrum of deterrence."[77] It deprived NATO of its new capacity to punish Soviet aggression by hitting military targets on Soviet territory. There were, to be sure, bombers and submarine-launched weapons to do this job, but the former were vulnerable to air defenses while use of the latter allegedly lacked credibility because they were "strategic" weapons that would invite retaliation against the American homeland.[78] Rogers was likewise unhappy about the treaty's second provision barring weapons with a range of 500–1000 kilometers, thus robbing NATO of "valuable escalatory options" against Central and East European targets. The new missiles, first proposed by Rogers in 1985, would restore some escalatory options: the new ground-launched missile reaching close to 500 kilometers as well as the air-launched missile again threatening targets on Soviet territory.

The avowed importance of "escalatory options" was underscored by a curious aspect of the debate: The United States opposed negotiations even though Soviets enjoyed a 1,400 to 88 numerical advantage in short-range missile launchers.[79] It might make sense to avoid negotiating away this disparity favoring your adversary, if by negotiating you severely limit your number of options for turning a conventional war (which NATO thought it would lose) into a nuclear one.[80] This argument was based on the familiar NATO dilemma: a conviction that conventional inferiority must be overcome by a threat to go nuclear; and a fear that the nuclear threat looked implausible unless it was based on restrained, militarily purposeful options. But as an argument against SNF negotiations it strained credulity, since NATO still wielded more than 4,000 nuclear weapons in Europe with which to start, prolong and escalate nuclear war.[81]

The real reason for reluctance to negotiate was stated openly by U.S. officials: They thought NATO was too weak, politically, to enter such talks without being swept away by a wave of West German antinuclear feeling. "If you can't resist the political pressure to get into the negotiations," argued Defense

Secretary Richard B. Cheney, "how do you resist the political pressure that is clearly going to be there to accept the first Soviet offer, which is going to be not 50, but probably zero?"[82] "The Soviets clearly want to denuclearize and undermine NATO's flexible response and forward defense strategies," said State Department spokeswoman Margaret D. Tutwiler at the same time. "Negotiations would provide them an opportunity to promote a third zero."[83] Americans and Britons adopted the phrase "Genscherism" as a new term of abuse for the forces they saw themselves combatting: weak will, naïveté, and deference to Soviet desires bordering on appeasement.

The best thing to be said for the U.S. position is that, with regard to short-range missiles, it had some logical basis in numbers. With only 88 Lance launchers, it was argued, what level could NATO seek other than zero?[84] The U.S. might propose equal ceilings of 50 launchers, but what incentive would the Soviets have to eliminate 1,350 missile launchers in exchange for a U.S. cut of 38? In other words, did not entering negotiations on SNF imply a willingness to eliminate it entirely?

But even this line of argument was ultimately unconvincing. It certainly did not appeal to Paul H. Nitze, the 40-year advocate of distrusting the Soviets, for whom it made both military and political sense to negotiate mutual SNF reductions.[85] In military terms, he thought NATO would "be in a hell of a lot better shape" if it could persuade the Russians "to come down to two or three hundred warheads"[86] as opposed to the 3,000 short-range missiles that by his estimate the Soviets currently deployed.[87] Nor did he accept the reasoning that the Soviets would never agree to such grossly asymmetrical reductions unless it meant the complete elimination of NATO's short-range nuclear forces (SNF).[88] Nitze also rejected the Rogers plea that a large SNF force was required to give the United States sufficient escalatory options.[89]

Even more telling was Nitze's rejection of the Bush administration's political assumptions. The administration, according to Nitze, was both too optimistic and too pessimistic, in precisely the wrong mix. Its unreasonable optimism was in assuming that "somehow or another we're going to be able to deploy these weapons against the total opposition of Germany. . . . How are you going to get support for it in Germany if we refuse to negotiate?" The unreasonable pessimism was in assuming a channel of transmission whereby German antinuclear feeling would force American negotiators into a bad bargain.

> After all, these negotiations would be U.S.-USSR negotiations; if you're worried about being led on some path that the United States doesn't agree with—certainly the United States doesn't have to agree to a goddamn thing unless it wants to. They talk about the negotiators selling us out and

we wouldn't be able to resist. The negotiator can't do anything the president doesn't want him to do . . .[90]

Nitze thought that the United States was fully able to pursue both its own and NATO's true interests by entering negotiations with a position worked out in advance with the West Germans.[91] He assumed that American negotiators would be able to stick to that position. He did not view German antinuclear sentiment as an unstoppable force of nature that must inevitably break down the walls of resistance to Soviet hegemony. And he did not believe, as many of his Reagan and Bush administration colleagues appeared to believe, that accommodating U.S. policies to West German political constraints would be tantamount to adopting the agenda of the European peace movement and thus start an unstoppable slide toward appeasement.

Nitze helped create the Finlandization image, but he was not prisoner to it. In contrast, the image held the Bush administration captive and led it to a position that seems rather odd. Paradoxically, it was very close in its logic to the arguments for a NATO no-first-use declaration. Both the Bush administration and no-first-use advocates considered nuclear deterrence too divisive to be the basis of a unified NATO policy. The difference was that no-first-use advocates felt its preeminent place in NATO strategy should therefore be abandoned. The Bush administration apparently felt it could be preserved through the sheer force of American (and British) will.[92]

CONCLUSION: THE ILLUSIONS OF NUCLEAR BLACKMAIL

The great debate over nuclear blackmail involved a subjective argument about the reliability of the West European allies and a more objective argument (though, in truth, still entirely speculative) about the nature of nuclear weapons as instruments of political coercion. These two arguments were mixed together in the neoconservative alarm about the failure of containment. But in judging them, it helps to look at each argument separately.

The reliability argument is one of the central themes of this book: the view that Soviet hegemonic ambitions would be helped by the endemic moral, psychological and political weaknesses of West European societies. In the context of this chapter, the argument was that the Europeans were so eager to avoid a confrontation that they would assent to the establishment of clear Soviet nuclear superiority in the European theater.

But the evidence of the Euromissile crisis casts doubt on this proposition. Despite considerable social and political trauma, European governments enjoying at least tacit backing from their publics *did* go through with the Euromissile deployments. A review of the entire Cold War, moreover, shows that repeated Soviet efforts to influence West German decisions with military threats have invariably failed. "No country in the world has been the recipient of more direct Soviet threats to burn it to a crisp than the Federal Republic of Germany," wrote former U.S. arms negotiator Jonathan Dean. The Russians tried such bullying to forestall the FRG's joining NATO, the creation of the Bundeswehr, the Bundeswehr's deployment of nuclear-armed aircraft and Pershing I missiles (both with American-controlled bombs), the Multilateral Force project, acceptance of neutron bombs on German territory, and finally, the deployment of Pershing IIs and GLCMs. In every case, the Germans ignored these threats (the MLF and neutron-bomb projects were dropped and the Euromissiles negotiated away by the United States). Their behavior was unflinching even where the issues were murky. The Bundestag's final vote in favor of the INF deployments, Dean notes, "took place under adverse conditions in a situation where the original decision to deploy INF missiles in Europe was flawed, a technical response to a crisis of political confidence, and where U.S. conduct of the INF talks was not fully convincing to the Europeans." The Soviets also were ultimately unsuccessful in their attempts to intimidate West German voters. They tried to do so in the elections of 1957, railing against the Adenauer government's plans for partial German control of U.S. nuclear weapons; voters responded by giving Adenauer his largest electoral margin ever. And the Russians intensified a campaign of public intimidation against the INF deployments as the German 1983 elections approached; Kohl's government won on a prodeployment package.[93]

American neoconservatives might have replied that this history of resistance to Soviet intimidation was not reassuring, because there was in Western Europe a pronounced, recent trend toward neutralism. They could point to the burgeoning peace movement, and especially its growing hold over the SPD, as evidence of this trend. There was and is, in fact, a disturbing prevalence of pacifist vocabulary in the German political discourse (the reasons for which are not very mysterious). This situation, a real problem in the author's view, will be discussed in later chapters. But the narrower question here is whether Western Europe's response to the INF deployments justified such grave pessimism about the viability of the NATO alliance. Were such American critics as Richard Pipes justified in viewing the mass opposition to INF deployments as evidence that an alarmingly large and growing share (one-third to two-fifths) of West German voters were neutralist in their basic instincts?[94]

Such a judgment would be justified only if the strategic principles underlying the deployments were clear and clearly presented. This was definitely not the case. In fact, the morass of confused rationales for deployments justified much of the peace movement's rhetoric.

American critics frequently denigrated the European fear that the Euromissiles were meant to give America a capability for fighting a nuclear war limited to Europe. This was an outrageous canard, the Americans said, since the deployments were designed expressly to couple Europe's and America's fates by triggering the superpowers' strategic systems.

And yet the rhetoric of the Reagan administration, the deterrence philosophy of the neoconservative movement, and the Pentagon doctrine of "prevailing" in nuclear war all lent more credence to this European fear than to the American rebuttal. The neoconservatives who staffed Reagan defense-policy positions had been loudly arguing for over five years that America needed to establish credible plans for limited nuclear war. They believed that deterrence depended on threats that the Soviets would find credible. That required, in Edward Luttwak's words, "that the act of retaliation be in itself purposeful, and less catastrophic rather than more."[95] "Purposeful" retaliation did very logically suggest a nuclear war limited to Europe. And the Pershing IIs, whatever their original purpose (and whatever one's views on the dynamics of escalation), could plausibly be interpreted as fitting this requirement.

Neoconservative warnings about Soviet nuclear blackmail, although related to negative judgments about West European reliability, also stood on their own as more general predictions about the way nations and people would behave under certain strategic circumstances. These were circumstances of alleged Soviet nuclear superiority at both the European-theater and global-strategic levels.

The most conspicuous development at the theater level was the deployment of the SS-20. In a world of nuclear redundancy, did the SS-20 really provide a margin of usable theater superiority?

If we accept the possibility of a nuclear war with realistic war aims short of the extermination of civilians, then we are imagining a situation where the Russians would have tried to cripple NATO's capacity to fight a theater nuclear war. The Committee on the Present Danger described Soviet plans for "withholding of nuclear weapons at the onset" of an armored attack against West Germany, but added:

> . . . it is clear that pre-emptive strikes would be launched against NATO's nuclear arsenal if it were determined that NATO was preparing a nuclear riposte to Soviet conventional attack. This is clearly the Soviet gambit for deterring NATO's first use of nuclear weapons and blunting such a riposte if it were executed.[96]

What would such preemptive strikes have entailed? In line with statements from Pentagon officials, Stephen Meyer identified about 285 NATO targets in Europe that the Soviets would have needed to destroy (these included roughly 150 air bases, 50 army bases, 5 naval bases, 50 nuclear-weapons storage dumps, and 30 troop-staging areas and command, control and communications facilities).[97] For this task, the SS-20s were powerful weapons indeed. Using median estimates for reliability and accuracy, Meyer reckoned that 55 missiles would be enough to ensure the destruction of the 50 hard NATO targets (hardened nuclear storage sites), and another 166 SS-20s would be required to destroy with confidence the remaining 230 soft targets. This meant a required total of 221 SS-20s (bearing in mind that each missile carried three warheads). In 1984, when Meyer published these estimates, there were roughly 240 SS-20s within range of Western Europe. Thus, on its own the SS-20 force could have dealt this crippling blow.[98]

However, a principal argument for the view that the SS-20s did not add materially to the threat against NATO came from the fact that these targets were already well covered. By using, at most, one-tenth of its ICBM force, the Soviets could have disarmed NATO theater nuclear forces (TNF) without the help of a single SS-20.[99] Perhaps, despite this destructive redundancy, the SS-20 did have characteristics that would have added significantly to the Russians' ability to manage the battle, or more likely the threat of battle, for political gain. But anyone who made such an argument was adopting, explicitly or implicitly, a set of assumptions about the way that nuclear war and the fear of nuclear war could operate. These assumptions start to appear dubious when we examine the SS-20's supposed advantages:

- *Damage Limitation.* The SS-20's greater accuracy and lower yield meant that it could be used against NATO military targets with fewer civilian deaths and less damage to Western Europe's economic infrastructure. This, according to alarmist scenarios, implied a number of benefits. If the Russians intended to conquer Western Europe, they presumably hoped that something in the way of industrial plant would be left standing when they got there. They would also hope to limit the fallout threat to their troops that were marching in. By the same token, they could not be indifferent to the fact that from Western Europe prevailing winds blow east. Finally and most importantly, it was argued that the capacity to destroy military targets while limiting civilian deaths made the threat of attack more plausible.
- *Operations.* A second alleged advantage of the SS-20 force can be dubbed "operational." The missiles were said to have the charac-

teristics needed to bolster Soviet confidence in their ability to carry out a preemptive strike against NATO TNF sites. Previously some 700 missiles of several distinct designs had to be directed against the targets. Now, owing chiefly to the SS-20's multiple warheads, greater reliability and accuracy, only 240 missiles of the same design had to be coordinated. Related to this reliability was the missile's reduced vulnerability and greater readiness. The SS-20 was mobile, making it less vulnerable to NATO preemption. There would be less pressure for panic launchings early in a crisis.[100] On the other hand, once the Soviets decided to strike, with the SS-20 they could do so almost immediately. The old SS-4s and SS-5s, being liquid fueled, required a long period for preparation. Once fueled, they had to be used within several hours, or else the fuel had to be drained. During this period, the preparations would be easily visible to U.S. spy satellites. "Their use was only really conceivable in a massive group firing—that of a nuclear apocalypse," wrote Michel Tatu.[101] The SS-20s, solid fueled, overcame such awkwardness. Not only could they be hidden and set up and fired quickly, but then their launchers could be reloaded and refired in the space of an hour.[102]

• *Theater Distinctions.* The operational advantages cited above made the SS-20 superior to the previous generation of intermediate-range missiles, but not to state-of-the-art ICBMs such as the SS-19. However, it was argued that the Russians might have preferred not to use ICBMs against Europe. First, there was always the danger that America's early-warning system would interpret ICBM launches as the beginning of a first strike against the United States. Second, the Soviets perhaps could not contemplate with equanimity the loss of one-tenth of their intercontinental force in strikes against Europe.[103]

In broader terms, the Soviets might have preferred the SS-20 to ICBMs because the former defined a clear rung on the escalation ladder. In combination, the SS-20's operational, theater-distinguishing and damage-limiting features were considered significant because they not only defined the rung but also established Soviet dominance on it. Thus the debate returns to rest on how seriously we take the concept of escalation dominance.

In fact, imagining the role of escalation dominance on a European battlefield makes it difficult to take it very seriously at all. To say that the SS-20 posed a significant new threat via the establishment of escalation dominance must mean that it gave the Soviets an advantage at the "theater" level—a lower rung than would be consistent with the use of ICBMs. However, was theater nuclear war really to be carried out in a manner described by game theory: formal, controlled nuclear exchanges in which the use of an SS-19 instead of an SS-20 against a given European target would constitute a violation of the implicit rules governing the exchange, thereby provoking the Americans to respond with ICBM strikes against Russian territory?

Such a scenario suffered from the "fallacy of misplaced concreteness," in Leon V. Sigal's words. To imagine "a ladder of escalation . . . with discrete rungs perceptible to both sides and discernible in battle"—a ladder, furthermore, of such technical formality that the rungs "supposedly correspond to weapons classified by range"[104]—was to assume that the "fog of war" was a condition peculiar to the gunpowder of Clausewitz's days.

Perhaps it is too easy to parody this idea of game rules proscribing the use in battle of a missile exceeding a certain *potential* range even when it is actually fired over a much shorter range. However, the image of an escalation ladder with rungs defined by a weapon's destructiveness makes little more sense. Why should the Soviets have wanted to minimize the collateral damage caused by their nuclear weapons? Paul Bracken argued convincingly that in a European battle, Soviet incentives would have worked entirely the other way. "The Soviet Army would have every reason *not* to engage NATO in a controlled, precise manner"—because to do so would be to cooperate in its own destruction.[105] It was more obviously in the Soviet interest to make clear that nuclear war would rapidly engulf European cities in order to terrify European peoples and inhibit European governments from responding. Soviet forces could be expected to hug urban centers with the intent of using them as a shield against NATO nuclear attack. At the same time, "although it is possible that the Pact would not engage in completely uncontrolled attacks with nuclear weapons against Western European cities," the invading forces might very well want to impress NATO with nuclear explosions "that 'accidentally' missed suspected military targets and happened to explode in a West German suburb in the course of a 'controlled war . . .'"[106]

From NATO's perspective, the concept of escalation dominance posed another problem, which I have already discussed. By basing its nuclear policies on a determination to deny the Soviets escalation dominance at the theater-nuclear rung, NATO might only have succeeded in convincing West European publics that they faced nuclear war limited to Europe. Such a conviction would, in turn, enhance Soviet power to "blackmail Europe by threatening it separately with nuclear war," in Kissinger's words.[107] Under such circumstances, the knowledge that NATO outgunned the Warsaw Pact in theater-nuclear fire-power could be of little comfort to the West Europeans.

That, of course, was one of the stated reasons that NATO did *not* respond to the SS-20s with a program aimed at establishing theater-rung escalation dominance or even parity. The Pershing IIs and GLCMs were limited in number and envisioned as a "bridge" between theater and strategic nuclear war. Yet, as I suggested just a few pages ago, this "coupling" rationale profoundly contradicted the American doctrine of "prevailing" (or, for that matter, "countervailing") at levels of nuclear war well short of mutual superpower destruction.[108] The Committee on the Present Danger had pointed to this contradiction when it accused former defense secretary Harold Brown of having "rationalized" NATO's theater inadequacy "by references to the strategic nuclear umbrella and escalation to strategic war."[109] The Committee believed that the bluff of escalation was self-evidently hollow, because the Soviets enjoyed escalation dominance at the strategic level as well.[110]

This alleged dominance stemmed from the supposed vulnerability of U.S. ICBMs. The debate over this notorious window of vulnerability, as Robert W. Tucker noted,

> has never turned primarily on the narrower technical considerations each side has advanced but on the assumptions each has made about the political utility of any marked asymmetry in strategic nuclear forces, and, of course, the willingness of the Soviet government to exploit such asymmetries to achieve its expansionist goals. The view that the present disparity in land missile forces seriously threatens the stability of mutual deterrence evidently assumes that such disparity can be turned to political advantage and likely will be so turned by a government willing to run considerable risks in pursuit of its interests.[111]

Tucker's own answer seems persuasive: Soviet behavior demonstrated caution, not recklessness, even "during years when the window was if not open then opening."[112] There was always abundant reason for such caution. A Soviet first strike, even one as successful as that envisioned by the Committee on the Present Danger, would nonetheless have left the United States with a robust retaliatory force.[113] That surviving force might not have been sufficient for the elaborate counterforce missions deemed necessary by the Committee. But it would have been sufficient to destroy the Soviet Union.

Admittedly, America's possession of such a powerful retaliatory force did not, by itself, refute the window-of-vulnerability thesis. The Committee considered the prospect of America's massive retaliation against Soviet cities to be inherently irrational and therefore insufficiently probable for the requirements of deterrence. And American supporters of minimal deterrence lent some unwitting support to this thesis, by insisting, as Tucker noted, that in the event of nuclear war "the overriding duty of the statesman is to try to bring the war to an end as quickly as possible and without regard to other considerations."[114] On the face of it, that duty does not seem consistent with an American presidential decision to launch a retaliatory second strike.

However, this apparent contradiction was really trivial in relation to the far more profound reality of nuclear weaponry's absolute destructiveness. And this was the fundamental, false note in the neoconservative alarm. The threat to retaliate might be illogical, but in the calculations of a potential aggressor, this illogic must be dwarfed by the potent combination of annihilating power and residual uncertainty as to whether the American president *might* use that power in retaliation. We must also understand that even in the event of a successful first strike against U.S. ICBMs, America would still have retained options for continuing a nuclear war without launching an all-out attack on Soviet cities.[115] In military terms, these options might not have been optimal, or even very effective. But by prolonging the war, while retaining submarine forces capable of total destruction, the United States would have prolonged the risk that the whole adventure would end very badly—as badly as can be imagined—for the Soviets. Indeed, it is not clear what meaningful form an American "surrender" could take under circumstances where an American leadership still possessed nuclear-armed submarines and the capacity for second thoughts. Uncertainty thereby rescued a deterrence that was "existential"—it flowed from the very existence of such destructive power.

Some advocates of a minimal deterrent suggested that it also met the requirements of extended deterrence for Western Europe. At times, even the leading no-first-use advocates seemed to imply as much, though their case was not very consistent.[116] Robert Jervis gave a more straightforward defense of extended deterrence. His basic point: A U.S.-Soviet confrontation over Europe would have been a "competition in risk-taking." Since the risk was the possibility of national annihilation, local battlefield superiority (or escalation dominance at successively higher levels up to but not including all-out strategic war) could be only one factor among many that each side had to weigh in assessing the other side's willingness to risk destruction. More important was the perceived stake of each antagonist in the outcome. Much, of course, was made of the danger that both allies and enemy would perceive the American interest in Europe as less than vital. But this preoccupation obscured a compensating factor: Under most scenarios that we can imagine, the Russian interest in attacking Western Europe was far less than vital. Furthermore, the single objective factor relevant to assessing these respective stakes accrued to the advantage of NATO: It, presumably, was defending the status quo. Finally, we should remember that the onus of starting this war would have fallen on the Soviets. While NATO planners worried that they had the exclusive burden of initiating nuclear war, the Soviets had to consider that their aggression against Western Europe would have entailed some finite chance of starting a process that ended in nuclear catastrophe.

The situation might have been less reassuring had an international crisis put the Soviets in a position where they felt they must strike in order to defend the status quo. Likewise, a conviction on either side that war was inevitable might have restored the attractiveness of short-term military gain, even if it remained impossible to deny one's opponent the means for devastating retaliation. These melancholy reflections applied to the military balance on the European central front as well as to the balance of strategic nuclear capabilities. The problem of crisis instability made it impossible to dismiss the window-of-vulnerability thesis completely.[117]

Yet even if one had a pessimistic view of crisis stability, one need not thereby accept the neoconservative diagnosis of the Soviet nuclear threat against Western Europe. There was no straightforward connection between crisis instability; a concern that the Soviets had achieved European or strategic escalation-dominance; and a Soviet capacity for nuclear blackmail against the West Europeans. For it is one thing to say a crisis might reach an acute stage where the Soviets were desperate and felt they must use ICBMs to preempt an inevitable U.S. attack, even though they expected that the likely end was nuclear catastrophe anyway. It is quite another to say that in times of relative peace, the Soviets, by virtue of a putative theater-nuclear or strategic-counterforce advantage, could manipulate the prospect of a mutual catastrophe that they themselves *clearly did not want* and thereby gain political leverage over Western Europe. It was conceivable that the Western Europeans would be more afraid of nuclear war than the Soviets and therefore more eager to make concessions. But their fear had no logical connection to Soviet nuclear forces that were fundamentally redundant.

Michel Tatu may have been right to argue that the SS-20s demonstrated a long-standing Soviet vocation for coercing the West Europeans. But surely George Kennan was also right to argue that "it takes two to make a successful act of intimidation; and the very improbability of the actual use of these weapons means that no one in Western Europe needs to be greatly intimidated by them unless he wishes to be."[118] The Committee on the Present Danger was therefore wrong to picture the Soviet Union on the verge of success with a patient, measured, grand strategy to control Western Europe by nuclear blackmail.

In all of this, the fundamental neoconservative error was an unreasonable hostility to mutual assured destruction. Mutual assured destruction was not a choice, much less a declaration of surrender, but a recognition of reality.[119] It perhaps transformed extended deterrence into a more difficult burden. It perhaps created a distasteful necessity to accept a modus vivendi with despots. But these were not excuses to deny its truth.

5

The Political Threat:
Europe's Slide to the Left

It was easier to take nuclear blackmail seriously if one assumed that the West Europeans suffered from weak nerves. And American critics imagined that the pressures on European leaders were not just external ones: A robust fifth column of Marxists and Marxist sympathizers would be agitating for conformity to Moscow's every demand. There was a process of analogy going on here, made explicit by, among others, Henry Kissinger, who drew parallels to the conditions of confusion and fractured confidence among democrats as well as newly polished prestige among Communists in Western Europe just after World War II.[1] At that time, of course, nervous American officials could point to a whole series of East and Central European object lessons in how the combination of external Soviet bullying and internal Communist subversion might help Stalin to subjugate all of Europe. The Czech case was perhaps most illuminating. In early 1948, the time of the Czech coup, there were probably no more than 500 Soviet troops in all of Czechoslovakia.[2] But the Communists, more popular in Czechoslovakia than anywhere else in Eastern Europe, had won 37 percent of the vote in the free elections of 1946. Communist ministers controlled the police, whom they used to intimidate opponents. Meanwhile, the Soviets had just promised with considerable fanfare to ship 600,000 tons of wheat to make up for the disastrous 1947 harvest. President Eduard Benes, oppressed by all too recent memories of the West's abandoning his country to Hitler, saw the writing on the wall. When 12 non-Communist ministers resigned, apparently expecting the president to call new elections, Benes instead invited the Communist prime minister, Klement Gottwald, to form a new government. Two weeks later, Foreign Minister Jan Masaryk jumped or, more likely, was pushed from a bathroom window to his death. Almost immediately a series of arrests and executions gathered momentum, reaching their grisly apotheosis in the bizarre and shocking show trial of November 1952.

It showed what a Communist minority, ruthless and organized, could achieve in the face of democratic disarray. The Soviet saber in the background obviously helped, but it did not need even to be rattled. "There was no evidence of any Soviet troop concentrations on the borders of Czechoslovakia," reported Laurence Steinhardt, the U.S. ambassador to Prague, two months after the coup.[3]

To save those capitals west of the Elbe from a similar nightmare became the burden of American foreign policy. In the face of French and Italian Communist parties looking as formidable as the Czechs, that policy succeeded. And yet, during the 1970s, American leaders came to see this success as fragile and uncertain. Communist parties in Portugal, Spain, France and, above all, Italy once again were making disquieting advances. And the disarray of the democrats seemed ominously familiar. Indeed, whereas conditions after World War II had been seen as temporary and remediable consequences of the war's disruptions, the crisis of the 1970s appeared deeper and more intractable. The student movements of 1968 revealed a profound alienation from postwar Western liberalism, reminding some critics of the nihilism that helped bury the Weimar Republic. A thesis of "ungovernability" attempted to explain how welfare capitalism carried the seeds of its own destruction, because it generated accelerating, incompatible and ultimately unlimited demands from undisciplined special interests.[4] Chronic inflation was one of the dismal consequences. Most dramatic was the parade of terrorists—again, especially in Italy, where civil war appeared a real possibility. Could it be that Moscow would pluck the prize denied to it a generation earlier?

The answer to this rhetorical question is an obvious and resounding no. In a very significant failure of comprehension, U.S. policymakers interpreted Western Europe's domestic troubles as a significant source of Soviet strength. There was a great flaw to comparing the crisis of the 1970s to that of the late 1940s. Whereas in 1947 Soviet Communism enjoyed tremendous political appeal but suffered profound military-industrial weakness, in 1977 the situation was reversed. Its military power was immense (though limited in utility, for reasons analyzed in the preceding chapter). Its political power—that is, the appeal of Soviet Communism as a model to be emulated elsewhere in the world—was approaching a nadir from which it would never recover.

In this chapter's conclusion I will argue that the American failure to perceive this terminal decline in Soviet political appeal was tied up with a general ignorance or distorted understanding of the history and political traditions of Western socialism. Having said that, I must repeat with special emphasis the need for an historian enjoying hindsight to show some humility. Without question, the political situation in southern Europe during the 1970s *looked* ominous at the time.

The Communist way of revolution, as Alain Besançon once noted, was almost invariably to seize power within somebody else's more democratic revolution.[5] So it was with Lenin's Bolsheviks. Six decades later, Portuguese Communists tried to repeat the trick. On April 25, 1974, the 50-year-old Salazar dictatorship fell to a peaceful coup by army officers who had been radicalized through their bitter and doomed fighting in the African colonial wars. Jubilant soldiers with rifles sprouting carnations marched into Lisbon. But behind the ensuing counterculture carnival, Henry Kissinger saw an old-fashioned Communist party, fanatically disciplined and subservient to Moscow. "You are allowing excessive Communist Party influence in the government. You are a Kerensky," he lectured Foreign Minister Mario Soares when the Socialist leader came to Washington that October. "I certainly don't want to be a Kerensky," Soares answered. "Neither did Kerensky," said Kissinger.[6]

In subsequent months it looked as though the American's fears might prove justified. A right-wing countercoup failed, and the Soviets poured in money.[7] Lisbon's main bullring was turned into a political prison. Kissinger spoke gloomily as though Portugal were already lost. Steps were taken to keep sensitive intelligence from Portuguese representatives to NATO, and both Kissinger and President Ford talked about the possibility of isolating the country economically and politically.[8] Yet by the summer of 1975, following elections in which the Communists fared badly but that the more extreme leftist officers chose to ignore, there was an increasing popular resistance to the Communist takeover.[9] When Kissinger and Ford returned from Helsinki in August, they met with the U.S. envoy to Lisbon, Frank Carlucci, who argued that more optimistic expressions of support from the United States could make a difference for the anti-Communists.[10] A few days later Kissinger warned the Soviets to keep their hands off.[11] Meanwhile, European Socialists, led by the SPD, had channelled considerable financial aid to help the Portuguese Socialists resist a Communist takeover. It worked.[12] The Moscow-oriented prime minister, Vasco Gonçalves, and the Maoist security chief, General Otelo Saraiva de Carvalho, fell from the ruling troika. The leftist Armed Forces Movement was suppressed. Press and other media were grabbed back out of the hands of

Communist propagandists. Portugal went on to enjoy, as of this writing, nearly two decades of fairly stable Social Democratic rule under Soares, its supposed Kerensky.

Kissinger saw scant cause for relief, however. The Soviets immediately shifted their attention to the loosened Portuguese colony of Angola.[13] And in Europe itself another threat—this one potentially far graver—was on the rise.

THE RENAISSANCE OF ITALIAN COMMUNISM

The Italian Communist Party was the largest in Western Europe and had grown throughout most of the 1970s. Toward the end of the decade, the prospect of a coalition government that included Communists appeared increasingly likely; the idea was supported by growing numbers of Communists and non-Communists alike, including the former Christian Democratic prime minister Aldo Moro, who would later be murdered for his troubles. The government and the Communists engaged in an increasingly intimate collaboration: At one point, Communists were accepted into the government's formal parliamentary majority. During this period of so-called historic compromise with the Communists, the Party's claims of independence from Moscow were subjected to considerable scrutiny. We might start by doing the same.

In 1921 the Partito Communisto Italiano (PCI) was born out of a dogmatic rejection of social-democratic reformism. It split from the Italian Socialists because it refused to abandon basic Leninist principles. The existing regime had to be overthrown by force and replaced with a dictatorship of the proletariat. The party had to remain in strict control of the revolution and, at the same time, completely subservient to Moscow.[14] However, despite these orthodoxies, Italian Communism developed a certain distinctiveness owing to the philosophical writings of one of its founders, Antonio Gramsci. Gramsci was possibly the most ingenious of twentieth- century Communist thinkers, "the one who gave to Marxist thought its most subtle and original turn—the one who attempted the most difficult synthesis of its contradictory impulses toward freedom and toward compulsion."[15] Subtlety and originality do not equal clarity, however. His writings, produced in a Fascist prison under difficult conditions, are full of code and ambiguities and are vague enough to be used to support a description of Italian Communism either as liberal-democratic or as totalitarian.[16] The decisive commitment to parliamentary democracy came at the end of World War II, when the PCI found that its prestige was high, owing to a leading role in the resistance, but its options limited by British and

American occupation. Party leader Palmiro Togliatti returned to Italy from Moscow in 1944 to announce what has become known as the *svolta di Salerno* (roughly, the Salerno turnaround). The party would turn itself into a "mass" party (thus abandoning the Leninist model of the party as a dictatorial vanguard for the masses); it would accept the monarchy and Mussolini's concordat with the Catholic Church; it would work with Socialists and Catholics to transform society within parliamentary rules. True to Togliatti's word, the PCI helped bring Alcide De Gasperi to power in 1945, played an important role in drafting the Republican constitution, and participated in coalition governments until thrown out in 1947.[17] Even after its ejection from government, and notwithstanding the damaging wave of strikes it instigated under Stalin's orders, there is no obvious moment when the PCI as a whole departed from the spirit of the *svolto di Salerno*.

The years of Italy's economic miracle were years of beleaguered isolation for the Communists. Deserted by the Socialists (who joined a Christian-Democrat–dominated center-left government in 1963), the PCI struggled to regain legitimacy and a positive role (as opposed to a certain veto power it always held) in Italian political life. In this struggle for legitimacy, the PCI was helped immeasurably by its performance in administering a large number of municipal and regional governments. As a result of the June 1976 elections, the PCI (either by itself or in coalition with the Socialists) governed every major Italian city.[18] Its reputation for competence and honesty in local government contrasted sharply with the disreputable norm of Italian public life.

The PCI's democratic legitimacy continued to be tarnished, however, by the undemocratic form of the party's own internal structure. Throughout the postwar era, it rarely deviated from the Leninist principle of "democratic centralism"—permitting free debate up until the moment of decision, but then demanding dissent-free adherence to the party line. In 1968 the party purged a large group of leftist dissenters, founders of the newspaper *Il Manifesto,* for their relentless criticism of the PCI's undemocratic structure and links to Moscow.[19]

And it must be said that those links to Moscow were, for most years of the PCI's existence, strong and untroubled. Precisely *because* of these links, the party found many new recruits for whom Russia's prestige had grown during World War II. Certainly Stalin had no strategic objection to the *svolto di Salerno*; on the contrary, immediately after the war he ordered the PCI to disarm its partisans so as not to challenge the Anglo-American sphere of influence. In 1956, the PCI welcomed Russia's crushing of the Hungarian rebellion. Over the next eight years until his death, Togliatti did make some timid efforts to test the room for PCI autonomy, playing with such ambiguous ideas as "unity in diversity" and "polycentrism." But he never overtly challenged Moscow's authority.

The first open breach came in 1968, when the PCI criticized the Soviet invasion of Czechoslovakia. Over the next several years Italians took the lead in trying to organize, together with the French and Spanish parties, a formal structure of "Eurocommunism." The idea was to create a separate pole of Communist ideology, independent of Moscow (and Beijing). The effort was not notably successful, not least because the French Communists would only briefly soften their rigid devotion to the Soviet Union.[20]

Moscow remained fairly tolerant of PCI ideological nonconformity throughout the 1970s. The fundamental split came in 1980 and 1981. The Italian party condemned the invasion of Afghanistan. Three months later PCI general secretary Enrico Berlinguer travelled to Beijing and established formal relations with the Chinese Communists. The PCI refused to participate in a Moscow-sponsored disarmament conference in Paris; the following year Berlinguer boy-cotted the Soviet Party Congress. In December of 1981, the Italian Communist leadership vehemently attacked Polish martial law and the suppression of Solidarity. The PCI attacked Moscow for imposing its system in Eastern Europe and repressing every reform. The Italian Communists, for the first time, articulated the vision of an "independent socialist Western Europe" that, as Joan Barth Urban put it, would "serve as an inspiration both to socialist advances in the Third World and to reform of the Soviet-bloc systems themselves." Moscow fired back with a sustained volley of anti-PCI invective that indicated the Soviet leadership had no hope and no desire to repair the rift.[21]

This final break came after PCI political fortunes had already started their decline. Through the 1970s, Communist statements about East-West relations were suffused with ambiguity. This ambiguity certainly extended to the PCI attitude toward NATO. In 1972 Berlinguer declined to issue "a simple pro-nouncement for or against the military alliance," but he urged "a general move-ment of European liberation from American hegemony and a gradual overcoming of the opposing blocs, ending with their liquidation."[22] In 1975, Giorgio Amendola offered a grudging and strictly limited concession to the idea of continued Italian membership in NATO. "Communists consider Italy's presence in the Atlantic Alliance and in NATO a negative fact which is a danger to peace and national security," said the high-ranking Communist Party official. "But they are not raising Italy's withdrawal from this system of alliances as a point of order, because their aim is the obsolescence of the military and political blocs within a perspective of peace and gradual, controlled and balanced disarmament."[23]

In June 1976, just before the PCI election triumph (discussed below), Berlinguer gave an interview to the *Corriere della Sera* in which he seemed to go considerably further, endorsing NATO as a shield to protect Italian socialism against Soviet intervention. "I want Italy not to quit the Atlantic Pact also for this reason, and not only because our exit would upset the international balance. I feel more secure remaining here."[24] Needless to say, the proximity between this statement and the elections aroused the suspicions of numerous skeptics. It is also obvious, however, that an intelligent person (which Berlinguer was), who surveyed the history of "fraternal relations" between Moscow and various Communist parties, might easily conclude that he needed some protection. That conclusion would certainly have been strengthened after the rhetorical fireworks of 1981, when *Pravda* charged the Italian Communists with "direct aid to imperialism."[25]

Speculations about the "democratic soul" of Italian Communism took on increasing urgency as leading Italian non-Communists concluded that to save Italy from chaos some sort of a deal had to be struck with the country's second largest party. The crisis they faced was at once political, social and economic. It was mainly against the economic turmoil, however, that they thought they needed Communist help.

Italy's economic descent had been all the more shocking because for two decades it had been in the lead of Western Europe's economic miracle. But when the fall came, Italy fell fastest. There was in fact a link between this rapid rise and precipitous decline. Until the late 1960s, the steady growth of Italian wealth was based largely on plentiful cheap labor. Labor unions were weak. Most unions were linked closely to the PCI through their major union confederation, the Communist-dominated General Confederation of Labour (CGIL). The PCI's main concern was regaining the political power it had lost after its 1947 expulsion from coalition government. High wages and improved working conditions were at best secondary to the PCI's goals and at worst, detrimental, since the Communists did not want to encourage the notion that it was possible under an anti-Communist regime to improve the lot of the working class. Hence there emerged an unholy alliance of the PCI, management and Christian Democrats (who had their own reasons for wanting union power crushed), at the expense of industrial wages.[26]

Suddenly, however, Italian industrialists discovered that their managers' paradise had a serious drawback. When a variety of causes, including the general radicalization of West European students and workers after 1968, promoted serious labor unrest, these industrialists found that weak unions left them virtually no one to talk to. Real labor power resided on the shop floor, which is to say, it was diffused and unreachable. Between 1969 and 1970 a wave of strikes washed over Italy, propelling for the better part of a decade an advance of real wages at the expense of profits. Repeated attempts by industry (as represented by its national federation, Confindustria) to negotiate some moderation failed miserably.

Finally Confindustria president and FIAT chief Gianni Agnelli decided to go over the heads of union leaders with an offer of 100 percent indexation of wages against price inflation. He hoped this would help still labor unrest by calming the inflation-fed fears of workers, making them more willing to follow the more moderate leadership of union confederations in their real-wage demands. Despite some evidence that the full indexation mollified and moderated some workers on the shop floor, it could not avert the continuing crisis. In 1974 and 1975, the negative amounts by which growth of real labor costs per worker exceeded growth of real value-added per worker were the largest of the decade: 10.1 percent and 10.6 percent respectively.[27] Grudgingly, Italy's political and industrial leaders saw the necessity of a politically brokered, emergency incomes policy in which the PCI would have an explicit role. "The main problem is the working out of an emergency plan in which the Communists absolutely must take part," said Agnelli in 1976.[28]

Here was the preeminent symbol of Italian entrepreneurial capitalism, saying that Italy needed her Communist party to help deliver her from chaos. That gives some indication of how far the Christian Democratic image of a party capable of competent governing had fallen. From the Risorgimento up until the early 1990s, Italians have never acquired the habit of according automatic legitimacy to their state.[29] In decades of uninterrupted rule after the war, the Christian Democrats failed utterly to rehabilitate the image of national government, clear away the pervading stench of corruption, or disentangle Mafia tentacles from public life. Police and judges were accused of obstructing investigations. United States investigations indicated that millions of dollars in bribes had gone to Italian politicians, reaching, in the Lockheed scandal, the very pinnacle of state power.[30] Likewise "*clientismo*" (voters expecting favors in exchange for continued, uncritical support of their electoral "patron") and government patronage made effective government, much less reform, unlikely and unbelievable. One estimate in the late 1970s put the number of public jobs "colonized" by Christian Democratic supporters at 60,000.[31] A bloated, "parasitic" public bureaucracy came to "symbolize the malaise of the Italian political system and the disdain in which political institutions were widely held."[32]

Keeping this mess immobile was Italy's notoriously "blocked" Christian Democracy, deprived of motive for improvement because the nation's major political opposition was a Communist party "excluded by definition" from taking its turn in power.[33] Despite nominal "crises" and rotations of ministries, one real government essentially held the reins of power for the entire Cold War.

The low quality and reputation of public life had two unhappy consequences. First, the government lacked both the credibility and the capability to enforce a regime of wage restraint and fiscal austerity.[34] Trying to cut public spending was going to be very difficult in any case; this was a time of intense politicization when Italians were becoming acutely conscious that Italy's social services still lagged behind those of its European neighbors.

Second, the perceived illegitimacy of the state helped legitimize, and fractured authority could not control, violence—the most salient feature of Italian politics in the 1970s. Other European democracies were beset by violence and terrorism, but not of the ferocity, regularity, or deadly effectiveness seen in Italy.[35] The country moved by stages from factory strikes and campus agitation, to street fighting between Marxists and neofascists, to right-wing mass bombings, to the paramilitary organization of left-wing terrorist cells at war with police and secret services, to a final murderous campaign by left terrorists such as the Red Brigades against Communist "collaborators" and center-left politicians.

Terrorism was a tool of both the far left and far right. Though comparable in cruelty, their methods were different: Left-wing ("Red") terrorists went after individual targets, with guns; right-wing ("Black") terrorists used indiscriminate bombs in public places.[36] Leftist terrorism, at least in its earlier, less brutal phases, enjoyed the support of a significant stratum of Italian society.[37] This at least tacit support appeared in part to stem from the widespread notion that civil authority was disintegrating, civil war imminent, and that leftist groups had to prepare for an armed battle against a repeated fascist seizure of power. According to a popular interpretation, government security forces were collaborating in a "strategy of tension" to foster a climate of chaos under which popular anxiety would bring in an authoritarian right-wing government.[38]

But after 1974, as the neofascist threat became less credible and right-wing terror abated,[39] left-wing terror kept growing. Such groups as the Red Brigades shifted their focus to the "betrayal" of Communist compromise with Christian Democracy. More and more as the decade went on, Red terrorists targeted the PCI itself.[40] Communist officials were maimed in the legs and killed. In the most spectacular and wrenching single act of terror, the Red Brigades kidnapped, held and finally murdered former prime minister Aldo Moro. Moro was kidnapped on his way to the investiture of Italy's first Communist-backed government since 1947—an event he had made possible.

Was Italy on the verge of a revolution? If the Communists thought the answer was yes, they seemed far from elated. Whatever one thinks about the PCI's ultimate democratic sincerity or goals, its strategy of "historic compromise" indicated that the Party saw more peril than promise in the prospect of a violent revolution. The strategy found its first complete articulation in a 1973 statement by General Secretary Enrico Berlinguer. Not only did the left not seek violent revolution, said Berlinguer, but it did not consider itself capable of governing Italy alone even if it won the electoral backing of a thin majority of Italians. The transformation of society could be accomplished only in collaboration with the Christian Democrats. The PCI was ready to start this collaboration.[41]

Berlinguer based this strategy on the conviction that Italy was a country where neither revolution nor conventional competition and alternation between political parties could work. Leftist victory by either means would only bring on the disaster just witnessed in Chile, where Salvador Allende had been toppled by a military coup. The ingredients for a similar disaster in Italy seemed abundant: a fragile economy bereft of domestic natural resources; American influence and disapproval of any leftist government that included Communists; survival of low-level fascists and fascist sympathizers in the state apparatus; a swarm of "infantile," out-of-control radical movements to the left of the PCI; and an already apparent right-wing reaction against the left-wing advances of the period following 1968. (Besides right-wing terrorism and violence, this reaction included neofascist electoral gains in 1971.) Under these circumstances, leftist electoral victory could provoke capital flight, runaway inflation, right-wing reaction and a military coup.

While PCI leaders preached the virtues of compromise over victory, the party's support among Italians grew. From 1974 through the summer of 1976, Italy saw a string of Communist successes in the fiercely contested divorce referendum, regional elections and national elections (where the Communists received 34.4 percent of the vote; the Christian Democrats 38.7 percent). This growing PCI electoral power combined with the worsening social/economic crisis to convince leading Italian non-Communists that some sort of collaboration was required. Agnelli's appeal for a Communist-brokered incomes policy has already been noted. After the June elections, Ugo La Malfa, the highly respected head of the Republican Party, also endorsed the idea of a historic compromise.[42] Within the Christian Democratic Party itself, the Aldo Moro–Guilio Andreotti faction (actually a group of factions) argued that Italy in her present predicament could not afford open conflict between her two largest parties.[43]

There ensued a series of complicated negotiations (conducted by Moro) to create governments (headed by Andreotti) designed to ensure Communist collaboration without actually granting the PCI any ministries. A few weeks after the June 1976 elections, a first agreement gave the Communists the presidency of the Chamber of Deputies, plus chairmanships of 8 out of 26 parliamentary committees. In return the Communists joined four smaller parties[44] in abstaining from the vote of confidence that installed an Andreotti government composed only of Christian Democrats. The Communists pressed for more. A second agreement reached in July 1977 reaffirmed the *monocolore* Andreotti government but gave the Communists a formal role in negotiating and approving the government's program. But by winter, the Socialists and Republicans along with the Communists were complaining about Andreotti's performance. Another round of negotiations produced, in March 1978, a third compromise under which the Communists were admitted, for the first time in 30 years, to the government majority that formally votes for a new government and has a say in its program. (Once more, however, this Andreotti government was composed entirely of Christian Democratic ministers.)[45]

A program of austerity, based on deflationary policies and wage restraint, lay at the center of the Communist–Christian Democrat collaboration. PCI authority over labor was limited—the same diffusion of power on the shop floor hindered Communist efforts to deliver the working classes to the table.[46] Nonetheless, during this period between the 1976 and 1979 elections, the PCI obtained from the unions an ambiguous form of wage restraint.[47] Certainly there was a calming effect on industrial disputes; strike statistics show that "from 177 million man-hours lost in 1976, industrial action declined to 15 million hours lost in 1977 and 71 million in 1978."[48] A January 1977 "social pact" between Confindustria and the labor confederations provided greater labor flexibility.[49] In early 1978, the three major unions formally endorsed the government's austerity program. Luciano Lama, head of the predominantly Communist General Confederation of Labor (CGIL) was notably outspoken in favor of labor moderation.[50] In addition, the PCI backed a series of deflationary steps that, starting in late 1976, reduced demand by an estimated 3 percent of GNP.[51]

The package had its effect: Real wages rose an average 2.6 percent per year from 1976 to 1978, compared to an average growth exceeding 10 percent for each of the previous six years.[52] It would be difficult to determine whether Communist- and union-backed wage restraint or the government's deflationary macroeconomic measures deserve most of the credit. But PCI and labor-union acceptance of the government's macroeconomic tightening was itself an integral part of the overall incomes policy.[53] For its economic content, the historic compromise must be deemed at least a moderate success.

KISSINGER AND THE EUROCOMMUNISTS

From Washington, however, the experiment in Rome looked like dangerous lunacy. American officials did what they could to stop it.

For Henry Kissinger a most exasperating aspect of the whole affair was the gullibility of those Europeans and Americans who were again ready to swallow Communist declarations of commitment to democracy. Such promises were "not significantly different from what East European Communist leaders declared with equal emphasis in the 1940s," said Kissinger, "just before they seized the total power which they have never relinquished since."[54] To make the point, Kissinger repeated the reassurances that Communist leader Klement Gottwald had offered his fellow Czechs months before the coup that reenslaved them. "The Communist coalition with other parties is not opportunism," Gottwald had promised. "With regard to parliamentary institutions, they will have no more vigilant guardians than the Communists, when they are written into the new constitution."[55]

After the 1976 Italian national elections—in which the Communists came within three percentage points of the electoral share that their Czech comrades had achieved three decades earlier—Kissinger sounded truly alarmed. Whereas he had seemed ready a year earlier to write off Portugal, the prospect of Communists sharing power in one of the four major European members of the Atlantic Alliance moved him to conduct a sustained public attack on the historic compromise, its apologists and their wishful illusions. His campaign continued after Gerald Ford lost the presidency and Kissinger lost his job. Taken together, these 18 months worth of speeches and statements constituted a powerful and elegant (if, for reasons argued below, flawed) analysis of a continuing Communist political threat.

At the first level of analysis lay the simple proposition, already noted, that Eurocommunist leaders might be lying. Their entire Weltanschauung practically required such lies. For Communists, politics was an extension of war by other means. Those means might be legalistic and bloodless for now, but the ends were total—they were war aims. Communists were willing, of course, to use democratic elections to take power. But could they allow elections "to reverse what they saw as the inevitable path of 'historical progress?'"[56] Indeed, the much-ballyhooed contribution of Gramsci to Communist doctrine had nothing to do with the manner of exercising power once the Communists held it. Kissinger discounted the supposed distinction between Gramscian and Leninist doctrine, saying that Gramsci's "hegemony of the working class" was just a "more elegant phrase" for the "dictatorship of the proletariat."[57]

Kissinger's second major point was that, in a very practical sense, the Communists were already well on the way to achieving this Gramscian "hegemony" over Italian society. This fact, above all, made the current Italian case uniquely dangerous. Nowhere else in the West did Communist parties have comparable sway over labor unions and workers, in local and regional governments, in the press and other media and among cultural and intellectual elites. Nowhere else was there a comparable contrast between the vaunted efficiency, discipline and incorruptibility of Communist cadres and the notorious inefficiency, disorganization, clientelistic self-interest and sheer corruption of their principal opponents. Nowhere else was the country in such chaos.

In certain respects, as a matter of fact, Kissinger considered the current Communist threat to be *greater* than that of 1947–48. "In 1948," he said, "the Communist party was far smaller, with little regional or municipal power. It had to contend with a younger and more united Christian Democratic party, a strong Socialist party, and a determined Western Alliance alarmed by Stalin's adventures in Greece and Czechoslovakia." In 1978, by contrast, the PCI had "enormous" reserves of support among trade unions, intellectuals, and in the popular culture.[58]

The changed circumstances that made the PCI now more dangerous would change further, to the greater peril of the Western Alliance, as a result of Communists joining an Italian coalition government. Such a development, said Kissinger, would have a "major psychological effect" on the rest of Western Europe by "suggesting that the tide of history in Europe is moving inexorably in [the Communist] direction."[59]

Since it was the basis of much of his global strategy, Kissinger could not deny a further and more reassuring difference between 1948 and 1976: The nature of world Communism had changed radically. Sino-Soviet antagonism was the most dramatic emblem of a general fragmentation in the Communist world. However skeptically he treated PCI professions of a democratic "soul," he could not plausibly claim that the Italians were faithfully and uncritically following Moscow's bidding.[60] But Kissinger insisted that his pessimistic analysis in no way depended on Western Communist parties that were subservient to Moscow.[61] "For the key issue is not how 'independent' the European Communists would be, but how Communist," said Kissinger. Italian Communist "foreign and domestic policies are not likely to be consistent with the common purposes of the Atlantic Alliance."[62]

This inconsistency would erode the Alliance from both sides of the Atlantic, he said. On the American side, "the permanent stationing of American forces in Europe could hardly be maintained for the object of defending some Communist governments against other Communist governments."[63] The American people would not support that commitment. To be sure, Kissinger recently had been insisting that America "must learn to conduct foreign policy as other nations have had to conduct it for so many centuries . . . knowing that what is attainable falls short of the ideal, mindful of the necessities of self-preservation."[64] And certainly the United States might have an interest in defending Communist European states on balance-of-power grounds. But there are political and moral limits to realpolitik, and it would be unrealistic to expect Americans to go far beyond those limits. Over the long run, Eurocommunist governments would erode "the moral and political basis" for U.S. troops in Europe.[65] After their withdrawal, Europeans would be left alone to make what accommodation they could with the Soviets. That would be the crucial first movement of Soviet hegemony in Western Europe.

The second movement, the rationalization that prepares a foreign policy for bowing East, would be supplied readily by the Eurocommunists. Among the whole catalogue of values, visions and assumptions that Eurocommunists did not share with the Alliance, the most important was a belief in Soviet aggressive intentions. In recent years, the center of PCI orthodoxy had shifted, but only so far as to concede, perhaps, that the balance of power should not be disrupted by anyone's *premature* withdrawal from either NATO or the Warsaw Pact. This was a short-term concession for avoiding conflict. In the long run the goal was to dismantle both alliances. Such a goal meant that Eurocommunists saw the threat to peace not from Russia, but from the confrontation of blocs. Such a vision, according to Kissinger, meant that the Eurocommunists were fundamentally blind to the danger from Russian intimidation and Russian hegemonic ambitions.[66] By extension, those center-left Socialists and Democrats in Europe and America who underrated the Eurocommunist threat were also blind to Russian hegemonic ambitions. That was the only plausible explanation of the center-left's applause for Eurocommunist neutralism. Neutralism might be marginally better, in some abstract sense, than pro-Soviet activism. But in a real sense it was more dangerous, because it was more seductive to the wishful thinkers who declined to face the hard realities about East-West conflict. Such wishful thinkers somehow failed to grasp the basic point that "it makes a great deal of difference whether there is an independent Communist government in Eastern Europe or an independent Communist government in Western Europe."[67]

Independent Communist governments might pose new problems for Russia, but "they would pose far more serious problems for the West." Even if the schism between Eurocommunism and Moscow should turn out to be as deep as the one between Beijing and Moscow, it would "hardly diminish the danger to current allied relationships," according to Kissinger. "By the time it occurred the damage to the NATO structure would probably have become irreparable."[68] As Moscow maintained its grip on the Warsaw Pact while NATO unravelled, "the freedom of many European countries, allied or neutral, to chart their own future would be diminished in direct proportion to the growth of fear of Soviet power."[69]

When he was Secretary of State, Kissinger often prefaced his remarks on Eurocommunism with a disclaimer: The role of Communist parties in various West

European governments was "essentially a decision that the country has to make"; if asked, the Ford administration would give its opinion, "even if we can't do much about our views."[70] But most left-wing Italians knew (even if they tended to embellish their knowledge with rather lurid exaggerations) that the American role went well beyond such friendly advice. With the possible exception of Greece, no other European country saw such a sustained and intimate involvement of U.S. officials in its domestic politics—for a period spanning almost four decades after the 1943 Anglo-American invasion of Italy. In the beginning, of course, there was nothing particularly sinister about American efforts to direct the political and economic reconstruction of a country that U.S. troops occupied. One should remember, moreover, that the earliest U.S. political intervention came on the side of the leftist antifascist coalition and against the British preference for maintaining the monarchy and Badoglio government. This disagreement provoked one of the sharpest Anglo-American clashes of the war.[71] By 1947, however, with the Cold War intensifying, the Communist–Socialist–Christian Democratic coalition governing Italy seemed like an anomaly, to put it mildly. Alcide de Gasperi, the Christian Democratic prime minister, got the signal from Washington that further U.S. aid depended on curbing the Communists' power. (Actual expulsion of the PCI from government does not appear to have been an explicit American demand, but the Christian Democrats somehow made it seem so, prompting a recent historian to remark: "To this day, it remains difficult to say precisely who was using whom.")[72] As a result, de Gasperi kicked the Communists *and* the Socialists out of the governing coalition. In national elections the following year, the United States poured in funds and sent Ambassador James Dunn out on the campaign trail against the left, while Secretary of State George Marshall explicitly threatened the end of American aid if the Communists won. Over the next two decades the United States spent something on the order of $65 million to influence Italian elections.[73] Thus America shared complicity in the Christian Democrats' virtual colonization of national government from 1948 onwards. By the early 1960s the Americans could not fail to observe some baleful effects of this single-party rule, and so the Kennedy administration helped engineer an "opening to the Left." The Socialists, heretofore nearly as anathema as the Communists, were brought back into a coalition government. This experiment, however, failed in its putative purpose, which was to replace the Communists as the major left-wing party in Italy. As the Communists' electoral share grew, the Socialists' electoral share continued to decline.

The Nixon administration responded rather eccentrically to this problem. Its ambassador to Italy, Graham Martin, funnelled $800,000 in CIA funds to the extremist chief of Italy's Defense Intelligence Service, Vito Miceli, who was later arrested for involvement in a rightist coup plot. In the global sweep of things, CIA connections to right-wing radicals were hardly unprecedented. In the current situation, however, with neofascists embarking on a campaign of terrorism, Micelli's connection to "antidemocratic elements" was sufficiently bizarre to embarrass the CIA station chief in Rome, who complained to his superiors in Washington. This 1972 dispute reached the level of high farce when Martin threatened to lock the CIA station chief out of the embassy.[74]

Four years later the United States, West Germany and Great Britain agreed to withhold future loans from Italy if Communists were given cabinet posts.[75] It was a dire threat, considering Italy's disastrous economic situation. In the short run, it embarrassed the Christian Democrats, accused once again by the Communists of depending on outside interference to stay in power. And in America it provided ammunition for those Kissinger critics who viewed the secretary's self-proclaimed "philosophical deepening" of American strategy as just fancy new clothing for old-fashioned anti-Communism. Typical was the reaction of Anthony Lewis who, in a *New York Times* column titled "Mr. Kissinger's Folly," charged that Kissinger would rather see Italy in chaos or under neofascism than with Communists in its government. The "crude threat," Lewis added, would backfire.[76]

Because the national elections in Italy coincided with a presidential campaign in America, Eurocommunism became an issue in American politics in 1976. Democratic presidential candidate Jimmy Carter, while hardly welcoming the prospect of an Italian Communist government, attacked Kissinger and the Ford administration for interference in Italian domestic affairs. "We may not welcome these changes; we will certainly not encourage them," said Carter. "But we must respect the results of democratic elections and the right of countries to make their own free choice if we are to remain faithful to our own basic ideals."[77] Elsewhere he argued, "If Communist leaders do obtain major roles in allied governments, it need not necessarily be a catastrophe."[78]

But the Carter administration showed more concern than Carter the candidate about the prospect of Italian Communists in power. In the early months of Carter's term, his national security adviser, Zbigniew Brzezinski, wrote to the president that the Communist advance in Italy was "potentially the gravest political problem we now have in Europe." Carter subsequently approved a decision memorandum that stressed two principles of policy: no direct interference but firm opposition to a Communist role in the government. In December 1977, U.S. Ambassador to Rome Richard N. Gardner reported that the PCI was again pressing for ministries in the Andreotti government and that some leading Christian Democrats were warming to the idea. Gardner also warned "that our emphasis on non-interference was being deliberately misinterpreted by the PCI and others favorable to their case and that a strong reinterpretation of our policy was urgently needed." In response, Carter approved a January 12, 1978 State Department statement: "Our position is clear: We do not favor such [Communist] participation and would like to see Communist influence in any Western European country reduced."[79]

In his memoirs, Brzezinski claims that "U.S. diplomacy as well as the carefully tuned policy toward Italy which the President approved in March 1977 were a distinct help" in ending the historic compromise. He claims this as "one of the less-known success stories of the Carter years."[80]

However, without discounting the American role, what seems more decisive is the masterful manner in which the Christian Democrats manipulated their Communist partners. Collaborating in the austerity program was a heavy political liability for the PCI. The Andreotti government managed to give the Communists very little in return. Union dissatisfaction with this situation led the Communists to press more forcefully for cabinet posts, leading to an open split between the two major parties.[81]

The role of Moro's murder in ending the historic compromise remains one of the murkier aspects of the whole affair. Moro was a leftist Christian Democrat who had come to see the historic compromise as the road to national salvation as well as to the reform of his own hopelessly corrupt party. Certainly Moro's Red Brigade kidnappers considered Communist moderation, which Moro had done so much to promote, to be a kind of heresy, and they had no compunctions about the killing of heretics.[82] Allegations have recently surfaced that there were also opponents on the right, among politicians and within the security services, who refused to bargain and even arranged to avoid finding the Red Brigades' hideouts because they found it convenient to let a troublesome Moro die.[83] But these allegations remain nebulous; it should be remembered, moreover, that the Communists themselves were among the fiercest opponents of any kind of bargain with the kidnappers.

It appears likely, in fact, that the kidnapping preserved Communist–Christian Democratic unity for some additional months as a climate of siege descended over Italy. Finally, in December 1978, eight months after the murder, the PCI for the first time voted against a major government initiative (on a technical vote involving Italian membership in the European Monetary System).[84] In January the PCI told the government that unless granted government posts, it would leave the majority; a week later, rather than agree to the demand, Andreotti resigned, bringing the period of historic compromise to an end. Subsequent elections suggested that the experience had compromised the PCI in the eyes of its supporters: The party suffered a decline in national election votes for the first time since World War II.[85]

NEOCONSERVATIVES VERSUS EUROSOCIALISTS

Eurocommunism had its rather pathetic last hurrah in 1981, when a Socialist-Communist alliance triumphed in France's presidential and parliamentary elections and the new president, François Mitterrand, promptly appointed four Communist ministers to his government. These Communists came from a party that had none of their Italian cousins' democratic gloss; on the contrary, the Parti Communiste had proven itself time and again to be a dull and dogmatic Soviet parrot.

But the American protests, in contrast to U.S. alarm over Italy, were perfunctory. It rapidly became obvious—even to the fiercely anti-Communist Reagan administration (itself only months old)—that France's new Socialist government would take a *harder* line against the Soviet Union than had Mitterrand's center-right predecessor, Valéry Giscard d'Estaing. Foreign Minister Claude Cheysson immediately visited the White House and delighted the Americans with his anti-Soviet views, and Mitterrand pursued a rapprochement to NATO that led to the first meeting of the North Atlantic Council in Paris since 1966. Most dramatically, in January 1983, the French president stood before the Bundestag and urged wavering German Socialists to accept deployment of the American Euromissiles.[86]

What is more, it also became apparent that Mitterrand, in a patient, measured strategy that included a series of on-again, off-again Socialist-Communist electoral alliances, had managed to maneuver the Parti Communiste into political oblivion. It was an astonishing achievement considering that as late as 1978, the Communists had received some 20.6 percent of the national vote; in 1973 they were still the largest left-wing party in France. By the early 1990s, however, the Communists were a marginal force. The Socialists were also in deep difficulty, but only after a decade of almost uninterrupted rule.

One would imagine that this Mitterrand example might have led American neoconservatives to reexamine their assumptions about an inherent Socialist vulnerability to Soviet stratagems—the highly dubious notion that relative proximity on some abstractly conceived political spectrum somehow rendered Socialists less vigilant against the Soviet threat. But while acknowledging the Mitterrand case, neoconservatives treated it as an anomaly.

The reason is no mystery. When they looked at Western Europe, neoconservatives saw all their favorite villains—an obsession with arms control, fashionable neutralism, and romantic Third Worldism—in particularly grotesque form. Added to these were highly developed welfare states, whose raison d'être was to be found in the concepts and traditions of European Socialism. Actually, these welfare states were built mainly under the conservative regimes that governed the major West European countries for most of the postwar period (the West German Soziale Marktwirtschaft being the most successful example). But in the years of this book's focus, European Socialist parties came to power one after another: the British Labour Party from 1964 to 1979 (with a four-year break in the early 1970s); the German SPD in 1969; the French Socialists in 1981. In Italy, as we have seen, there was throughout the 1970s the astonishing prospect of Communists sharing power.

Neoconservatives interpreted these left-wing triumphs as bad news for NATO. Thus Richard Perle, when he became point man for the Reagan administration's campaign against European détente policies, argued that a principal explanation for détente's unnaturally long life was its nurturing in what he considered the appeasement-oriented ideology of European socialism. "In all of this there was and is an important political dimension," he told the Senate in hearings on the energy-trade dispute discussed in chapter 6.

> Many Europeans, particularly of the left, saw the emergence of an energy relationship with the Soviets as a useful device for fostering détente: And détente, in turn, was seen as a process that could transform an essentially hostile relationship between East and West into a more cordial, and less volatile political arrangement that would lessen the need for burdensome defense budgets. In Germany especially these elements fit neatly together with the political vision of the left wing of the Social Democratic Party—a vision captured by the German term, 'Ostpolitik,' which had become a prominent feature of German socialist politics.[87]

Perle's identification of *Ostpolitik* with Democratic Socialism was accurate enough, but also politically explosive insofar as he made no secret of his view that *Ostpolitik* was tantamount to appeasement. It was a short step to attacking the development of West European Social Democracy in general. Similarly, Irving Kristol blamed West European pacifism on the growth of the welfare state itself since World War II. "Perhaps," Kristol wrote, "one can sum it up, roughly and vaguely, by saying that, in the intervening three decades, the social-democratic temper, the inward-turning politics of compassionate reform, has largely replaced the patriotic temper, the politics of national self-assertion."[88]

Such arguments were extremely popular among America's right-wing social critics—not least because they fit snugly with ingrained prejudices about European pusillanimity. European Social Democracy, in this view, bred social and economic flabbiness, which in turn produced an aversion to any serious military efforts to counter the Soviet threat. The "absence of a will to self-assertion" engendered a political attitude in which there was an ever present desire to escape from international politics.[89] Conveniently, Social Democracy, with its leftist view of the world, could provide a hundred rationalizations for discounting the evils and perils of Soviet Communism—or so went the neoconservative critique. Such excuses revealed a readiness to submit to Finlandization, the implicit foreign policy of Europe's Socialists and nuclear disarmers.[93]

CONCLUSION: "THE TYRANNY OF RIGHT-LEFT THINKING"

How, finally, should we judge American antipathy to leftist political movements? In the case of Kissinger, it is certainly difficult to dismiss his concerns about the Eurocommunists out of hand. It is hard to argue that an even partly Communist government in Italy would have been good for NATO.

But that hardly settles the matter. For in Kissinger's strategy toward Italy, one sees a manifestation of his general attitude toward domestic political economy: indifference. As Richard Barnet justly observed:

> . . . unlike . . . Acheson, McCloy, and the other architects of Atlantica, Kissinger had no vision of how domestic structures in the United States or in Europe would or should evolve. The first postwar generation of American statesmen, politically conservative though they were, were sensitive to the connections between the expanding welfare state and foreign policy even if they did not always know how to make the connections work. For Kissinger, on the other hand, domestic structures were a given. Those who were in power were by definition more predictable, more reliable, and more orderly than those who were waiting to take power—unless they were perceived, like Salvador Allende in Chile, to be a subverter of order.[91]

Many critics have attacked Kissinger's seeming preference for the stability of right-wing, authoritarian regimes, such as those in Chile, Iran, Greece and so on. This preference has often been made to seem sinister, but there was nothing sinister about it if one shared Kissinger's worldview. Kissinger's "conservatism" had nothing to do with domestic politics and everything to do with geopolitics. It was derived from the familiar view of containment as organically unstable—the West as decadent and fractured, facing a more disciplined East. In this light it is understandable that radical political change in the Western world should be feared.

But if one did not share his geopolitical pessimism, if one had a Kennan-esque concept of containment's stability, then a different idea about the acceptable range of Western political systems presented itself. Italy is a good example. It is arguable that the historic compromise, which Kissinger fiercely opposed, saved Italian democracy. Leading non-Communist Italian politicians certainly believed at the time that collaboration with the PCI was necessary to stave off chaos. And Communist appeals for wage moderation were a distinct help in weathering the economic crisis of the late 1970s. Again, Kissinger's indifference to domestic political arrangements is glaring. What alternative solution could he have proposed?

Moreover, the anti-Communist imperative thwarted what might have been a long-term solution to Italy's political malaise: the PCI's transformation into a genuine social-democratic party that, perhaps in combination with the Socialists, might have provided Italy with a real multiparty system. Instead, for the remainder of the Cold War, Italy was saddled with the virtual single-party rule she had suffered since 1947. It is an iron law of politics that such political immobility breeds corruption—in Italy's case, a corruption so deep and so venal as to threaten democracy itself. Left-wing terrorism was beaten, but the Mafia remained free to terrorize and murder judges.

Only after the end of the Cold War, with the car-bomb killings of the most prominent anti-Mafia magistrates, did a kind of revolution come to Italy. It was a historically unique revolution, led by a class of public prosecutors whose tolerance for the state of affairs seemed to snap. Their suddenly zealous investigations into government-Mafia collusion and more general habits of kickbacks and bribery swept up virtually the entire ruling class of political and business elites.[92] Christian Democrats and Socialists were wiped off the political map. The former Communists, renamed the Party of the Democratic Left, emerged briefly in late 1993 as the country's single strongest political force. But a right-wing coalition of southern neofascists, northern separatists and the followers of Thatcherite media tycoon Silvio Berlusconi defeated the left in the spring 1994 national elections and, despite deep political tensions, managed to put together Italy's first distinctly post–Cold War government.

The moral of this continuing saga is hardly to blame Kissinger, or any other American, for Italy's many problems. (Such anti-American demonology has too often been an excuse for political elites around the world to avoid facing their homegrown political ills.) But it is to argue that on the level of ideas, an exaggerated view of the Soviet threat has not been helpful to the country's political development.

Yet if Kissinger's approach to European domestic politics was flawed, neoconservative views were generally absurd. Fanatical in their apostasy, neoconservatives were ready to cast European Socialists as Soviet dupes and fellow travellers. Yet the truth is that West European Socialism was among the bulwarks of anti-Soviet containment.

The Social-Democratic welfare state, derided by neoconservatives for allegedly sapping Western will, was in fact the West's secret weapon. The most plausible Soviet threat, very real in the first years after World War II, was the extension of Stalinist power by political means. Hunger and associated miseries presented ripe revolutionary situations in France and Italy with popular Communist parties and also in the Western zones of occupied Germany, where the totalitarian impulse might have readily reemerged. Class consciousness was sharp, while the valiance of the Soviet war against Hitler tended to obscure the horrors of Stalinism. With considerable help from the United States, the social democracies of Western Europe succeeded in defusing this class conflict. Soviet expectations of Western crisis based on a Marxist-style conflict between labor and capital became more and more fanciful. In the 1970s, flurries of infantile leftist enthusiasm demonstrated not the strength but the inexorable decline in Communism's prestige. Certainly the terrorist left was reacting with murderous rage to the realization that left-wing parties and the working class in general had been converted to the benefits of welfare capitalism.

"Social Democracy" can be a slippery term, and it is true that the European welfare state was also in large measure the creation of conservative parties: Gaullists in France and Christian Democrats in West Germany and Italy. But it is nonetheless wrong to argue that Western Europe's success therefore had nothing to do with genuine Socialism. Democratic and reform-minded Socialists had long ago anticipated their ideal societies as melding market and socialist elements. One of the early, great Socialist revisionists, for example, was the German Social Democratic theorist Eduard Bernstein, who in the 1890s not only anticipated but also welcomed the survival of capitalism. Bernstein's observation of late nineteenth-century economic development led him to conclude that capitalism, far from imploding upon the progressive pauperization of the working class, was creating the prosperity upon which a just social democracy might be built. Revolution was not only unnecessary: it would destroy this progress. The enemy was not capitalism itself, but the greed of certain capitalists. Democracy could defeat this greed as "the common interest gain[ed] in power to an increasing extent as opposed to private interests."[93] Bernstein celebrated ethical freedom, not class struggle; a "democratic Socialist party of reform" instead of the Marxist "Calvinism without God."[94]

> Unable to believe in finalities at all, I cannot believe in a final aim of socialism. But I strongly believe in the socialist movement, in the march forward of the working classes, who step by step must work out their emancipation by changing society from the domain of a commercial,

landholding oligarchy to a real democracy which in all its departments is guided by the interests of those who work and create.[95]

With such comments, Bernstein stands out as a remarkable prophet of the West European welfare state, which was built together after World War II by Socialists, Christian Democrats and Gaullists, members of a coalition that had resisted Hitler, spent time together in concentration camps, and shared a conviction that after all the suffering and struggle, postwar society had to be better than prewar society.[96]

The German case bears some attention. Throughout the Cold War, the German Social Democratic view of Soviet Communism was shaped by a conviction that the SPD was the true and authentic party of the left[97] and that Communists were thuggish heretics. The "Great Schism," in which Communism broke off from Socialism, produced an immediate and lasting hatred, which can be traced from the bitter polemics between Lenin and Rosa Luxembourg, to the feisty contempt of Kurt Schumacher ("Communism is Nazism varnished red," he once said), to the vitriolic Soviet propaganda against Western Socialists.[98] (Other European Socialists nursed similar antagonisms born of intimate knowledge: Ernest Bevin, the foreign secretary in Britain's first postwar Labour government, learned to hate Communists fighting them for control of the British Transport and General Workers Union.)[99]

It is true enough that Schumacher feared, presciently, that his country would be interminably divided: two pawns for the two superpowers. To avoid this fate he wanted to avoid close identification with an American-led alliance. But once the Cold War alliances were clearly drawn, the German Socialists were strongly Atlanticist; Social Democrats collaborated enthusiastically with the CIA during the Berlin "spy war" of the 1950s.

One has to acknowledge that a change came over the SPD by the 1970s, a change in the party's moral clarity vis-à-vis Communism.

To some extent, of course, what happened was the same confusion and anger that the Vietnam war brought to center-left parties throughout the West. The student radicals of 1968 were unaffected by the residual loyalties of such Socialists as Brandt, who felt he owed and needed the Americans too much to voice his own deep misgivings about Vietnam.[100] These new leftists were not in favor of complication. Having aged a little and entered mainstream politics, many gravitated to the SPD and brought their simplistic pacifism with them.

Something similar happened to the Democratic Party in the United States, although antiwar slogans were never really allowed to become conventional wisdom. Complacent moralism was shaken by a turbulent intellectual struggle, in which the neoconservatives certainly played an honorable part, and which resulted in Bill Clinton—the anti-Vietnam student protester—leading fellow Democrats to accept the idea that there are some things worse than war.

The SPD, by contrast, has failed to this day to unload some heavy pacifist baggage, a failure that admittedly complicates any general defense of the West European Socialists. It is important to be clear, however, about the causes and effects of this pacifism. One general cause has been Germany's historical experience of war. The uniqueness of that experience is best understood if we look at the American contrast, which is stark. *Our* fundamental experience of war has been an experience of military and moral success. Although introduced in 1917 to the European battlefield, Americans were largely spared the postwar disillusion and despair that haunted the European consciousness. The real American introduction to world responsibility came with the war against Hitler. Thus, the postwar generation of American leaders (and every Cold War president until Bill Clinton) was conditioned by a war of historical singularity. Almost universally, by losers as well as winners, World War II was judged a "just" war. More important, it ended in a peace that was successful beyond the wildest Allied hopes. It is not only the famous cautionary lesson of Chamberlain's appeasement, but also the enormity of this postwar success that leaves its imprint on the American consciousness. George Bush, for example, as he went to war in the Persian Gulf, knew from personal experience that war need not lead inexorably to disaster. (This conviction survived, tarnished but essentially intact, the anguish of Vietnam.) Small wonder, then, that many American elites lack what might be called a "European" appreciation of the tragic dimensions of the exercise of power. Not that they love war, or are blind to its human costs, but rather that they have a diminished perception of tragic hubris—the sense that catastrophe can result not only from appeasement of evil, but also sometimes from overconfidence in defending good.

The Germans are prone to an opposite mistake. The major wars of recent history were uniformly catastrophic for them and their nation. They tend therefore to read this century as a moral parable against war in general, forgetting that it required not peaceful diplomacy but total war to defeat Adolf Hitler.

A second general cause has to do with the German experience of peace since 1945. In a position of utter dependence on the Americans, with considerable economic power but constricted international sovereignty, the ultimate questions of war and peace were out of their hands. This odd and artificial condition, though considerably happier than what came before, has also had a distorting—one might even say degenerative—effect on the way the Germans debate the rights and wrongs of military force. The most useful comparison here is with France: The kind of pacifist arguments that one hears too often in Germany are precisely what de Gaulle wanted to avoid among the French. A central tenant of Gaullist foreign policy is that there is a critical link between national independence and the capacity to act responsibly on the world stage. When de Gaulle removed France from the NATO commands, he indisputably damaged the Alliance in operational military terms, subtracting not only the French army but also French territory as a rear staging area for West Germany's defense. But de Gaulle, convinced that the Soviet threat was adequately checked, had broader concerns: the preservation of French national unity and will. He believed that only in full control of its national destiny could France be ready to make the difficult choices of war and peace, which, in a nuclear age, might mean life and death. And it does seem clear that formal independence from NATO has deprived French political parties of certain easy rhetorical temptations. Of course left-wing anti-Americanism has had its fashionable seasons in Paris. But for politicians in positions of responsibility, American domination could not be used as an alibi for avoiding serious thought about the nature of the world. More than anything else, the French Socialist experience proved de Gaulle right. When Mitterrand's party came to power, it was constrained to judge the Soviet military threat realistically. One noticeable result was Mitterrand's firm support for the deployment of American intermediate-range missiles in Europe in the early 1980s. (Ten years later, after some eleventh-hour maneuvers for peace, Mitterrand resolutely sent French forces under American command into war against Iraq.)

The causes, then, of German socialist-pacifism are much more complicated than the neoconservative criticisms would lead you to believe; but so were the effects. I will argue in the final chapter that German pacifism is a very harmful factor in the post–Cold War world. *During* the Cold War, on the other hand, it did not significantly weaken the West's position, although it certainly did a lot of harm to the SPD. The Socialist chancellor Helmut Schmidt was deposed as SPD chief after he failed to rally party support for the deployment of American Euromissiles. The pacifists' victory over Schmidt was followed by their immediate political defeat. The small liberal party, a member of the governing coalition, switched sides in late 1982 and brought Helmut Kohl's CDU into power. In early 1983 German voters confirmed this turn to the right. In electoral terms, then, the basic German consensus for standing up to Soviet bullying was unchanged. And we should recall from chapter 4 that this entire drama concerned an American missile deployment whose strategic rationale was fuzzy, to say the least. Soviet nuclear blackmail, already senseless in military terms, was ineffectual politically as well.

Jeane Kirkpatrick used to complain about the "tyranny of Right/Left thinking," by which she meant the tendency of many liberals and socialists to ignore the evils of Communism while attacking the abuses of various right-wing regimes.[101] The complaint was hypocritical, coming as it did from someone who had developed an elaborate theoretical framework for explaining why right-wing dictatorships, such as Argentina's murderous military junta, were more acceptable than Communist regimes. But for all its inconsistency, the complaint was no less astute, and it should be remembered as we sit down to write and to understand our recent history. We should not allow "right/left thinking" to confuse us. An ideological perspective is simply not very useful for explaining the role of various West European political parties in winning the Cold War.

6

The Economic Threat:
Energy and Jobs

A long with the specter of nuclear blackmail and Communist political gains came warnings about a third tool of Soviet hegemony: economic coercion. Given what we now know of the disaster that was the Soviet economy, this way of imagining Soviet power seems preposterous. But it was argued at the time that Soviet political discipline more than compensated for the economic flaws. "A key to economics," wrote Paul Nitze in 1980, "is politics, both domestic and foreign." While he conceded that Soviet-bloc economies suffered "serious problems," Nitze argued that "their system is already tightly managed from the center. . . . Their economies are less productive but may be better able to weather a storm."[1]

Nitze's colleagues in the Reagan administration were more explicit: Economic ties with the Soviets automatically placed the West European democracies in a subordinate position, because the latter were politically weaker (unable to resist the accelerating demands of electoral constituents for uninterrupted benefits of Eastern markets and resources) and in awe of Soviet military power.

Neoconservatives warned of Western Europe's emerging condition of economic Finlandization, involving two intertwined but distinguishable elements. First was the element of economic exploitation: Russia's use of Western finance and technology to support its military effort and its political system. Second was the element of the political exploitation of economic relations: Russia's use of economic leverage to achieve diplomatic purposes.

These warnings were the basis of an angry transatlantic dispute over the joint Soviet–West European undertaking to build a gas pipeline from Siberia to Western Europe. Americans said the pipeline project featured both elements of economic Finlandization in almost obscene measure. It also contained a third element of energy security, which seemed highly relevant to the Finlandization scenario, given West European economies' high dependence on imported energy. It is significant that the decade after 1973, during which a heretofore latent Europessimism came to dominate the Weltanschauung of U.S. elites, was punctuated by two energy crises. In both cases, a stark revelation of the vulnerability of Western economies to hostile oil suppliers came in tandem with a general diminishing confidence in the stability of the economic and social order. The energy crises, and related political disagreements, inspired more bitter resentment and distrust between America and her allies than possibly any other postwar controversy.

Chapter 2 discussed the reflections of an embittered Kissinger following what he saw as Europe's craven, *sauve-qui-peut* response to OPEC's first use of the oil weapon. Starting in 1979 a second oil crisis again transmitted shock waves through the structure of NATO relations. Iran's revolution, the proximate cause of this second oil-price increase, was followed by the Soviet invasion of Afghanistan, sharpening American perceptions of a Middle Eastern "arc of crisis" toward which Russia was now directing its grand strategy. When, in direct response to the 1979 price hikes, the Europeans looked to Siberian natural gas as an alternative energy source, the Americans were appalled. Nothing, in their view, could fit more neatly into Russian plans for controlling the rest of Europe.

The dispute pitted the four major Western European countries (including Thatcher's Britain) against the Reagan administration. U.S. officials considered the Europeans to be willfully blind not only to the Soviet threat, but to the lessons of 1973 and 1979—indeed, blind to the whole concept of economic power and influence. "Is there any doubt," an incredulous Richard Perle asked a Senate committee in late 1981, "that our allies listen more carefully to Kings and rulers who supply them with energy than to those who do not?" Even barring any explicit Soviet threats to cut off gas supplies, "there is the day-to-day influence that must flow, like the gas itself, through a pipeline to which there is no practicable alternative," Perle insisted. "Practical men will find alternatives to angering their suppliers more easily than they will find new suppliers."[2]

In more general terms, the American critics saw Europe succumbing to an economic relationship whereby Russia would gain hard currency, virtually limitless financial credit, advanced Western technology, and political leverage directly usable for Finlandizing Western Europe. In the neoconservative analysis, Russia was already gaining most of the benefits of conquest with virtually none of the costs.

WESTERN EUROPE'S TRADE WITH THE EAST

Chapter 3 described how the American debate over détente had started with the Kissinger-Jackson battle over Soviet-American trade. The Europeans seemed immune to these poisonous battles. There was in Western Europe a general consensus that trade with the East was a good thing. In the late 1940s and early 1950s, British, French and Italian governments had managed to keep their Eastern trade links alive even while nominally cooperating with an American policy of virtual economic warfare. In West Germany, even as the Adenauer government maintained its posture of diplomatic intransigence toward the East, it signed an April 1958 trade agreement and promptly allowed its trade with Moscow to double.[3] A decade later, the Brandt government began consciously to develop East-West economic relations as a principal engine of *Ostpolitik*.[4]

The inducement of trade does appear to have been one factor that brought the Soviets to sign the Renunciation-of-Force and Four-Powers Agreement of 1970. And the influence this had over popular West European attitudes about economic détente was rapid and enduring. Normalization of Berlin's status, and the more general rapprochement between the two Germanys meant improved conditions for citizens of the German Democratic Republic as well much increased contact across the border—this, at least, was one of Bonn's stated rationales. Western Europe's leaders also believed that their exports to the East, while only a small share of total trade, had a significant marginal impact in cushioning certain vulnerable sectors during the 1970s, a decade of increasingly injurious economic cycles. West German chancellor Helmut Schmidt resolutely defended Eastern trade for just this reason. The Communist bloc, Schmidt said in 1977,

> . . . offers markets which are especially attractive for the West because they are not, or not fully, involved in the synchronization of Western business cycles. In 1975, for instance, due to the world recession, German exports dropped by almost 4 percent in nominal terms whereas the exports to the Soviet Union rose by 46 percent, thus making a valuable contribution towards improved use of capacities and a better employment situation in my country.[5]

It rapidly became clear that the best match of Soviet and European needs, resources and capabilities would be in the field of energy trade. In 1979 the Soviets accounted for 9.1 percent, 4.9 percent and 9.1 percent, respectively, of total West German, French and Italian energy imports.[6] The largest share of these imports was in the form of oil, which Russia had been exporting to the Europeans since the nineteenth century. Throughout the 1970s, however, purchases of Soviet gas also took on increasing importance for both sides.[7]

The Russians needed the West not only as an energy market but also as a source of energy technology. The Russians faced diminishing returns for both oil and gas from existing wells as well as formidable climatic and geological obstacles to exploiting vast new fields in Western Siberia. Although independent estimates varied, there was general agreement with 1971 and 1977 CIA findings that the Russians "urgently" needed Western equipment in order to extract both oil and gas with enough efficiency to meet world market prices. The 1977 CIA report predicted so rapid a decline in oil production that the Soviet Union would be a net oil importer by 1985.[8] If true, this was a dismal prospect for the Soviets, given various estimates that they depended on energy exports for more than half of their hard-currency earnings.[9]

Aside from obtaining the requisite oil-extraction technology, the other obvious solution to this Soviet dilemma was the development on a massive scale of Siberian gas reserves. The potential was enormous—Soviet reserves were a third of the world total. Western Siberia's Urengoi field, the biggest natural gas field in the world, was half again as large as the Netherlands' Groningen field. Such a solution also fit nicely with market trends in Western Europe. Already before 1973, natural-gas consumption had grown to 10 percent of Western Europe's primary energy use. Following that year's oil embargo and price explosions, the Europeans consciously accelerated this trend to gas. They turned first to their own gas sources, especially Dutch, Norwegian and British reserves. But the Dutch, fearful of depleting their fields, were cutting sales; French, Italian and German domestic production was declining; anticipated increases in Norway and the United Kingdom were not expected to make up the difference. Other sources, such as Algeria, were also problematic.[10]

THE TRANSATLANTIC FEUD OVER SIBERIAN GAS

The single great exception to this diminishing supply seemed to be the Soviet Union, with 27 billion cubic meters of gas reserves. During the 1970s the Soviets had signed a series of complicated supply contracts with the Italians, the West Germans, the Austrians and even the French, who became frustrated with their traditional Algerian suppliers. The 1979 oil crisis, with even tighter supply shortages and steeper price increases, made it seem all the more urgent that the Europeans diversify away from their still alarmingly high dependence on OPEC oil.

It was in this context that negotiations unfolded to build a 5,000-kilometer pipeline able to carry an annual 40 billion cubic meters of natural gas from Siberia's Yamal Peninsula, over the Urals, through Russia, the Ukraine, and Czechoslovakia into Western Europe.[11] Cost estimates varied between $10 and $15 billion—it was, at any rate, sure to be the largest single project in the history of East-West economic relations.[12] Governments, banks, manufacturing companies and state-controlled gas-import firms from Germany, France, Italy and the United Kingdom were involved. The most important technology exports were 25-megawatt turbines to power the compressor stations, but the deal also involved massive quantities of wide-diameter pipe, computerized gas-flow equipment, refrigeration stations and truck-mounted cranes.

Initial plans were that gas would flow through the pipeline to West Germany, France, Italy, Belgium, Austria, Finland, the Netherlands, Switzerland, Sweden and Greece.[13] The largest share of the gas was destined for the major countries who were constructing the pipeline; a large part of their investment was to be repaid in the form of guaranteed gas deliveries. In addition, the Germans and especially the French provided generous interest-rate subsidies.[14]

The whole package was undeniably an attractive one for the Soviets. With very little in the way of start-up costs, they hoped by 1985 to enjoy a yearly stream of $8 to $10 billion from gas sales.[15] Aside from the concessionary financing, they drew on Western engineering and experience for the daunting task of constructing and maintaining an advanced pipeline on permafrost terrain where winter temperatures regularly hit -50 degrees centigrade. They might theoretically have come up with the technology on their own, but as an economically sensible engineering and managerial project, it seemed beyond their capabilities.[16]

This does not mean, as American critics alleged, that the Europeans accepted a bad deal out of deference to Soviet political and military power. The Europeans were in the habit of financing exports to maintain employment, a practice not unknown in the United States. The construction of the pipeline itself would take a vast amount of steel from the depressed European steel industry.[17] Such companies as Scotland's John Brown Engineering and France's Creusot-Loire expected the Siberian project to keep up to half of their employees occupied for years.[18] And the gas itself looked to be attractively priced, particularly in the early 1980s, when the extent of the oil-market slump had not yet become apparent.[19] Writing in the midst of the controversy, energy consultant Jonathan P. Stern defended the deal from a simple business perspective:

. . . the essential point is that the favorable interest rates offered by the West Europeans—7.8 percent—are offset by the high prices charged for the equipment sold to the USSR, the employment the project will create in Western Europe, and the low prices to be paid for the gas. Gas projects concluded with the USSR in the past have been structured in the same manner. The eagerness of West European companies to conclude new contracts would seem to indicate that those past projects have been highly profitable.[20]

Three factors turned the underlying disagreements between America and Europe about East-West trade into an acute NATO crisis. One was simply the vast scale of the pipeline project. A second was the political victory of Ronald Reagan. His neoconservative backers felt they had successfully discredited the American proponents of economic détente; now, as with nuclear strategic policy, they saw the familiar errors driving policy in Western Europe. Third was the accelerating series of crises in East-West relations: the Soviet invasion of Afghanistan, the ongoing Euromissile battle; and Poland's imposition of martial law. Western Europe's continuing enthusiasm for Eastern trade in general and the pipeline in particular dramatized the wide gap in American and European thinking on how to handle the Soviets.

The invasion of Afghanistan had shaken President Jimmy Carter's confidence in the prospect for Soviet-American harmony, prompting an array of trade sanctions that included the fateful grain embargo. American exports to the Soviet Union fell by half in 1980, and in the same year French, West German and British exports to the Soviet Union all *increased* by more than 30 percent.[21] French president Valéry Giscard d'Estaing met Leonid Brezhnev that year and offered the kind of conciliatory comments that moved both French and American critics to accuse him of "self-Finlandization." German chancellor Helmut Schmidt left his rancorous meeting with Carter at the June 1980 Venice Summit and travelled almost immediately to Moscow, where he signed the initial pipeline agreement.[22]

The Carter administration expressed some unease about the pipeline, but it was neither loud nor aggressive. The Reagan administration, by contrast, was both. It pushed for a review of the COCOM embargo list, for reclassification of the Soviet Union under OECD guidelines as a "rich country" to which higher export-finance interest rates had to be charged, and for an end to the pipeline. Reagan raised these issues in July in Ottawa at his first summit with fellow G-7 leaders.[23] European leaders agreed to the COCOM review, and a year later they accepted the export-credit reclassification. But the pipeline negotiations with the Soviets continued. That November Undersecretary of State Myer Rashish led a delegation to Europe for the purpose of selling the Europeans on alternatives to the Soviet natural gas, principally Norwegian gas and American coal.[24] Neither alternative seemed very credible. Norway had only recently decided—for social, economic and environmental reasons—that it wanted to avoid rapid development of its gas and oil fields. American coal, though the reserves of it were massive, was hardly more available. There was environmental opposition, both to digging it in America and burning it in Europe, and serious constraints to shipping it via America's already overburdened Eastern ports. Some other American suggestions were almost outlandish in their implausibility, such as Europe's further reliance on Algerian natural gas.[25]

On December 13, 1981, the Polish army imposed martial law. In response, President Reagan announced a list of sanctions against the Soviet Union, including suspension of licenses for "an expanded list of gas and oil equipment." If applied retroactively, and to American subsidiaries abroad or to equipment manufactured under American license, the sanctions could have interfered with West European plans for the pipeline. That was precisely what a number of administration officials intended. However, at the urging of Secretary of State Alexander Haig, Reagan delayed imposition of the measures pending further discussions with the allies.[26] In January an emergency meeting of NATO ministers agreed to some sanctions against both Poland and the Soviet Union, but none of the pipeline contracts were included. For the next six months the Americans continued to press for collective sanctions; the dispute became a principal source of tension at the Versailles G-7 summit in June. Reagan and French president Mitterrand also quarrelled over the specific matter of credits and subsidized interest rates for the Soviets.[27] Tensions were already high for strictly economic reasons—the Europeans blamed high U.S. interest rates and a strong dollar for inhibiting their recovery from recession. The French were particularly disgruntled because they believed that American economic policies were adding to pressures on the franc and thus thwarting their socialist programs. The summit ended with a loose compromise under which, according to Haig, the United States would help support the distressed franc in exchange for a commitment of "restraint by the other governments on future credits to the Soviet Union." Implied in the agreement was an end to the threat of American pipeline sanctions.[28]

The agreement immediately unravelled.[29] A few days later the Reagan administration moved unilaterally, imposing extraterritorial and retroactive sanctions to block the pipeline. The retroactivity covered contracts that were already signed. The extraterritorial extension of these sanctions was intended to cover the pipeline compressors, which constituted the critical export technology. The European contractors for these compressors were either American subsidiaries, under license for American technology, or depended on American-made components, General Electric rotors in particular. Threatened penalties included ten-year jail sentences, $100,000 fines for each violation, and the prohibition of all trade with the United States.[30]

Western Europe's leaders were outraged. Schmidt declared defiantly that "the pipeline will be built." French foreign minister Claude Cheysson described a "progressive divorce" of transatlantic partners who "no longer speak the same language." Mitterrand added, "We wonder what concept the United States has of summit meetings when it becomes a matter of agreements made and not respected." Even Thatcher bristled at the notion that "one very powerful nation" would try to overturn existing contracts.[31] The German, French, British and Italian governments ordered their companies to carry out the contracts. As Dresser-France, Creusot-Loire, Nuovo Pignone, John Brown Engineering and AEG-Kanis obeyed their own governments and made good on their contracts, President Reagan issued a series of executive orders imposing on each company countersanctions barring trade with the United States.[32]

The transatlantic bitterness was intensified by the fact that America continued to sell grain to the Soviets. Reagan had fulfilled his campaign pledge to lift the Carter embargo. Administration officials defended the sales, claiming that "grain is not a strategic commodity" and even suggesting that grain trade actually hindered the Soviet military effort by using up their precious hard currency.[33] The Europeans were little impressed by such arguments. "To us," a leading French security expert told American senators, "this looks like a joke."[34]

Experienced observers of Atlantic affairs judged this one of the most serious crises in the history of NATO relations.[35] It had a parallel (if less dramatically) divisive impact on the Reagan administration itself, accentuating the tensions between neoconservatives and such traditional conservatives as Alexander Haig and George Shultz. The imposition of extraterritorial sanctions was a clear victory for the neoconservatives and a proximate cause for Secretary of State Haig's resignation.[36]

It was not a victory that could be maintained, however, at any bearable cost in terms of Alliance solidarity. European leaders continued to make clear that they considered this a test of national sovereignty and that they would not relent. Schmidt's successor, the Christian Democrat Helmut Kohl, pledged to stick with the pipeline. On November 13, 1982, the United States backed down, lifting the countersanctions in return for European participation in several studies on the security implications of East-West trade. The Europeans did not agree to abide by any of the findings.[37]

AMERICA'S CASE AGAINST THE PIPELINE

Little or nothing had changed in Poland to justify the American reversal. At any rate, a close reading of the history and arguments of the Reagan administration's campaign against the pipeline deal makes clear that the controversy was related only tangentially to Poland's troubles. The administration's case rested on more universal principles. Administration spokesmen assailed the project as a manifestation of the inane and discredited détente fantasy. Confident of having demolished the fantasy in America, the neoconservatives professed amazement at its endurance in Western Europe. Before a series of House and Senate committee hearings, high-level Defense, State and Commerce Department officials cited the supposedly clear lessons of the 1970s. Richard Perle led the way. "It is simply no longer convincing to suggest that trade will moderate Soviet behavior or deflect it from its build-up of military power," said Perle in November 1981. "If anything, the reverse has proven true. Increased trade has enabled the Soviet Union to accomplish its military expansion faster and at a lower cost, as Western technology and industrial assistance has become increasingly available to them."[38]

The Reagan administration viewed the pipeline project as a key element of Soviet grand strategy against the West. Administration officials described detailed planning by Moscow to "firmly ensconce the Europeans in what may be an irrevocable dependency on Soviet energy supplies," as Assistant Commerce Secretary Lawrence J. Brady put it.[39] He spoke of the "ominous possibility" that Russia was pursuing a "two-track strategy to destroy the cohesion of the Western alliance," combining a skillful manipulation of its own energy resources with a political talent for stirring up trouble in the Persian Gulf.[40]

As far as the Americans were concerned, the pipeline project contained every ingredient in the formula for the economic Finlandization of Western Europe. First, its hookup would place Western Europe in a precarious position in which energy supplies critical to its economy would flow at the whim of the Russians. Second, the project would "help to forge an economic link"[41] of a more general nature: essentially a network of jobs, dependent on East-West trade, that the Soviets, with their centrally controlled political economy, were better able to exploit for diplomatic purposes. Third, the project's financing arrangements would create a financial link that, again, would favor only the Soviets. West European banks would assume all of the risk for the development of Siberian resources; not only would the Soviets enjoy the benefits of exploiting those resources, they could also exploit the debt risk itself as another political lever against Europe. Fourth, pipeline computers and compressors would join the deluge of Western technology that was already flowing to Russia's military-industrial complex and general economy, allowing the Soviets to evade the constraints of their intellectually and entrepreneurially deadening system. Finally, immense hard-currency earnings from gas sales would allow the Soviets to buy more advanced technology from Europe and directly finance their relentless military buildup.

Invoking the specter of vulnerable energy supplies, administration spokesmen lectured on two levels. First, they warned of specific aspects of natural gas, and of this proposed pipeline, that would give the Russians maximum possible leverage from a cutoff or a threat to do so. And second, they warned of an "energy relationship" that altered the political-power relationship even if the threatened supply cutoff never emerged into conscious political discourse.

Administration spokesmen also pictured the Siberian project diverting resources from potential energy investment that would make strategic sense for the West. The pipeline would come into service during a temporary period of slackening world energy demand, further forestalling the development of Western coal, oil, natural gas and nuclear supplies—investment projects that naturally would require very long lead times. But after the 1980s, with demand again growing faster than supply, the true strategic significance of Soviet sources would emerge.[42]

As to more immediate dangers, Perle and Robert Hormats argued that the technology of gas supply was inherently inflexible and therefore exceptionally vulnerable to supply manipulations. "It is much more expensive and technically challenging to hold large strategic stocks of gas than it is to hold stocks of oil," said Hormats. Unlike coal or oil, "there is no spot market for gas" to respond to fluctuations in supply and demand. And use of natural gas "requires large start up investments and pipelines."[43] The secondary, residential and commercial pipelines in themselves "create dependency," argued Perle, "because they are dedicated facilities, tied into an elaborate infrastructure of delivery networks and distribution facilities."[44] While overall, Soviet natural gas would make up only 5 percent of Europe's energy use, certain regions (notably Bavaria) already depended much more heavily on Soviet gas—and would burn even more of it once the pipeline was built.[45] And the character of those customers constituted a special political liability.

> ... residential and commercial consumers are particularly dependent upon gas. A cutoff of Soviet gas would be particularly onerous for these politically sensitive sectors. Thirty percent of the gas from the pipeline is earmarked for residential use. Residential and commercial consumers are the least able to absorb an abrupt fuel supply interruption. Homeowners have limited capacity to switch easily to another fuel. Furthermore, gas

prices would probably rise precipitously in the wake of a Soviet embargo and thus place a harsh financial burden on the homeowners and commercial business.

Hence, European vulnerability to Soviet gas leverage could be more substantial than the total energy share might lead one to believe. Recognizing this, users of Soviet gas would be likely to urge their governments to avoid any action which could provoke a Soviet cutoff or sharp price increase. It is this sort of leverage which, even without a direct Soviet threat of a cutoff of flows, could have an important impact on Western European political behavior.[46]

Much of this argument was a straightforward description of natural gas as a strategically significant commodity, with a delivery system whose technical characteristics added to its strategic significance. However, the second paragraph quoted above moves into an area of murky political and psychological assumptions. Residential and commercial users of Soviet gas, conscious of their energy source, were going to pressure their governments to anticipate and satisfy Soviet desires even if the Russians never mentioned the words "supply cutoff." This assumes that the natural response of a democratic society to foreign blackmail is a kind of reflexive impulse to surrender. This latter assumption was *not* supported by a directly analogous and very recent experience with which these administration officials were familiar—indeed, an experience to which, arguably, they owed their current jobs. Two years earlier, American streets had been clogged by cars waiting in long lines to buy gasoline. Perhaps some motorists did use their ample time before inching up to the gas pump to reflect on the wisdom of America's Middle Eastern policies. But it would be difficult to argue that frustrated motorists were joining together to press Washington for a pro-Arab, anti-Israel policy. Nor did they do so in 1973–74, when an actual oil embargo was explicitly declared by OPEC for the purpose of changing U.S. policy.

The assumption seemed to be that the Europeans would prove more receptive to similar blackmail, for reasons not of greater vulnerability, but lesser moral fiber. Consider Richard Perle's statement, already quoted above: "Is there any doubt that our allies listen more carefully to Kings and rulers who supply them with energy than to those who do not?" Clearly the reference to "Kings" was neither accidental nor mere poetic flourish: There was one place in the world where a modern-day kingdom supplied energy to "our allies"; and it was the conventional American interpretation that those allies had cravenly abandoned Israel rather than face the economic consequences of Arab displeasure. In chapter 2 I argued briefly why that interpretation seems overstated. It is certainly not so obviously right as to justify the argument that Europeans would preemptively submit to the subtlest forms of Soviet blackmail.

And yet, without offering any real evidence that this was how energy dependence fed into political behavior, administration officials presented their model as a matter of simple common sense. Call it "sensitivity or solicitousness or simply reality," said Perle. There was a "day-to-day influence that must flow, like the gas itself."[47] Hormats first conceded that "vulnerability is a hard thing to measure," but then went on to the remarkable assertion that "simply rattling the saber a little bit can lead countries to take actions in the political or the economic area that they would otherwise not be willing to take."[48]

These officials made similarly casual assumptions when they extended their vulnerability arguments to the prospect of Soviet trade subsidizing Western European jobs, thus creating constituencies in Europe with a vested interest in détente. Gas revenues, recycled by Soviets into further economic links with Europe, would "*inevitably* increase Moscow's influence among our allies," according to Perle.[49] This notion that economic intercourse "inevitably" generated more political leverage for the Soviets than for their European trading partners rested on a peculiar understanding of the relationship between the two political economies. It assumed that totalitarian political discipline gave the Soviets virtually unlimited latitude in every foreign-trade decision. "A centrally controlled economy like the Soviet Union can place orders where it likes," said Perle. By contrast, capitalist democracies were virtually without choice:

> There is not a Senator on this, or any other committee, who does not feel an obligation to do what he can to promote the well-being of his constituents. That is as it should be. But the same holds true of governments and parliamentarians in the democracies of Europe . . . where jobs and profits in Europe emanate from Moscow, it would be naive to believe that politics will stay far behind.[50]

To this scenario of European gas consumers and steelworkers serving as effective political hostages for the Soviets, Perle added West European bankers, whose financing of the project is described above. "The creation," he said, "of a community of interest between Western banking circles and the Soviet Government is hardly what is needed to arrest the troubling neutralist trend that we detect in some European countries."[51]

The large Western financial credits were themselves cited as evidence that the Soviets already enjoyed considerable power to force the Europeans into bad bargains.[52] That bargaining power would only grow, and as it grew, Soviet economic (as opposed to political) exploitation of trade relations with Western

Europe would grow ever more profitable. It was precisely this economic exploitation of Western Europe that would allow the Russians to continue their military buildup unabated.

In the short term, the gas deal relieved the Soviets of any hard economic choices between military and energy investment. Western Europe had in effect agreed to "save them the pressure on their military budgets," said Fred C. Iklé, "because, for the short term, important for the next several years, they build the pipeline on the back of Western credits."[53] Numerous other administration officials invoked this specter of the Soviets achieving unambiguous military superiority over the West with the active collusion of the West. "We are facing a 10-year window of opportunity in which the Soviet Union may attempt to assert essential military superiority over the United States," Lawrence Brady told senators. Under normal circumstances, "energy shortages in the U.S.S.R. in the 1980s would impose serious constraints on the Soviet economy and quite possibly on the military potential."[54] Yet Western Europe was now proposing to remove those constraints.

In the longer term, hard currency earnings from the pipeline would continue to feed not just the Russian military machine but various other aspects of Soviet power and influence. Oil and gas exports to West Germany, France, Italy and Austria—one million barrels per day of oil and the energy equivalent of about 400,000 barrels per day of gas—already accounted for one-half of Soviet hard-currency earnings.[55] Iklé imagined the added Siberian gas revenues leading to a mushrooming of Soviet power, analogous to "the influence that countries like Libya or, for that matter, Saudi Arabia have gained because of their acquisition of currency."[56] Brady anticipated that "such large supplies of hard currency could give the Soviet government potentially significant competitive advantages over Western companies and financial institutions." Russia might also "use its hard currency surpluses to intervene in Western monetary and banking systems."[57] In addition, the Soviets would have new wealth with which to tempt defections from COCOM.[58]

The direct transfer of technology was a minor point in the administration's case against the pipeline deal. The specific complaints concerned French computers (and associated equipment for gas-flow control), wide-diameter pipe, and the compressors produced by European companies who were either American subsidiaries, under license for American technology, or users of American parts. Of these, only the computers were alleged to have serious military value.[59] But even if only a limited amount of advanced technology was directly involved in the pipeline deal, the Americans saw it as a major expansion of an already highly developed system of imperial tribute paid by the Europeans to the Soviets in the form of technology. Energy trade provided the Soviets with their major source of hard currency for importing technology. The American critics regarded this technology flow as perhaps the most ominous element of the East-West economic relationship, for two related reasons. First, they considered it indispensable for the modernization of the Soviet military system.[60] Its transfer negated the West's single outstanding military advantage.[61] Second, Western technology helped the Soviets to ease their domestic problems, enabling them to maintain a system that might otherwise be insupportable. "Expanded commercial ties with the West," said Brady, "have traditionally been the means by which chronic problems in the economy could be overcome." He cited chemicals, claiming that Western equipment produced at least two-thirds of Soviet polyethylene, polypropylene, polyester fiber and acrylic fiber. For more than a decade the Soviet computer industry had "essentially been a replication of Western experience." And Soviet truck and automobile production "surged ahead with infusion of Western capital equipment and know-how in the 1930's and again in the 1970's." The Russians used Western imports "to infuse technological and financial quick-fixes" into their troubled economy—without paying the political price of capitalist democracy. It enabled them, said Brady, "to redirect resources from the civilian to the military sector and to alleviate persistent problems of declining labor productivity and other production bottlenecks that retard growth in the Soviet economy."[62]

CONCLUSION:
FINLANDIZATION AND THE SOVIET ECONOMY

"What does the Soviet Union want of Western Europe?" asked an American historian in 1981. His own answer:

> At this stage, the Soviet Union clearly does not seek to add Western Europe to its political and military empire. The Soviets have enough to cope with for quite a while. What the Soviet Union wants for the time being is to make Western Europe serve Soviet purposes in the struggle for power against the United States.[63]

Western Europe, according to this historian, already served Soviet purposes in two ways. First, it served as a ready conduit for Western wealth and technology to the East, on a scale not seen "since the early years of the Soviet regime. Western help was then needed for the Soviet regime to survive; it is now needed for the Soviet regime to gain ascendancy."[64] The second way in which Western Europe allegedly served Soviet purposes in the struggle against America was simply by opting out of that struggle. In numerous practical instances, European "independence" amounted to "the removal of an American ally."[65] These two strands of the West European attitude toward the Soviets—economic aid and political neutralism—were said to be inseparable.

> For West Europeans, the compensations for not unduly disturbing the Soviet Union are concrete, lucrative and immediate; the compensation for maintaining a friendly alliance with the United States in the event of war is hypothetical, uncertain, and abhorrent to contemplate. It is all understandable and even in the nature of things. The one thing not easily forgivable is the pretense that such a state of affairs does not exist, that it does not strengthen the Soviet Union, and that Soviet demands on Western Europe will not rise with the changing "balance of forces."[66]

Aside from his considerable eloquence, I have a particular reason for quoting this historian, for Theodore Draper was in most respects a harsh critic of Reagan administration policies. He nonetheless took the prospect of Soviet economic hegemony over Western Europe very seriously. Despite all that has happened since, should we also take it seriously?

As discussed earlier, American critics pictured Western Europe's economic Finlandization as a kind of double helix: Moscow's political exploitation of economic relations being one strand, and its economic exploitation of political relations being the other.

The question of energy security was an element of the first strand. With the Siberian pipeline, were the Europeans putting themselves in an irresponsibly vulnerable position? From the perspective of late 1994, this is perhaps the most difficult question to settle. The Europeans made a number of claims about how they intended to protect themselves against excessive dependence on Soviet energy.[67] Their most fundamental claim, however, was that Soviet gas was at least as reliable as OPEC oil; since these were their only real choices, it made sense to opt for diversity of supply.[68] The years following this controversy saw the virtual collapse of OPEC and world energy markets. Since its low point of 1985–86, OPEC has struggled to restore oil prices and has enjoyed some mild success. But the happy revelation of the 1980s—that world energy demand was far more elastic than previously believed—has remained valid.[69]

As a general consequence, scarce energy no longer threatened the stability or confidence of Western economies. As a more specific consequence, West European contracts for Siberian gas were immediately scaled back in both price and amount, which cut projected Soviet hard-currency earnings from the project in half, from $10 to $5 billion a year.[70] In fact, according to the CIA, *total* Soviet hard-currency earnings from all natural gas sales never reached even $4 billion per year.[71]

In general, it would be ridiculous to deny that political leverage can grow out of economic relations. But in criticizing West European economic relations with Moscow, American policymakers seemed reflexively to assume that the leverage in such cases always accrued to Moscow. This was a curious assumption. As a general proposition, it is not clear why primitive economies should be able to dominate more advanced ones. It seems particularly doubtful when the primitive economy is also a Socialist, that is to say, a full-employment economy. The Soviet Union was a sellers' market characterized by overemployment and chronic excess demand over supply. This was, to put it somewhat differently, a condition of chronic domestic inflation. Had Soviet enterprises been able to trade freely, the Soviet Union would have been troubled with chronic balance-of-payments deficits. That is fundamentally why the ruble was not convertible. Such a condition implies serious disadvantages. Since producers did not have to compete to sell goods at home, they were poorly conditioned to do so abroad. And since, in a system of carefully planned material balances, trade also had to be planned, the system was ill-suited to adjust to the vagaries of world supply and demand.[72]

To suggest that the Soviets, with all their inherent disadvantages, could manipulate a capitalist trading system like a political accordion seems a tremendous exaggeration of their economic flexibility. It can be argued, after all, that the Soviets, with their elephantine bureaucracy and rigid system of planned material balances, were far more vulnerable to trade dependence than the market system of the West. To begin with, the Soviet system was much poorer, and it already suffered from chronic bottlenecks that severely disrupted its functioning and impeded its improvement. In general, Western economic systems were far more resourceful in the face of sudden disruptions.

The larger historical question concerns the second strand of the double helix. With a bit more luck, might the Soviets have been able to tap into West European technology and resources in order to cure what ailed their economy? Did economic Finlandization offer Moscow a way out of its economic and historical dead end?

The answer depends largely on our understanding of Soviet economic development. The Soviet Union was an industrial behemoth with a backward economy. It was committed to improving the lot of the consumer, but in a political economy in which "metal-eaters" continued to hold great power and where agriculture remained a comparative failure. It justified its existence with an ideology that promised to surpass the West economically, but its leaders watched helplessly as the economic gap grew wider. Meanwhile, the Soviet leadership tried to maintain a military balance and a global rivalry against an opponent whose gross national product was nearly twice its own.[73]

Since Khrushchev's fall, Soviet leaders had become increasingly frustrated by these dilemmas. They responded with a measure of economic reform, but this reform was defeated by vested economic interests and intractable political barriers. Hence the leadership appears to have become captivated, starting in the early 1970s, with the idea of East-West trade as a kind of big fix that would satisfy consumer demands for food, exploit Western technological advances, and use its own natural resources to the best advantage a time of what looked like impending scarcity in energy and raw materials. In this regard, American neoconservatives were right to argue that the Soviets would try to use East-West trade to compensate for the failings of centrally planned economies. The debate lies in how successful they could hope to be, and whether their effort constituted a threat or an opportunity for the West.

To make this debate seem somewhat less surreal, it helps to remember that the Soviet industrial behemoth once appeared, and in certain respects really was, formidable. But the success of Soviet industrialization under Stalin, and the rapid recovery from the ravages of World War II, were triumphs with inherent limits. The dynamics of postwar recovery contributed to impressive growth rates through the 1950s, as the Soviets repaired damaged plants with relatively little new investment (and looted physical plant from their newly extended empire). By the 1960s these artificial factors were exhausted.[74]

In more general terms, Soviet central planning, despite its inherent inefficiencies, was probably well-suited to direct the transformation from a peasant to a heavy industrial society. The Stalinist model of industrialization relied on "extensive" as opposed to "intensive" development. When there remained unexploited resources of labor, land, raw materials and other inputs, the command from on high to bring them into service worked effectively, if brutally. But as the economy became more complex, requiring horizontal coordination between firms, and when resources such as labor turned scarce, coercion and planning proved clumsy in efforts for more "intensive" exploitation, that is, greater and greater productivity.[75]

With the Soviet Union's collapse, previous estimates of economic growth rates were revealed to be highly suspect. Subject to the caveat that almost all the figures are controversial, economic growth fell from between 6 percent and 7 percent annually in the 1950s, to 5 percent in the 1960s, to 4 percent, then 3 percent in the 1970s, and 2 percent in the 1980s. Afterward it collapsed entirely.[76] Before this catastrophe, Soviet growth rates were perhaps not wildly out of proportion to rates in the United States and other Western economies. But the Soviets *needed* faster growth. As mentioned earlier, the Soviet Union had set itself the task of at least matching the United States in military power, despite the latter's much larger economic base. With "resource allocation to defense . . . well insulated from competing claims," Robert Campbell argued in the early 1980s, one could expect defense spending to continue growing at 4 percent to 5 percent per year.[77]

At the same time the Soviets were ideologically committed to the goal of "overtaking and surpassing the advanced capitalist countries."[78] Thus the standard for growth was pegged to the performance of capitalist rivals. Though the leadership struck an embarrassing reminder of this promise from the party program in the early 1980s, there was little sign, even before Gorbachev came to power, that the regime was indifferent to economic stagnation. Promises of improved consumption levels suggested the opposite.[79]

It was because of this commitment to the lot of the consumer, according to Abram Bergson, that the Soviet leadership accepted a slowdown of capital investment, "despite the fact that such expansion has been the primary means by which the government has over the years endeavored to achieve a rapid growth of output."[80] But Bergson also suggested, writing in 1973, "that if productivity [were to grow] rapidly enough—say by 3.0 percent—the capital stock, and with it output, could continue to grow at high rates even while the needed improvement in consumption standards is realized."[81] The necessity for productivity growth was further underscored by the sorry state of agriculture in the Soviet Union, a veritable sinkhole of investment.[82] But in fact, marginal factor productivity (the increased output per increased input of labor and capital) fell steadily after Bergson wrote that article.[83]

Throughout the Brezhnev years, the Soviet regime was desperately seeking the elusive source of productivity, at home and abroad. The domestic search put the leadership on what Gertrude Schroeder once called the "treadmill of reforms."[84] It could not move forward on that treadmill. Innovation and technological progress remained the almost exclusive domain of space and military programs, where secrecy kept the benefits away from the civilian sector. Prices, though perhaps inherently irrational in the absence of a free market, might theoretically have been reformed, at least partially, to reflect scarcity and encourage efficiency.[85] But in a centrally planned economy there remained a fundamental discouragement of innovation. An enterprise's main responsibility was fulfillment of the plan. Innovation implied uncertainty, and uncertainty was bad for the plan.[86]

The other potential source of innovation was imported technology. But the Soviet leadership had unrealistic hopes and American critics overblown fears for how such imports might improve productivity. In their tendentious campaign to discredit détente, Reagan administration spokesmen seemed momentarily to forget about the magic of free markets. It was a little bit funny to hear them talk as though a few imported machines could compensate for the inherent irrationality of Socialist central planning.

The Soviet economy was vast, and technology imports relatively meager. The same absence of competition that inhibited innovation in general also blocked the diffusion of foreign technology throughout the economy. The Soviets purchased foreign technical publications, tried to copy technology directly from imported machines, and engaged in wholesale industrial espionage.[87] Such methods were no doubt very helpful to rocket scientists, who had their own process of experimentation and did not depend on the adjustment mechanisms of free markets. But against a complex economy's underlying dysfunction, the work of spies was next to useless.

As Western economies grew more interdependent and more complex, Soviet dilemmas worsened. For the vitality of modern "information economies" is largely a matter of human capital.[88] The only effective way to import human capital is through human contact: study in foreign universities, work in foreign firms, academic exchanges and simple conversation. In pre-Gorbachev Russia, such contacts were discouraged when they weren't forbidden. And even where allowed, the intellectual climate to exploit them—the readiness to embrace new systems and new ideas, to critically examine old assumptions—was lacking. An "open society," in Karl Popper's terms, is a prerequisite for the advanced development of human capital.

Economic pressure was not nearly all of what went into the revolutionary transformations of the 1980s. But it was one critical element and a concrete historical example of the "magic of the market." It would be complacent and sentimental to suggest that, in a contest with totalitarianism, liberal democracy will always emerge victorious. Yet once a military balance was established, and Western political stability assured, the Cold War became a particular kind of contest between open and closed societies on a playing field of post-industrial economics—where closed societies had no hope of winning.

Part III

The Threat Vanishes

7

Who Won the Cold War?

In the late spring of 1979, Karol Wojtyła came home to Poland. It was the beginning of the end for European Communism.

Millions turned out for the open-air masses conducted by Wojtyła, who eight months earlier had been elected Pope John Paul II. One prominent Catholic journalist recalled his reaction at seeing the hundreds of thousands standing and cheering in a meadow south of Kraków: "We were counting each other and realizing how many we were."[1] The consciousness and confidence inspired by those numbers gave direct impulse to the Solidarity trade-union movement of the following year. Here was history's answer to Stalin's sneering question about an earlier pope: "How many divisions does he have?" This was 1979, a time when the neoconservative alarm was at full blare. The Western alliance was supposed to be falling apart. Western Europe lay in a web of political, military and economic power relationships that was drawing it into the Russian sphere.

The conclusion of the preceding chapters was that this pessimistic view of power relationships in Europe was not only exaggerated but the reverse of reality. For the better part of two decades, the popularity of the Finlandization idea distorted the American understanding of this reality. In truth, the weakness of the Soviet empire far exceeded any difficulties the Atlantic alliance might have been suffering. Wojtyła was a son of Poland, but in 1979 he represented the West. Can one imagine Brezhnev enjoying a similar reception in Paris or Bonn?

The essential weakness of the Soviet position was acknowledged by some neoconservative writers but turned on its head in such a way as to make it indistinguishable from unlimited danger. The Soviet rulers could not tolerate free societies on their peripheries, because freedom itself constituted a mortal ideological challenge to their rule at home. Hence, even a defensive glacis had to expand constantly until, logically, it covered the globe. The idea—simple and persuasive enough in the abstract—shared some logic with Kennan's early assessments, the Long Telegram and "Sources of Soviet Conduct." Kennan had been trying to show that assuaging Soviet security anxieties was useless, because the Soviet leadership needed an external enemy to justify despotic rule at home. But Kennan added a crucial qualification: If the Soviet expansion by political means was contained, then the independent complications, forces and aspirations of both Russian and European society would regain vitality. These forces included nationalism, religious conviction, material ambitions and the simple aspiration for freedom. Given time, to be purchased by a successful policy of containment, these forces would "mellow" both the Soviet regime and international Communism.

This second part of the containment argument stood in stark contradiction to the thesis of an enduring Soviet political threat to Western Europe. For if one believed Kennan, it was the Soviet system that would suffer a steady erosion of power and influence so long as it shared a continent with Western Europe's wealthy, capitalist democracies. The neoconservative denial of this more optimistic aspect of containment was connected to one of their more dubious assumptions: the "irreversibility" of Communism. "Irreversibility" did indeed figure prominently in the Soviet worldview. If taken seriously, it did imply a considerable Soviet political advantage over Western Europe. Once irreversibility was accorded the status of a natural law, any change to the status quo must, by definition, accrue to the Soviets' advantage. That gave the extension of their influence into Western Europe a certain gloss of statistical inevitability. The Soviets could sit secure in their irreversible East European empire and eventually wear down the resistance of the West Europeans.

To suggest that neoconservatives accorded irreversibility the status of a natural law may be an exaggeration, but not a very great one. The theoretical elaboration came from Jeane Kirkpatrick in her famous distinction between "totalitarian" and "authoritarian" regimes.[2] Totalitarian regimes exercised total control over every aspect of society—police, economy, culture, media—and used it to ensure their permanence in power. And they had been uniformly successful—their power had never been undone.[3] By contrast, according to Kirkpatrick's distinctions, authoritarian regimes, though undemocratic, exercise more limited control over society, and they are capable of peaceful evolution to democracy.

Within a few years of its publication, the Kirkpatrick thesis that "totalitarian" regimes would never evolve to democracy proved spectacularly wrong.

It may seem unfair to judge the neoconservatives for failing to anticipate this development, since hardly anyone else did either. But it is curious that their pessimistic assumptions were taken so seriously even a decade ago. After all, the authoritative statement of "irreversibility"—the so-called Brezhnev Doctrine—rationalized the 1968 invasion of Czechoslovakia, a move that became necessary when Soviet-style Communism started to appear all too reversible.[4]

THE TOTALITARIAN ILLUSION

Westerners' concept of totalitarian power was itself misleading. We imagined the world depicted by Orwell, whose primary, grim insight in 1984 concerned the terrible power of debased language: "War is peace." His second insight, concerning the helpless atomization of civil society—Winston and Julia as mere pawns against the overwhelming force of state control—was still acute, but not an accurate prediction. To be sure, countless individuals who dared oppose the regime, both before and after Stalin's death, found themselves trapped in the nightmares depicted by Koestler, Solzhenitsyn, Milosc and Kundera. But if Orwell meant to predict the future (and one can reasonably doubt that this was his intention), he got one thing very wrong: the impact of technology. Perhaps technology offered some specific innovations in police-state surveillance, but in general it had a liberalizing effect. Postindustrial progress turned out to require a wide diffusion of information. Centralized Communist control—under which even photocopiers had to be guarded and locked up at night—became the enemy of progress, by almost any definition. By the 1980s it was Communist societies that most resembled the oppressive, clanking, industrial behemoths of Marx's age.

Václav Havel used the more helpful "post-totalitarian" to describe European Communist regimes in the 1980s. The term suggested an ambiguous evolution away from Stalinism toward a system in which state control was still oppressive and ubiquitous, but nonetheless hedged in by the trivia of daily life. The regime's power had something less to do with state terror and something more to do with individual complicity in "the canvas of ideologically determined lies that really holds the system together—and keeps society in thrall to the state" (to borrow Timothy Garton Ash's paraphrase).[5] Havel's celebrated example of this mundane apparatus of lying was the greengrocer who affixes a placard with the words "Workers of the World, Unite!" in his shop window. No one—not customers, nor passersby, nor the Communist authorities—would have mistaken these words for genuine enthusiasm "about the idea of unity among the workers of the world." The real meaning of the sign was clear, yet "if the greengrocer had been instructed to display the slogan 'I am afraid and therefore unquestioningly obedient,' he would not be nearly as indifferent to its semantics, even though the statement would reflect the truth."[6]

Lies can be very powerful instruments, of course, especially when endowed with the passion of hatred, as in Nazi Germany or in former Yugoslavia. Yet the most salient aspect of posttotalitarian lying—as in the Central European greengrocer's sign—was its essential flabbiness. The greengrocer's habit of conformity was a depressing phenomenon, and yet the very transparency of the lie revealed something about the regime's inherent weakness. Simply refusing to "live within a lie," unquestionably a difficult and heroic act, could contribute significantly to transforming that regime.[7] This assertion, so at odds with the pessimism of a Kirkpatrick, may sound utopian, yet the events of 1989 proved it to be utterly realistic.

In assessing the Soviet threat, one error went virtually unchallenged: the notion that the mendacity and unpopularity of totalitarian regimes was essentially irrelevant to their domestic and international power. Poland, by itself, refuted this notion. Of course, Poland was an extreme case, but it was more than just an embarrassing anomaly. With some 35 million people, a third of the Warsaw Pact's non-Soviet population, it was the geographical heart and largest dominion of Russia's Central European empire.[8]

In a 1976 campaign debate, President Gerald Ford embarrassed himself by denying that Poland was "dominated by the Soviet Union."[9] Yet Ford was on to a basic truth. The Sovietization of Poland had always looked like a losing struggle. Special reserves of resistance included Catholic piety and a centuries-old distrust of the Russians. Stalin, like Hitler, could subdue the country with overwhelming force and brute terror. But after Stalin, with the terror lifted and a conscious project of liberalization without democracy begun, the Poles' anti-Communist character reasserted itself.

The Communist regime had little choice but to seek deals and accommodations with its people. After 1956 the Catholic Church had to be accepted more or less on its own terms. "The authorities couldn't *not* allow [religious activities] for pragmatic reasons, but they tried to enclose it in a kind of Catholic ghetto," observed Jerzy Turowcz, editor of the highly respected *Tygodnik Powzechny* (*Catholic Weekly*) in 1985 in Kraków. "This was paradoxical because it was a ghetto that included 90 percent of the population."[10]

The regime made its other main effort at accommodation in the economy (where Communists always preferred to confine their concessions). Farmers were hemmed in with state prices and other regulations, but the smaller farms were not collectivized. Most Polish farmland remained in private hands, another gaping paradox for a largely agricultural society that also claimed to be Socialist.

The idea that economic demands might be appeased while political demands were repressed assumed an unreal distinction between the two. Failure to satisfy economic demands invariably gave rise to new political demands. And failure was programmed into the system. Inflation was an intrinsic product of constitutionally guaranteed full employment (with controlled prices, inflation generally showed up in shortages and lines). The Stalinist regime could deal as brutally with this problem as with any other—by confiscating the inflationary part of the peoples' incomes. But post-Stalinist regimes were reduced to coaxing and cajoling their workers with unrealistic promises and ineffectual threats. A 1970 spasm of workers' revolts on the seacoast toppled party chief Władysław Golmulka and brought in Edward Gierek, who proceeded with desultory economic reforms and heavy borrowing from the West (and set ticking a time bomb of external debt). Gierek also tried to promulgate a "propaganda of success," centered on nightly stories of economic achievement on the television news—"the prosperity hour," as Poles called it. "This propaganda led to Gierek's downfall," a Polish media expert has argued. "We saw consumer goods only on TV. It created a frustrated population that knew that the official press told too many lies."[11]

On July 1, 1980, the government raised meat prices. Sporadic strikes followed—nothing, at first, that the authorities were not used to. But this time the unrest did not sputter out and die. On August 14, striking workers locked themselves into the Lenin Shipyards in Gdansk, named electrician Lech Walesa as their leader, and issued a set of demands having little to do with the price of pork. Gierek went on television four days later to reiterate that "political" issues would not be negotiated. By this time, however, workers across Poland had risen up to support the demands for free trade unions, an end to censorship, release of political prisoners and freedom of expression. And unlike in past disputes, the country's intellectuals and church leaders this time made effective common cause with the workers. The Polish people were in open revolt.

On August 31 the government caved in. The "Gdansk Agreements" signed that day contained specific provisions, including pay raises and shorter hours; Sunday Mass on the radio and the opening of the press and airwaves to "a variety of ideas, views and opinions;" the freeing of political prisoners and the legal right to independent trade unions. But their essence was the earth-shaking, official recognition of Poland as a pluralistic (though hardly demo-cratic) society. The strikers themselves made only minimal concessions. They recognized the "leading role of the Communist party" and pledged that their unions would shun that role—which was something of a joke, given that this "nonparty" had just achieved the most radical political transformation of any opposition group in the history of Communism.

There was one concession by the strikers, however, that was no joke at all. They acknowledged that Poland had to remain a member of the Warsaw Pact. For the shadow of a question—when might Moscow intervene?—was to darken the political landscape for 15 months after the "Polish August." The Soviets obviously preferred not to invade: It would upset relations with the West and once more make a mockery of the pretense that the Warsaw Pact was a genuine alliance of sovereign states. And if they did send in troops, they faced a real prospect of full-scale war (the Kremlin, it was rumored, had received warnings of likely resistance from the Polish army). Although Soviet victory would be certain, it would also be followed by the headache of occupying and running the country. But forbearance was not inexhaustible, as the Soviets constantly hinted, and as they had amply demonstrated in Hungary in 1956, Czechoslovakia in 1968, and, for that matter, Afghanistan in 1979.

Yet the Polish revolution continued in a bloodless frenzy. Gierek was driven from office six days after the Gdansk Agreements and soon faced formal charges of corruption. Ten million Poles joined the new "Solidarnosc" (Solidarity) umbrella union. Communists left the party in droves, while the top echelons of both party and state were in a constant turmoil of turnover. Strikes continued, further concessions followed, and the economy imploded.

The revolutionaries needed to learn the art of "self-limitation," warned a nervous Tadeusz Mazowiecki, the Catholic intellectual and adviser to Solidarity (and later Poland's first post-Communist prime minister). The Soviet army conducted ostentatious maneuvers on both sides of the Polish border. But freedom was intoxicating. The Polish Communist Party Congress of July 1981 featured the unprecedented spectacle of freely elected delegates, a sizable minority of whom were radical reformers. And Solidarity itself became increasingly radical in its demands, despite the warnings of such moderates as Mazowiecki. At a September national congress the union invoked the Kremlin's worst nightmare, calling on "the working people of Eastern Europe" to emulate the Polish example.

In the night from December 12 to 13, the regime made its move. General Wojciech Jaruzelski, prime minister since February and party chief since October, formed a supreme military council and declared martial law. Thousands of Solidarity activists were jailed while Poland's own army seized its snow-covered streets.

Interpretations of what followed played an important role in the continued misunderstanding of Soviet power. The swift success of Jaruzelski's coup shocked Poles and foreigners alike. It was meticulously planned and well-executed. The army, far from resisting a Soviet invasion, obediently followed orders that relieved Moscow of any *need* to invade. Despite sporadic demonstrations and strikes in 1982, open resistance was easily crushed. In the shadow of Soviet power, it appeared, pluralism could be extinguished and totalitarianism reimposed with the ease of turning a switch.

But the appearance was false. "In this system you have to touch everything to see what it is," cautioned a Polish journalist.[12] To touch Polish society was to realize that although martial law had suspended the revolution, genuine counterrevolution was not possible. "Though the police rule the streets, this country cannot be 'normalized'—i.e., returned to Soviet norms," as Timothy Garton Ash observed in 1983. "Though the totalitarian communist system remains in outward form, in reality it is still being dismantled from within."[13]

The Jaruzelski regime jailed Solidarity's leaders but, anticipating embarrassment, it repeatedly put off a planned show trial for the top 11. It then offered to release them in exchange for their temporary emigration. The offer was rejected. "We very much want this trial to go ahead," said the Solidarity intellectual Adam Michnik. "A trial cannot compromise us, but it may compromise the regime. Jaruzelski counts on the discipline of the judges who will be sentencing us. But he should not rely on the discipline of the accused." Finally, in July 1984, the 11 were amnestied; Michnik, still demanding a trial, had to be dragged from his cell.[14]

In the summer of 1985, I accompanied a group of Western graduate students on a six-week tour of Kraków, Warsaw, Prague and Budapest. Although we could not know it at the time, this was a fateful moment in the history of Communism. In the space of less than three years, the Kremlin had buried three Soviet leaders. All three had started their careers under Stalin. In March, a fairly young Politburo member named Mikhail Gorbachev had become, in this sense, the first post-Stalinist Soviet Communist Party secretary.

None of the Poles we met expected anything hopeful from the change in Moscow. Two years after the lifting of martial law, they all seemed tired, cynical and bitter. But one thing was missing: fear. The disdainful and fearless openness with which they cursed their national catastrophe made an astonishing impression. "My belief is that you have as much freedom as you want to have," explained Maciej Kozlowski, the *Catholic Weekly* reporter. "We don't know that the things I'm telling you today will be regarded next week as a crime. Today not. Freedom of expression is total."

Even the press managed a real debate. In December 1981, after 18 months of "the greatest freedom of the press that Poland ever saw," all but three official newspapers were closed down. But an underground press soon flourished that the authorities were helpless to suppress. "With an enormous police apparatus it would be possible," said Kozlowski. "But there might be 50,000 people involved. It is not technically easy, or politically easy, to put 50,000 people in prison." The officially sanctioned Catholic press, small but influential, started publishing again at the end of 1984. Once again, Poland was the only Soviet-bloc country with a legal, independent press.[15]

Jaruzelski tried to appease and enlist the Church as a more moderate alternative to Solidarity. The radio still played Sunday mass. The state continued its unprecedented program of new church construction. At the highest level, this strategy seemed to pay off, with Cardinal Josef Glemp making conciliatory noises—arguing, for example, against a November 10, 1982, strike.[16] But whatever the compromises at the top, the Church at its base was a sanctuary of revolution, and parish priests were its firebrands.

That July 1985, members of my group visited a prayer meeting at a church next to the massive steel works of Nowa Huta, a Kraków suburb. It was a raucous political rally: Chanting, cheering workers, festooned with Solidarity banners, crammed into the sweltering church. They *had* to fit inside, because that's where their protest was privileged. A few days later we met an aide to Jaruzelski, who ruefully acknowledged what was happening. The priests "use the Church to attack the state system, Soviet Union, socialism, whatnot," he complained. "It is illegal, of course. If an ordinary citizen did it, he would be arrested. . . . In Gdansk the Church built a monument to John Paul II overnight. What could the government do? Tear it down? We'd have great unrest."[17]

This cabinet official's 45-minute talk to us was emblematic of the government's general plight.[18] Leszek Zapotowski made no attempt to explain or defend any positive program. Instead, he appealed to our sympathy. The Polish people, he said, were "to a considerable degree disappointed with the performance of previous governments," still "shocked by the introduction of martial law" and generally "fed up with politics." The only small victory he claimed was a sullen "return of realism," based on the fact that "people cannot strike all the time." And the only defense of repression was a barely coded version of the defense Jaruzelski makes to this day: It was a choice between martial law and a Russian invasion. "What did they want next?" Zapotowski asked of Solidarity. "The Finlandization of Poland? Forget it! . . . We won't be lifted and placed in Madagascar. We have to stay right where we are. . . . We live in a certain place in the world. We live on the banks of the Vistula."

The bankruptcy of Communist authority was palpable. "In terms of daily, viable politics, the party is very weak," Andrzej Bryk, an assistant professor of history at Kraków's Jagiellonian University, told us. "In terms of defending its position, it is strong, which Solidarity fatally failed to recognize." Bryk was trying to explain Solidarity's December 1981 debacle, but the deeper significance of his statement requires turning it around. A nomenklatura's stubborn ability to hold on to its position did not mean it could effectively run an economy or a society. Polish Communist power, like Soviet power, was essentially negative. A few years later, in so-called Round Table talks, the regime once again courted the same Solidarity leaders whom it had banned and jailed. To be turned around, Polish society had to be appeased.

The same was true in the Soviet Union. Except the Soviet leadership—with no organized opposition to talk to; no tradition of individual responsibility to refer to; and an overextended, multinational, sullen, impoverished empire on its hands—was to find its own predicament to be far graver.

DID REAGAN SAVE THE WEST?

Apologists for the neoconservative pessimism of 1970–85 have a second, third and fourth line of defense. The second goes as follows: The "present danger" was indeed grave. The Soviet Union was on the verge of global supremacy; fortunately America woke up to the danger in time, raised defense spending (under Carter and Reagan), and elected a president (Reagan) whose seriousness of purpose the Kremlin could not doubt. Thus was history made. A sophisticated variation of this argument would concede that the Soviet empire was already in serious trouble, but that is precisely what made it so dangerous: The combination of internal decay and global strategic ascendancy might have tempted Moscow to strike out to save its crumbling position. And finally: Maybe the West *was* already winning the Cold War in 1979, but Reagan administration policies accelerated and clinched the victory.

"It was correct that if we hadn't taken various steps [there would have been] evident an unambiguous change in the strategic nuclear balance of power, yes. We came very close to lacking the capability to keep them from being tempted to think that we'd become a paper tiger, [being] able to press us with outrageous actions that we would not find ourselves in a position to respond to." Thus did an "unreconstructed" Paul Nitze (his characterization) continue to defend the neoconservative alarm in May 1989.[19] One problem with this defense is that the alleged "window of vulnerability"—the vulnerability of American land-based missiles—was never really closed. But the more basic problem is that this argument can never be settled with reference to historical facts. It is all speculation, tangled up in conditional clauses. My refutation, elaborated in the conclusion of chapter 4, seems convincing, to me at least. But the refutation remains in the realm of the hypothetical as well. It is the nature of theological debates that they are never conclusively settled.

The next line of defense, regarding the dangers of empires in crisis, is historically plausible. From Rome to Austria-Hungary, empires have seldom been content to expire peacefully. In a 1980 *Commentary* article, Edward

Luttwak warned that the Soviet invasion of Afghanistan might be the prelude to an audacious coup: the insertion of overwhelming Soviet power into the Persian Gulf.[20] For the Soviets this high-risk gamble might look necessary, Luttwak argued, because Moscow enjoyed transient military superiority but faced a grim future. Its long-term decline was dictated by a failed and unreformable economic system, stagnating Russian birth rate and shrinking life expectancy, and the demographic and national resurgence of non-Russian Soviet peoples. The United States and other Western powers, moreover, had finally roused themselves from their post-Vietnam stupor. They were raising defense spending and in other ways taking the Soviet threat more seriously. The iconoclastic twist in Luttwak's argument was that this reaction probably came too late; since it would take years before increased NATO expenditures could be translated into real power, the Soviets had every incentive—even a desperate need—to strike out immediately. Securing Afghanistan as a base opened up "various possibilities in and around the Persian Gulf, from the seizure of Iran's northern provinces to something on a wider scale; or else, starting from the Soviet base in Yemen, south-to-north political-military action, to change political structures in Arabia, if not the map."[21] One need only revise Luttwak's thesis slightly—in a direction away from fatalism—to explain why the Russians did *not* so flagrantly challenge the West. In 1980 the Soviets were not yet quite strong enough; once the resolute Reagan replaced the vacillating Carter, they lost all confidence in their ability to present the United States with a fait accompli without it leading to catastrophic war.

But there is a glaring flaw in all such explanations. The near-miss scenarios of both Nitze and Luttwak depend on a Soviet leadership that was positively Hitlerite in its recklessness, that would risk calling down the fire of the heavens rather than lose the Cold War. Indeed, a big part of the neoconservative alarm was an attack on the alleged liberal failure to understand that Kremlin leaders were in a fundamental way different from us—that they were so conditioned by a Leninist fanaticism that they did not necessarily view nuclear war as the worst of all possible outcomes.

But the evidence, in retrospect, points the other way. Even the Brezhnev leadership—while certainly seizing opportunities issuing in the 1970s from unravelling colonial relationships and America's loss in Vietnam—never shed its innate cautiousness about a direct confrontation with the United States. And the succeeding generation, under Gorbachev, proved willing to lose a great deal more than the Cold War rather than repeat an invasion of Prague—much less risk a shooting war with the West. Either Gorbachev and his cohorts considered it simply *wrong* to repress anti-Communist movements by force (a most likely explanation), or else they feared the consequent harm to relations with the West and their standing in the world. They certainly could not have feared war with NATO, which was never a prospect even if they had attempted to re-Stalinize Poland, Hungary, East Germany and Czechoslovakia. That things might have been different under different circumstances with a man other than Gorbachev at the helm cannot be denied. But the neoconservative thesis of extreme Soviet recklessness—which suffered from a paucity of evidence even at the time it was propounded—proved in the course of actual events to be groundless.

The final line of neoconservative defense is perhaps the strongest one. It is the argument that the Reagan administration was uniquely able to seize the moment. Ronald Reagan himself, though obsessed with the idea of a Communist menace in Central America and elsewhere, also seemed to have an intuitive grasp of the reality that the whole business was nearing its end. His prediction that the Soviet empire would soon crumble and fall into the "dustbin of history"—a prediction that upset many liberals because it sounded recklessly provocative—had the virtue of being true. European Communism *did* expire on the Reagan-Bush watch. And we have to acknowledge the coincidence between Reagan administration policies and the Soviet turn from confrontation to radical reform. Arguably, the Reagan administration's determination not to compromise its INF (intermediate nuclear forces) position denied Russia a diplomatic victory that would have lent Brezhnev-era behavior a few more years of credibility among Soviet elites. Moreover, the circumstances of economic dysfunction that impelled *perestroika* and *glasnost* seemed to fit at least superficially the controversial prescription published by Richard Pipes in 1984. Pipes argued that a "staunch resistance to Soviet expansion and military blackmail" would "have the effect of foreclosing for the nomenklatura the opportunity of compensating for internal failures with triumphs abroad." In addition, "by denying to the Soviet bloc various forms of economic aid," the West would "help intensify the formidable pressures which are being exerted on their creaky economies," thus accelerating a systemic crisis ending in radical political change.[22] Arguably, the Reagan rearmament and especially the technological challenge of SDI convinced Soviet elites that Pipes was correct and that to avert such a crisis they had best rethink their fundamental approach to politics, economics and society.

However, the opposite argument is equally plausible. Gorbachev and his close adviser, Aleksandr Yakovlev, both have claimed that SDI and the Carter-Reagan arms buildup made it more difficult, not easier, to pursue arms control and general reform. "Star Wars (SDI) was exploited by hardliners to complicate Gorbachev's attempt to end the Cold War," Yakovlev said years later.[23]

Such claims might be considered self-serving, of course. Perhaps Reagan deserves some credit after all. But so do seven presidents before him. If America contributed to Gorbachev's reform program, it was through four decades of containment. The fundamental positions of the two blocs came about over a long period. The decline of Soviet political and economic prestige, in Western strongholds such as Italy as well as in the East bloc itself, certainly predated the Reagan administration. And the renewed prestige of market economies was a global phenomenon. The economic success of West Germany, France and Italy was based on social-market principles that eventually had to be noticed east of the Iron Curtain.

If one is looking for proximate causes of the Gorbachev reforms, the most obvious candidate is a strictly internal one. The old guard died. A new, post-Stalinist generation finally took charge. Gorbachev's reforms were the continuation of a 30-year progression away from Stalinism. The progression was glacially slow, with setbacks that spelled horror for dissidents in the late 1960s and 1970s. But the lineage is clear. There is abundant evidence that the liberal impulses of Gorbachev and his colleagues were awakened already during the Khrushchev thaw.[24]

Khrushchev's "secret speech" revealing Stalin's crimes introduced a standard of legality in regime behavior. The standard was very loose, to say the least. No one can call the regime that crushed the Hungarian revolt and raised the Berlin Wall a liberal one. Europe's Communist *apparatchiki* could be thuggish, brutal and murderous, but it is simply false to say that they were unrestrained. These restraints mattered for all the years after Stalin's death: In the 1970s and early 1980s, for example, it was far safer to be a political dissident in Poland than in El Salvador or Argentina.

In the Soviet Union, after Khrushchev's fall, a government of "minimal reform" continued the political liberalizations of the Khrushchev regime in a selective, measured fashion—even as it made life hell for the more outspoken dissidents. With the explicit commitment to overtaking the capitalist world already appearing dubious, the leadership saw the need for a widening policy debate—so long as it never challenged the fundamentals of one-party rule or Socialist control over economic production, information or culture. The party established a "scientific approach to decisions, cautious, but amenable to going forward," giving some hope of respect for reason to an increasingly educated and intellectually ambitious professional, technical and managerial class.[25] For all of its stultifying conformity, this was a climate in which the paradoxical personality of Mikhail Gorbachev—an ambitious party functionary who was nonetheless intelligent, creative, free-thinking and well-meaning—could advance to the top.

Before 1985, however, this carefully dosed out liberalism was inadequate, and the conservative reformism it was supposed to support was simply incompetent. Minimal reforms that unsettled the system without improving it did actual damage: A washing machine without spare parts to repair it causes more dissatisfaction than no washing machine at all, as Timothy Colton perceptively argued in the early 1980s. There grew an "expectations gap" aroused by previous economic success and also by the population's rising educational profile. Consequent disappointments fed bitterness and pessimism about the future, lowering worker productivity in a deteriorating cycle that proved impossible to break.[26] The "inner migration" described by one of the intellectuals I met in Poland afflicted the Soviet Union as well. Even an extremely repressive system can do little about the kind of passive resistance of elites withdrawing from public life or failing to provide the talent that the system needs to cope with the complicated demands of modernity. Soon after Khrushchev was ousted from power, Zbigniew Brzezinski wrote about the weakness of a system that promotes conformity and thus burdens itself with a "decline in the quality of social talent the regime can enlist."[27] Nor was this exclusively an "elite" issue—the masses also withheld the effort and productivity needed to solve economic problems.

Here is where it proves impossible to support the case that Reagan's hard line gave the decisive push to topple the Soviet system. The most dramatic deterioration of Soviet society began in the 1970s, the very years in which Western appeasement was supposedly giving away the store. Unregulated industry poisoned the air, lakes, rivers, forests and soil on a scale beyond Western imagination.[28] The general deterioration in the quality of life was reflected in a declining average life expectancy—an unprecedented and shocking phenomenon for a supposedly advanced industrial society. Alcoholism, always a problem in Russia, increased stupendously; per capita consumption rose 50 percent between 1965 and 1979.[29] "The nation of drunkards I had left ten years earlier had become a nation of staggering drunkards," wrote *Washington Post* journalist Robert Kaiser, describing a 1984 visit to the Soviet Union.[30] Crime and corruption drained the system's lifeblood. (This lawlessness reached high places as well, as notoriously illustrated by a diamond-smuggling and illegal currency ring involving Brezhnev's daughter, her opera-singing lover, known as "Boris the Gypsy," and members of the Moscow State Circus.)

On top of these evident disasters came the rebellion in Poland. To repeat: The Solidarity uprising came *before* the end of Carter's presidency, and it is obvious that the Soviet leadership took it seriously as a challenge to their system and rule, without illusions of somehow being saved by American or West European appeasement. "Solidarity's success grew out of poor economic conditions in Poland, but every Soviet political leader knew that Polish workers actually lived a good deal better than their Soviet comrades," observed Robert Kaiser.[31]

Moscow's response to the Polish crisis combined repression, quarantine and reform. The repression, as we have seen, was spectacularly ineffectual in the long run. Attempts to quarantine Poland and its contagion meant that it became easier (legally if not financially) for Poles to travel to the West than within the Warsaw Pact. To keep out the bad news, Moscow also resumed jamming Western radio broadcasts, a practice they had ended with détente in the early 1970s.[32] Reform took longer, and it was mixed, at first, with bluster and hypocrisy. Much familiar claptrap issued from inside Kremlin walls. In his February 1981 report to the twenty-sixth Party Congress, an enfeebled Brezhnev blamed the troubles of "fraternal Poland" on "enemies of socialism, helped by foreign forces" who were "instigating anarchy" and "trying to turn the course of events in a counterrevolutionary direction."[33] Yet amid the cant, Soviet leaders could be heard to understand that the failures of their own system were to blame for the unrest and that the system had to perform better for the unrest to subside. In the same Party Congress speech, Brezhnev indicated that the regime did not count on the Soviet population remaining passive in the face of a sharp deterioration in living standards.

> The things we are speaking of—food, consumer goods, services—are issues in the daily life of millions and millions of people. The store, the cafeteria, the laundry, the dry cleaners are places people visit every day. What can they buy? How are they treated? How are they spoken to? How much time do they spend on all kinds of daily cares? The people will judge our work in large measure by how these questions are solved. They will judge strictly, exactingly. And that, comrades, we must remember.[34]

After Brezhnev's death, his ailing successor, Yuri Andropov, took up this theme of popular unrest as part of his campaign against endemic corruption of party officials. "If the party's bond with the people is lost," he warned in 1983, "into the resultant vacuum come self-styled pretenders to the role of spokesmen for the interests of working people"—a fairly obvious allusion to Lech Walesa and Solidarity.[35]

Then, after a second geriatric interregnum of Chernenko, came Gorbachev, a perfectly logical choice for a Communist establishment that could perceive, even through its ideological blinders, the gathering crisis. Like Khrushchev and like Andropov, Gorbachev was a committed Communist, moderately reform-minded. He came to save the Soviet system, not to destroy it. But he became progressively radicalized by the intractability of Soviet stagnation and by the vast gap between what Communism promised and what it could deliver. Gorbachev was a reluctant revolutionary who equivocated often and maneuvered, not always courageously, between radical reformers and the entrenched old guard. Yet when the moment of clarity came, when his out-of-control revolution devoured the system he had hoped to renew, Gorbachev's humanity and common sense prevented him from standing with the forces of reaction.

In the supreme Marxist irony, it was indeed through "internal contradictions" that history brought about a global, systemic collapse—of Communism, not capitalism. Among its many sins, Communism was a failure in its own terms. It could not provide what it promised: "an alternative road to modernity," as Paul Berman has written.

> Its moment of weakness arrives when, for political reasons or maybe out of exhaustion, critics can no longer be prevented from pointing out the failure. The truly powerful challenges, when they come, are offered by people who may not own a single gun, but who can convincingly claim to be more up-to-date than the communists, not less; more scientific and sophisticated, not less; better educated, more worldly, not less. Faced with people like that, communists are perplexed, and their perplexity is fatal.[36]

If we return to Ronald Reagan's role, we find his real contribution in the speed and ease with which he recognized Gorbachev as someone genuinely committed to the causes of peace and his own people's betterment. To embrace Gorbachev so quickly, Reagan had to shed a great deal of conservative and neoconservative baggage. But this was no great feat for a politician who had always been more amiable populist than ideologue. Hendrik Hertzberg reminds us of this critical distinction between Reagan and the Reaganites:

> When Reagan called the Soviet Union an "evil empire" and "the focus of evil in the modern world," conservative op-ed writers expressed their satisfaction that at last we had a president who had a moral vocabulary and a tragic sense of history, a president who recognized that some political systems are irredeemably tyrannical and aggressive, a president who rejected the contemptible claptrap that attributes every international conflict to "lack of understanding." These commentators, and many of their friends inside the Reagan administration, saw Gorbachev as simply cleverer than his predecessors, and therefore more dangerous. Reagan did not agree. When he said "evil," he just meant bad. He didn't really believe in immutable malevolence. The villains of Reagan's world were like the ones in Frank Capra's movies: capable of change once they saw the light. Reagan thought that Gorbachev was a pretty good guy.[37]

Reagan was a fairly ignorant optimist surrounded by knowledgeable and ideologically sophisticated pessimists. These pessimists had constructed a Manichaean worldview of great detail, inner consistency and plausibility. But Reagan, the sentimentalist, had a better grasp of reality.

DÉTENTE AND THE COLLAPSE OF COMMUNISM

It is worth recalling the specific role that neoconservative pessimism played in American politics. Neoconservativism was, above all, a critique of détente, that supposed snare and delusion that rationalized American appeasement and Western Europe's Finlandization. In terms of the actual American policy debate, this is what neoconservativism was about. It was wrong.[38]

If détente was a trap, it was the Soviets who got snared. SALT treaties, whatever imbalances they might have allowed, helped Russia not one whit in the real world. Economic relations made things positively worse for them. In the Soviet Union itself, such relations encouraged a counterproductive effort to substitute trade for reform. In Poland, détente provided the basis for Gierek's huge borrowing from Western bankers, which put Poland in roughly the same position as Latin American debtors, having to spend most hard-currency earnings on external debt service and hastening the economic collapse that aroused Solidarity.

On balance, détente probably encouraged liberal reforms and political dissent in the Soviet bloc. Admittedly, this judgement is a difficult one, for there were no doubt many occasions on which Eastern dissenters were demoralized by the spectacle of Western leaders shaking hands with their jailers. In a perceptive and finely balanced history of West German *Ostpolitik*, Timothy Garton Ash suggests that friendly contacts between leaders in Bonn and the Communist regime in East Berlin not only compromised Bonn morally, they also helped, at certain times at least, to legitimize the East German regime and reassure the Communists that radical reform was not necessary. But in the end, Garton Ash concludes, the mix of Western policy—an American emphasis on human rights and a German emphasis on East-West reconciliation—was probably the right one.

> Arguably neither the United States nor the Federal Republic achieved on their own that flexibility in the combined use of favours and injuries which George Kennan [has] identified as the prerequisite for successful economic statecraft. Crudely put, Americans remained too hooked on sticks while the Germans became too partial to offering carrots.
>
> Insofar as this aspect of Western Ostpolitik contributed to the achieve-ment of the desired results it was rather through the combination, as much by accident as by design, of the two contrasting approaches, in the overall policy of the West. Yet, to the very end, representatives of each approach denied the wisdom of the other; and, after the end, claimed that history had proved them right.[39]

Détente also gave extra space and political respectability to Communists in Western Europe. The consequences, from a Soviet point of view, were dismal. The Italian and Spanish Communist parties started to take seriously their own rhetoric about being independent from Moscow. Independence from Moscow entailed the right to criticize Moscow, which the Italian party exercised passionately after Moscow bullied Warsaw into cracking down on Solidarity.

Most significantly, détente created the climate of trust and stability under which European Communism allowed itself to be buried. Hungary's two momentous decisions of 1989, first to dismantle its section of the Iron Curtain and then to allow vacationing East Germans to travel West, were the decisions that effectively nullified the Berlin Wall. Aside from any humanitarian impulse, and aside from the understanding that Moscow under Gorbachev would allow such decisions, what had to motivate Budapest was the realization that it had more at stake in relations with its Western partners than with its ostensible ally, the German Democratic Republic.

Likewise, Moscow's decision to give up its piece of Germany and allow unification was only possible because Soviet leaders knew they need not fear a united Germany. As Garton Ash suggests, this realization had something to do with the trust stored up by 20 years of German *Ostpolitik.*[40]

Détente's Western proponents did not foresee all of these consequences, but their justifications for détente certainly came closer to the truth than did the neoconservative critiques. Among the most sweeping of these critiques was *How Democracies Perish,* a brilliantly sarcastic polemic from the French neoconservative Jean-François Révél, written just after the Polish government imposed martial law. American neoconservatives greeted the book warmly; Jeane Kirkpatrick, America's UN ambassador at the time, quoted with approval Révél's indictment of democracy as "the first system in history which, confronted by a power that wants to destroy it, accuses itself." Révél's theme, as Kirkpatrick correctly summarized it, was the "delegitimization of the West."[41] The tactical and strategic superiority of Communism, according to Révél, consisted of its enduring ability, even after the revelations of the Gulag, to dictate the terms of global, moral discourse. Détente was a Western disaster for this reason too: It encouraged the insidious assumption of moral equivalence between East and West. He cited as an example the Helsinki agreements, with their solemn human-rights pledges that were "merely a joke designed to liven up dull Politburo meetings."[42]

Révél, like many American critics of détente, had a superficially strong argument: Signing an agreement on human rights that no one expected the Soviets to honor would seem very plausibly to have the effect of generally debasing all standards and discussion of the subject. (The complaint recalls

Kennan's despair about the American eagerness to sign agreements with Stalin that included such words as "democracy.") It is likely that Kremlin leaders thought the same thing: In their intoxication with their own Orwellian power, they thought they could promise devotion to human rights, and it would not mean anything other than what they chose it to mean.

But a funny thing happened. The Helsinki accords required their publication in the national press of each signatory. East Europeans could read and understand what they were reading in plain Czech, Polish, Magyar and German. They saw the vast contradiction between what was being promised and what was being delivered. Communist regimes could not bend moral reality after all.

The English version of Révél's book appeared the same year that Mikhail Gorbachev became Communist Party secretary. The timing was embarrassing, for in 1985 it was not democracy that was about to perish.

8

Epilogue: America, Europe and the Shadow of a Vanished Empire

Many thousands have died in the Soviet Union's collapse.[1] This does not mean we should mourn the passing of the Russian empire. But we might have been better prepared.

The challenge, after November 1989, was to find some structure or structures of liberal stability to replace the Iron Curtain's brutal stability. Western Europe's political leaders recognized this challenge almost immediately, and decided that a strengthened European Community, in league with a solid Atlantic community, could help create the requisite climate of confidence and stability even among non-EC members in the East. Such was the logic behind the Maastricht Treaty for European Union. But Maastricht is in trouble and its troubles poses the single greatest threat to European order.

This point requires some explanation. Obviously, it is in Eastern and not Western Europe that the more dramatic disorder is emerging. A savage war rages in the Balkans. In Russia, the prospect of an aggressive revanchism has to be taken more seriously after the December 1993 electoral success of nationalist demagogue Vladimir Zhirinovsky, whose party received a share of the popular vote greater than Adolf Hitler's in 1930.[2] Increasingly, even moderate to liberal currents in Russian politics speak of a rightful Russian sphere of influence extending at least to Poland's borders. Uncertainty and turmoil extend from the Baltic nations, to the Ukraine, to the southern Republics of the former Soviet Union.

Yet this turmoil is more or less a given. It will take a generation or more to sort out the conflicting claims, inherited hatreds, economic confusion and physical rubble left over from the overlapping empires that were once governed from Istanbul, Vienna, Berlin and Moscow. With the exception of the former Yugoslavia, it is hard to argue that the inheritors of this rubble are doing worse than might reasonably be expected. In East Central Europe—that is to say, Poland, the Czech and Slovak republics, and Hungary—the reformers are doing *better* than expected. It is not here, but in the West, and especially in Western Europe, that fragmentation and political-economic malaise pose the most troubling uncertainties.

Such critical analysis may seem to be at odds with the burden of this book. For more than a decade and a half after 1970, U.S. foreign policy elites were spellbound by an image of Soviet strength and West European weakness that was strangely detached from reality. The European democracies were a decisive asset, not a vulnerability, in the struggle against Soviet Communism. Why should they collapse now?

What is evident is that the strategies that proved successful in the Cold War are inadequate for coping with its aftermath. For 45 years the Western democracies showed themselves capable of collective wisdom, perseverance and will. The overriding question for after the Cold War is: How to do it again?

THE CONTINUING CLAIMS OF GAULLISM

The Americans and the French were soon back to an old quarrel, specifically about the future of NATO, but more broadly pitting the concept of an American-led, Atlantic "community" against the Gaullist ambition of an independent, European superpower under French leadership.

The Gaullist moment had come—or so it seemed—with the end of the Cold War. In the East, Soviet hegemony had collapsed from within; in the West, consequently, much of the remaining rationale for U.S. hegemony had vanished. The opposing blocs had melted, just as de Gaulle had hoped and predicted. History appeared ready for a French-led Europe to emerge as an autonomous force in world politics.

This Gaullist epiphany was tarnished, however, by the simultaneous re-emergence of the German problem and by the severe disorientation that German reunification had inflicted upon France's political class. It became commonplace to argue that France, next to the Soviet Union, was the Cold War's loser. Not only was Germany now one-third larger; in addition, Bonn had recovered the trappings of full sovereignty. Paris could no longer count on a superior diplomatic status to compensate for Germany's economic dominance.

President François Mitterrand was in some respects like de Gaulle, a man of the nineteenth century, with "roots in an imperial age when international affairs were conceived in terms of power relationships, of alliances, counter-alliances, and the balance between them."[3] This perspective may continue to have considerable relevance, but it served France poorly in the first months after the opening of the Berlin Wall. French diplomacy was visibly off balance as it tried to slow Bonn's campaign for reunification.[4] Mitterrand met several times with British prime minister Margaret Thatcher, who was, if anything, even more alarmed at the prospect of Germany putting itself together again. The fact that U.S. president Bush supported the Germans unconditionally posed a major difficulty. Within a month after the opening of the Wall, Mitterrand flew to Kiev to meet Gorbachev. Afterwards Mitterrand issued a communiqué warning that "no country" could ignore "the situation deriving from the war." In Germany it was rumored that Mitterrand had asked Gorbachev for help in blocking reunification.[5] The affair was reminiscent of de Gaulle's comic-operatic visit in 1944 to Moscow, where he had tried to interest Stalin in a revival of the Franco-Soviet alliance. And just like Stalin, Gorbachev ultimately snubbed the French leader.[6]

Mitterrand recovered his balance, however, when he discovered that the Germans were willing to pay a high price in order to reconcile Paris to reunification. "The German government," according to Kohl adviser Horst Teltschik, "found itself in the situation of having to approve practically every French initiative for Europe."[7]

So Mitterrand abandoned his brief entente with Thatcher's Britain in favor of a new effort to bind German power in the webbing of an integrated Europe. This renewed cultivation of Franco-German relations bore fruit in December 1991 when EC leaders signed the Maastricht Treaty, the most tangible element of which involved transforming the European Monetary System into a genuine monetary union, with a single currency managed by a European central bank. From Germany's side, the treaty constituted an extraordinary, voluntary surrender of power: In agreeing to abolish the deutsche mark, the Germans were giving up both their primary symbol of postwar success and the source of their monetary hegemony in Europe. Granted, the new European central bank was to be modeled on the German Bundesbank. But "it makes all the difference in the world whether you serve as the model or whether you are actually in charge," as financier George Soros has observed.[8]

France's effort to restrain German power in the gilded cage of Maastricht was one with the strategy of trying, finally, to forge a European superpower. Along with monetary union, the Maastricht treaty contemplated a somewhat vaguer "political union" with a common foreign policy. President Mitterrand's government pushed for a new European defense community, capable of military intervention outside the NATO treaty area and independent of U.S. leadership. The Germans, always wary of being forced to choose between their American and French alliances, nonetheless tilted toward Paris and agreed to form a (largely Franco-German) "Eurocorps."

The Bush administration responded, as if by reflex, with the same pained exasperation that de Gaulle himself had provoked. U.S. officials warned darkly that if NATO's role were undermined, the United States might withdraw from Europe altogether (which, of course, tended to support the French point that an indefinite American presence in Europe could not be taken for granted).

Behind American pique was the fact that so many in Washington took for granted the emergence of a "unipolar" international system, managed by America as the single remaining superpower. This vision granted Western Europe, at most, an economic and political role in the stabilization of Eastern Europe, including the Soviet Union. But it remained, at bottom, disdainful of Europe's possibilities for sharing global leadership. Crisis and war in the Persian Gulf—from Iraq's August 1990 invasion of Kuwait to the American-led rout of Saddam Hussein's troops the following February—had reinforced the notion of a renewed *Pax Americana*. For such commentators as Charles Krauthammer, the war had taught a simple geopolitical lesson:

> We live in a unipolar world. The old bipolar world of the cold war has not given birth to the multipolar world that many had predicted. It has given birth to a highly unusual world structure with a single power, the United States, at the apex of the international system. Multipolarity will come in time. But it is decades away. Germany and Japan were to be the pillars of the new multipolar world. Their paralysis in the face of the Gulf crisis was dramatic demonstration that economic power does not inevitably translate into geopolitical power. As for the other potential pillar, "Europe," its disarray in response to the Gulf crisis made clear that as an international player it does not yet exist.[9]

Krauthammer's argument did not go unchallenged. An array of academic critics questioned whether a unipolar world structure was either desirable or sustainable for very long. They doubted, moreover, whether America—socially fractured, loaded down with debt, its infrastructure decaying and industrial competitiveness waning—really had the wherewithal to continue playing the role of benign world hegemon.[10] And a more bitter challenge came from the French, who were unwilling to accept a condition of permanent nonexistence on the international stage. Paris officials were particularly angered by the revelation of a draft Pentagon document that argued why it was in America's interest to prevent the emergence of any rival superpower.[11]

This dispute continued throughout the second half of the Bush presidency. It appeared finally to be over when Bush was replaced by Bill Clinton, whose administration was generally more receptive to European ideas and models, including alternative security structures.

EUROPE'S DISARRAY

Skepticism about France's superpower ambitions continued to feed, however, upon a series of setbacks in the Europeans' efforts to order their own continent. Two years after Germany's official reunification, a fin-de-siècle gloom was back in fashion. "[In] Western Europe a kind of frozen fascination exists before the spectacle of Europe plunging back into the worst of its 20th century past—a paralysed willingness to let anything happen, so long as it happens to others." William Pfaff, a Paris-based American newspaper columnist, was normally a strong defender of West European perspectives against Washington's frequently insular condescension. Yet by November 1992 Pfaff was discouraged. "This European debacle validates every one of the perceptions of Europe which lay behind America's isolationism in the 19th century, and in the 1920s and 1930s, and which motivated American hegemony politely but firmly imposed upon Western Europe in the 1950s, in the circumstances of the Cold War."[12]

How fair was Pfaff's indictment? To attempt an answer shows the hazards of writing contemporary history, for prevailing moods about nations and powers are notoriously ephemeral. At the time of this writing, certainly, there was reason for disappointment. Dreams of a new world order, bruited about casually in 1989 and 1990, were now looking laughable, especially in Europe. With its Maastricht Treaty, the European Community (now the European Union) had overreached and fallen on its face. Voters in Denmark rejected the treaty, French voters approved it by only the narrowest of margins, and the British Conservative government had to appease a revolt in its own back benches by putting off ratification repeatedly. Due in part to this spectacle, financial markets also revolted, knocking British sterling and the Italian lira out of the European Monetary System and putting downward pressure on the franc. A year later, when all 12 EC members finally did succeed in ratifying a modified Maastricht, their achievement was mocked by further disintegration of the EMS. France's currency could no longer be held to its deutsche mark parity: A radical enlargement of the exchange-rate bands meant that the exchange-rate mechanism was, in effect, temporarily suspended.

The main source of this monetary turmoil was a beleaguered Germany, which in the first few years after reunification had transferred hundreds of billions of deutsche marks in an effort to reconstruct and revitalize the poor and embittered new eastern states. Something fundamental then happened to Germany's role in the European economy. The reunited Germany remained the hegemonic anchor of the European Monetary System, but it went from being a benign hegemon supporting the system to an exploitative hegemon slowly destroying the system. The Bundesbank jacked up interest rates in order to compensate for the inflationary effects of Bonn's deficit financing of reunification. Germany thus sucked in financial capital from European partners who, entering a major recession with already high levels of unemployment, could not afford to give it up. The Maastricht plan for monetary union, laudable and even indispensable in its goal of embracing a larger Germany in a more solid EU, was nonetheless based on a fallacy: that the EMS would continue to transmit German economic virtue to the rest of the community, until their economies converged so far that they could tie themselves together with a single currency. In fact, the EMS has been transmitting German economic vices to the rest of the community, with damaging results.

The primary count in Pfaff's indictment concerned the European Community's failure to halt or even curb the astonishing slaughter in what was recently called Yugoslavia, a land that lies, embarrassingly, more or less inside the EC. Since the Enlightenment, with a predictability that evokes black comedy, humanity has professed amazement at its own capacity for murder on a horrifying scale. In this century some of the most stunning brutality occurred where Enlightenment ideals had supposedly prevailed: in the trenches of Belgium and France and in the extermination camps of Nazi Germany. During the winter of 1989–90 another horror was brewing. This was a time when European and American elites were congratulating themselves, with some justice, on their management of history's most peaceful revolution (the single ghastly exception to this peacefulness, at the time, was the toppling of Romania's Ceausescu). A celebrated academic debate, spilling over into political discourse, concerned Francis Fukuyama's recently published thesis that history itself had ended in the triumph of Western liberalism.[13] War, according to a slightly vulgarized version of this thesis, was or would soon be obsolete.

There was, to be sure, suspicion in some quarters that history had been merely frozen for four decades and that the thaw might be something torrential. Most of the worry was devoted to the Soviet Union, to the prospect of civil war or a reactionary coup. There were also some nervous glances toward Yugoslavia, where a Communist party hack turned Serbian demagogue named Slobodan Milosevic was already busy promoting a poisonous Serbian nationalism. It was worth remembering, as pessimists kept pointing out, that the European civil war of 1914–1945 had been sparked by a pistol shot in Sarajevo.

Diplomats in Belgrade were warning their foreign ministries about Milosevic and other assorted rogues.[14] One cannot say that the West was oblivious to the pressures building there. But the Western Europeans (and the Americans) were throughout this period curiously complacent nonetheless, at a time when they might have been able to influence events for the better. Why the embarrassing passivity?

In part, the answer is that they were overburdened—preoccupied with German reunification and Mikhail Gorbachev's high-wire act. Another answer is that they had internalized a version of Fukuyama's thesis even before he had written it. Intuitively convinced that Europe had changed utterly, they forgot the ancient truth that what has happened, can happen.

In the summer of 1991, after Croatian and Slovenian voters approved referendums for independence, the Yugoslav civil war began. The Serbs quickly gave up on Slovenia. But Croatia had a large Serbian minority that could not, in truth, feel very confident about minority rights under Franjo Tudjman, the Croatian leader whose postures were only marginally less demagogic than Milosevic's.

A series of desultory EC peace missions produced a series of cease-fire agreements that collapsed, literally, before they had been signed. This EC diplomacy was hobbled from the start by a diplomatic schism in Western Europe that recalled, ominously, the alliances of World War II. German and Austrian sympathies, both official and in the general public, quickly went out to Slovenia and Croatia, while France and Britain initially remained closer to their old ally, Serbia. Serb propaganda naturally had a field day with the fact that Germany and Austria were aligning themselves with the same Croatia where, during World War II, a Nazi puppet regime had murdered, by various accounts, some 200,000 Serbs, Jews and Gypsies.[15] Belgrade newspapers and politicians charged Bonn with planning a "Fourth Reich." This was nonsense, of course. The most salient feature of the German debate over Yugoslavia was the utter refusal, on the part of all political factions, to contemplate the involvement of German troops in any sort of international intervention there. But these World War II echoes were nonetheless highly unsettling to Western Europe's view of itself. The EC's handling of the Yugoslavia crisis was inevitably seen as a decisive test of its aspirations for a common foreign policy. Disunity in the matter would be bad enough, but disunity along World War II lines would be considered proof that the Old World had not, after all, changed very much.

So the major Western European powers struggled, with limited success, to put on a show of unity. The central issue was whether to extend formal recognition to the breakaway republics. Britain, France and the United States balked, arguing that such a step would widen the war and might encourage a violent unravelling of the Soviet Union as well. German officials were somewhat divided, but German public opinion was strongly in favor, as was most influential press commentary. Diplomatic recognition, it was argued, would internationalize the conflict and thus give the outside world greater legal standing to pressure Serbia. Hans-Dietrich Genscher, though he faced skepticism in his own foreign ministry, vigorously championed the recognition within the Bonn cabinet. Chancellor Helmut Kohl held back, hoping for a common EC position. In December Germany delivered France what amounted to an ultimatum: Either join in official recognition, or face the ignominy of an open split in EC ranks.[16] In January, on the basis of a somewhat farcical face-saving compromise, France and the rest of the EC went along.

There was much talk at the time that this diplomatic coercion meant that a reunified Germany was returning to the habit of trying to dominate its neighbors. But as John Newhouse has reported, the problem had little to do with a flexing of German muscle and much more to do with the fact that the European Community was making important foreign policy on the basis of internal compromises far removed from the problem of Yugoslavia. French officials were mostly concerned with reaching an EC-wide agreement on political union. EC ministers came together that same December in the Dutch town of Maastricht to hammer out final details and sign the treaty. The EC, it was felt, could not, at this of all times, afford the spectacle of an open row over Croatia. The French also recognized that the Maastricht treaty's centerpiece— plans for a common European currency under which the deutsche mark would disappear—was asking a lot from the Germans. Satisfying Germany's political needs vis-à-vis Croatia seemed like a fair trade.[17]

So the process of recognition was disorderly and, in a distasteful sense, political. Whether the result was also a mistake will be long debated. Some Germans continue to argue that recognition helped establish a real cease-fire in Croatia. Critics respond that this cease-fire took hold only after the Serbians had already achieved their strategic goals there. The same critics point out that Bosnian officials had, in fact, pleaded against Croatian and Slovenian independence, expecting that their multiethnic republics could avoid a brutal Serbian land-grab only if some sort of loose Yugoslav federation stayed together. (Germany's apologists respond that there is nothing in the Serbian record of the last several years to indicate that they required an outside provocation to commit aggression.)

Whoever was right, a second, more savage phase of the civil war began as Serb irregulars, backed by the rump Yugoslavia army, indeed set upon Bosnia-Herzegovina. France's remaining ties of sympathy for Serbia finally snapped as François Mitterrand flew, practically alone, into besieged Sarajevo. The personal gesture was impressive, even stirring, and it heralded a new attempt to use limited military force to bring food and medicine to besieged Bosnian Muslims. Under United Nations command, the French and British deployed troops to guard relief convoys wending their way through the mountains, from the sea to Sarajevo. But these troops could not intervene directly in the fighting or stop the murders. Muslims were herded into concentration camps, subjected to systematic rape, and massacred.

A case could be made, and it was made by American military officials, among others, that a significant intervention in this Balkan civil war would bring nothing but tears. These Pentagon officials feared a European Vietnam: The intervening troops would face mountainous terrain, a fundamental difficulty in distinguishing friend from foe and fanatically dedicated guerrilla opponents. And as in Vietnam, the Pentagon complained, an intervention would lack clear military goals—short of an unthinkable occupation of the country. Moreover, what moral principles could guide military intervention in a civil war where atrocities would surely be committed by all sides? Such is the nature of civil wars, and this one proved true to its nature. The moral clarity of the affair suffered when the Bosnian-Croatian alliance against Serbia broke down. In a three-sided war, the Croatian forces proved capable of their own rapacious land-grabs and of their own massacres.

None of this diminished the fact that the suffering of Bosnia was vast and largely unprovoked. By early 1993 pressures were building on both American and European leaders to overrule their generals and send in air strikes, if not ground troops, against the Serbian forces in Bosnia. But the Americans and Europeans could not agree on a strategy. American officials urged the European allies to agree to lift the arms embargo against the Muslims. (It is a historical rule of thumb that general weapons embargoes hurt the victims more than the aggressors, since the aggressors, almost by definition, already have enough weapons.) The Americans also urged air strikes to silence the Serb artillery that was pounding Sarajevo from the surrounding hills. France and Britain resisted the American arguments, for some of the reasons mentioned above and also because their peacekeeping forces on the ground in effect supplied hostages for Serb reprisals. The French and British expressed considerable irritation that the Americans, while apparently eager to join the war from the relative safety of the air, refused to deploy their own vulnerable ground troops.

In February 1994, a mortar shell exploded in a crowded Sarajevo market, killing 68 people and rousing the NATO allies at least partly from their passivity. United States and French officials pushed through a NATO ultimatum, threatening air strikes against any party that shelled Sarajevo or did not hand heavy artillery over to U.N. control within ten days. After some added pressure from Russia, the Serbs complied, but later that month, NATO fighters shot down four Bosnian Serb jets operating in the U.N. imposed no-fly zone over Bosnia. It was the first NATO combat action in its 45-year history, and it marked increased Western involvement, including more airstrikes around Sarajevo and Gorazde and an American-brokered agreement between Croats and Bosnian Muslims for a reconstituted confederation.

But there was still no readiness for the kind of decisive engagement that could change the facts on the ground. The most likely outcome, at this point, is a partition that ends the war more or less on Serb terms. Given what we now know about the democracies' willingness to intervene, it might have been wise to urge this solution on the Bosnians much earlier—simply ignoring the painful analogies to Munich. The horrors already committed cannot be undone. But the helplessness and passivity of the major European powers in the face of these horrors, however justified by prudence, constitutes a moral defeat of the highest order.

The Balkan crisis also represents a concrete political defeat for Europe, for it has revealed a grave constitutional weakness to the idea of common European foreign policy. The weakness is illustrated by EU-member Greece's refusal to let Macedonia call itself Macedonia. The absurdity was important because the progress of Serb aggression had followed a certain north-to-south logic. First, briefly, there were attacks by the Serb-led Yugoslav army against Slovenia, followed by the fighting in Croatia and then Bosnia. It seemed fairly predictable that the next targets would be Kosovo and Macedonia in the south—which might well be the spark to ignite a Balkan-wide conflagration engulfing Albania, Greece and, in some scenarios, Turkey. A strong warning to Serbia to keep its hands off, and the deployment of some cautionary foreign troops, seemed to be called for. Recognition of Macedonia's independence would help give the warning credibility (and did not raise the same dilemmas as the earlier recognition of Croatia, since

"Yugoslavia" was, by now, a purely historical concept). But Greece would not hear of it. Harking back to Alexander the Great, the Greeks claimed the name Macedonia for themselves, and they pretended to fear that Yugoslav Macedonia had claims on Greek territory. In early 1994, just after the market massacre in Sarajevo, Greek prime minister Andreas Papandreou announced a trade embargo, cutting land-locked Macedonia off from its vital link to the port of Salonika. The European Commission charged Greece with violating EU law, but as of late 1994, Athens would not relent. By committing a virtual act of war against a small republic whose independence the European Union strongly supported, Greece made a travesty out of the idea of a common European foreign policy.

GERMANY'S MORAL CONFUSION

Organizing Europe to do a better job in future crises means facing another obstacle in Germany. The German problem, in its current form, is a paradox of German weakness wrapped in German dominance. From November 1989 to October 1990, the year of reunification, the prospect of unbridled German power was setting off alarm bells from London to Moscow. But Bonn's more immediate offense was a maddening passivity. During the United Nations' war against Iraq, a blizzard of pacifist clichés descended over the German political debate, blurring sense and meaning. In chapter 5 I traced the pacifist transformation of the SPD's left wing and argued that this transformation was relatively unproblematic during the later years of the Cold War. Now it is a serious problem. Whenever the use of military force is even hypothetically at issue, there comes a repetitive mantra for "political solutions" (with rarely an acknowledgment that sometimes appeasement is the only "political" solution available). These pacifist assumptions affected the center-right government's wobbly response to the Gulf war. Germany was justifiably criticized, not for the absence of German troops (which no one really expected), nor for the size of its financial contribution (ultimately quite generous), but for the never-never-land quality of its political debate. That debate achieved its egregious apotheosis in the spectacle of legalistic public quibbling about whether Germany would be obligated to come to NATO-ally Turkey's defense in the event of an Iraqi attack.

The moral confusion continued after Saddam's troops retreated from Kuwait. Embarrassed by Germany's much-noted absence from the UN coalition against Iraq, the Christian Democratic leadership in Bonn proposed amending the federal constitution so as to allow the future use of German troops in UN-sanctioned military actions. It was a matter of debate whether Bundeswehr deployments outside the NATO area really required a constitutional amendment; clearly, however, establishing a political consensus for such deployments called for a national debate about first principles. Germans had come to take for granted that the mission of their military establishment could only be defensive, in the narrowest definition of the word. Again, this narrow definition was fully adequate at a time when Russian tanks were lined up on the inner German border. But in the present, more complicated era, it has led to such absurdities as the German constitutional court being called in to decide a dispute between the governing coalition partners about whether German crew members would have to be pulled from the NATO AWAC flights assigned to control the UN no-fly zone over the former Yugoslavia.[18]

In fact, the court ruled in July 1994 that there was no constitutional obstacle to German participation in foreign deployments along with other NATO allies.[19] But the effort to enlarge the Germans' sense of their international responsibilities still has far to go. Although there are still some realists in the party leadership, the SPD as a whole remains adamant that German forces participate only in traditional UN peacekeeping missions. Recent party resolutions promise that as long as the SPD maintains its veto power, "there will be no participation of the Bundeswehr in wars of the Gulf war model." Instead, conflict will be prevented by an international security system based on "the rule of justice" and "non-aggression."[20] Not spelled out is how this utopia will be attained.

Some of Germany's neighbors no doubt prefer this kind of passivity. The French, for example, abstained from criticizing Bonn during the Gulf war, probably because Paris appreciated every possible reminder that Germany was not quite yet a world power. But a pacifist Germany is no solution to the fear of German dominance. The pacifists' world is dangerous precisely because it does not exist. The Yugoslavia crisis shows that Germany is on the front line of real security threats: from turmoil in Eastern Europe, to nuclear confrontation between Russia and Ukraine, to a resurgence of Russian aggressiveness. In dealing with such perils, a romantic pacifism is hardly more reassuring than the old nationalist romanticism, for one leads easily to the other. Some Germans' pretense of moral superiority (under the cloak of "potentially we're so bad that we have to remain pure") has tremendous potential for alienating their allies. For example, much of the lingering bitterness in Western capitals over Germany's pressure to recognize Croatian independence stems from the fact that the Germans ruled out in advance any military measures to deal with the consequences. Under these circumstances, it is impossible to imagine Franco-German military cooperation as an effective tool against Balkan-style savagery.

AFTER CONTAINMENT

Western Europe has reached a point where the vagueness and contradictions of its movement toward unity can no longer be ignored. As William Pfaff has observed, by the early 1990s Europe "had run into the contradiction in its own ambition to create a 'union' of 'sovereign' states. Europe actually had to be one or the other."[21] The end of Europe's Cold-War division has only sharpened this dilemma. It seems imperative to extend the EU's economic and political stability eastward to Warsaw, Prague, Budapest and perhaps even beyond. But a decisive and cohesive EU, already a dubious proposition for 12 states, becomes well-nigh impossible after much further enlargement.

Logically then, any common foreign policy will have to be forged on a smaller scale—by a more decisive core of united, but still sovereign nations. In practical terms, this means Germany and France once again taking it upon themselves to lead the way. Their various European Union partners could then join in or stay on the sidelines, according to capability and whim.

Such a "two-speed" Europe would be divided between a core of advanced members with a truly common foreign policy and monetary union, and an outer ring of slower countries for whom the EU would be essentially just an economic union. This would mean giving up, for the foreseeable future, any notion of a true federal union. And the burdens to Franco-German partnership—German power and pacifism, French disorientation, Eastern chaos, America's partial withdrawal, economic malaise, to name just a few—are more difficult now than they have been for many years. But are they really more difficult now than at the beginning, as Adenauer, Schuman, de Gasperi and de Gaulle faced one another across the rubble of World War II?

And what, finally, of the future American role in Europe? American isolationists have almost always justified their insularity by pointing to the general hopelessness of the Europeans. Sometimes the contempt was justified, and there was invariably *some* objective basis to their disdain. But just as invariably, the isolationist vision has distorted Americans' reckoning of their interests and strategic position in the world. France and Britain were far from perfect in the 1930s, but they deserved American support against Hitler nonetheless. A strategically more sophisticated America would have provided that support well before 1941.

During the years of this book's focus, the 1970s and early 1980s, a new kind of contempt for the allies could be heard from America's rising neoconservative mandarins. Some liberals joined with George Ball in arguing that neoconservative ideology was "a kind of mutated version of American isolationism that flourished in the 1920s and 1930s."[22] This designation was somewhat tendentious, given that these "mutated" isolationists were actually quite eager for America to intervene all over the world. Yet the distorted strategic reckoning, product of an enduring Europessimism, definitely fit an old American pattern.

Since the end of the Cold War, there have been repeated warnings of an American return to isolationism. Yet how would we recognize American neoisolationism if we saw it? This is not a matter that can be defined by the number of troops the United States maintains in Europe. A complete withdrawal might signify an aggressive turning inward. But given the current strategic landscape, can one really argue that cutting U.S. troops to, say, 50,000 would represent a decisive return to isolationism? Nor can the Clinton administration's determination to concentrate on a domestic agenda be taken as isolationist. Renewal of American society and economy is in fact a prerequisite for maintaining the United States' world role. A virulent economic nationalism definitely would be isolationist. But aggressive negotiating tactics in GATT talks are nothing more than the negotiators' duty.

The American isolationist impulse *can* be identified by reference to one trace element that is almost always present: a bitter disappointment over Europe. If we examine this disappointment with any care, we must realize that it is the world as such—that is to say, we ourselves—that have invariably disappointed. This was true for the classic period of American isolationism in the 1920s and 1930s. America under Woodrow Wilson had raised the moral stakes in Europe by declaring a "war to end all wars," thus setting the stage for inevitable disappointment. The United States raised German hopes for an honorable peace and dashed them by joining in imposing a harsh surrender. Wilson legitimized the appealing idea that every people has the right to their own nation, but he failed to reconcile the neat principle with Europe's messy geography. One consequence was the breakup of East Central Europe—the Austro-Hungarian empire especially—into isolated, unworkable mini-economies. Another consequence was the bitter, overlapping territorial claims that are again ravaging southcentral Europe.

The United States was also responsible for the irresponsible use of its financial power between the wars. America had emerged from World War I as the world's preeminent creditor, holding most of its gold reserves. At that time of great fragility in the international economy, critical capital flows were driven by rather selfish American policies—framed, as David Calleo puts it "with little thought for the international consequences, and often [reflecting] rather eccentric economic theories and fitful coalitions of domestic interests."[23] And by the time of the failed London Economic Conference of 1933, American trade policy was set on an equally nationalistic course.

None of this means that America deserves the blame for Europe's twentieth-century catastrophes. What it does mean is that like Britain and France, America very often pursued shortsighted and counterproductive policies. And then, as the clouds of depression and war gathered, many Americans sought refuge in their country's splendid isolation, the arcadian refuge of Puritans and cowboys. In the 1930s American midwestern Republicans, Catholic anti-Semites, and socialist-pacifists all shared the illusion that this refuge still existed. They shared a sense of American "exceptionalism," which was an effort to deny, against all evidence, that they were products of a European culture with all its sins and foibles and that, moreover, they had a tremendous stake in what transpired there.

This stake has grown, by the simple measure of the immense blood and treasure Americans subsequently have invested. The payoff has also been large, albeit in a somewhat intangible currency. The defeat of fascism, followed 45 years later by the end of Soviet Communism, means that America's physical security is somewhat improved. But that was never the primary stake, since our physical security was rarely directly threatened.[24] Victory in World War II, followed by a seemingly permanent Atlantic Alliance system, did help preserve America's economic access to Western Europe. Yet it should not be assumed that this payoff was either commensurate with or even dependent on the military investment. For as Charles Krauthammer once put it, "A Finlandized Europe will trade with the United States. Finland does."[25]

America's greatest interest in Europe has always been a moral one. This interest can be understood only if we avoid making facile distinctions between an interests-based and a "moral" foreign policy. To be sure, there are often tensions between the two. Yet Americans have an overriding interest in the preservation of a world where they are not left alone with their ideals and conceptions of human society. More concretely, America has a broad interest in the preservation of a world where it can pursue its many specific interests without violating its ideals. For it is always difficult, and often self-destructive, for a nation to act at odds with its moral conception of itself. The experience of Vietnam offers ample evidence for this proposition.

The United States has a national interest, therefore, in the global enlargement of democracy. A world full of democracies might not mean the end of international conflict, but it would be the world in which American interests and ideals could be most easily reconciled. Outside North America, Australia and Japan, Western Europe is the only place where democracy is *solidly* established. It would bode ill for democracy's enlargement in the rest of the world if it could not be enlarged in Europe. And having struggled for the better part of this century against Europe's antidemocratic forces, Americans should have no difficulty perceiving that it would be against their interests if liberal democracy actually lost ground there.

The latest cycle of inflated and disappointed hopes for a "new world order" poses the greatest danger to Americans' healthy perception of their own interests in Europe. In 1989 and 1990 it was possible to believe that the agony of history had ended in the triumph of liberal internationalism. This belief was based on direct observation of how the Cold War ended: "In the years leading up to 1989 it was the magnetism of the democracies' cooperative successes which irresistibly drew Eastern Europe and the Soviet Union towards western political values."[26]

By the end of 1994 we knew that, while there may or may not be progress in history, it has not yet finished. To work for further historical progress, Americans must work with their European allies; encourage the more realistic plans for European union and world responsibility; discuss a sensible division of diplomatic, economic and military labors; and, above all, not retreat in disgust and exasperation at the inevitable setbacks that are still to come. Such a retreat, familiar but hardly inevitable in the American character, would pose a real threat to all that has been won.

NOTES

Introduction

1. A notable recent effort to give Reagan the credit comes from Patrick Glynn, special assistant to the director of the U.S. Arms Control and Disarmament Agency in the Reagan administration. See his *Closing Pandora's Box: Arms Races, Arms Control and the History of the Cold War* (New York: Basic Books, 1992).

2. On the level of literal analogy, "Finlandization" was a paper tiger, easily demolished by any serious analysis; see, for example George Kennan, "Europe's Problems, Europe's Choices," *Foreign Policy*, no. 14 (Spring 1974), pp. 3–16; Adam M. Garfinkle, *"Finlandization": A Map to a Metaphor* (Philadelphia: Foreign Policy Research Institute, 1978); and John P. Vloyantes, *Silk Glove Hegemony: Finnish-Soviet Relations, 1944–1974: A Case Study of the Theory of the Soft-Sphere of Influence* (Kent, Ohio: Kent State University Press, 1975). West European members of NATO shared few of Finland's specific weaknesses with regard to the Soviet Union. Except for northern regions of Norway, none shared a border with the Soviet Union. Viewed as a group, these nations possessed greater wealth, greater industrial capacity, and greater population numbers than did the Soviet Union. But Finlandization's larger significance has been in its wide currency as a symbol with which to tie up the bundle of fears about Western Europe's alleged, inherent defenselessness against a variety of Soviet pressures short of war.

3. Kenneth Rush, "The Nixon Administration's Foreign Policy Objectives," remarks before the national foreign policy conference for editors and broadcasters at the Department of State, March 29, 1973, Department of State Bulletin 68, no. 1765 (April 23, 1973), p. 478.

4. George F. Kennan, "Europe's Problems, Europe's Choices," op. cit., pp. 3–4.

Chapter 1

1. Except where otherwise noted, this account of American isolationism, exceptionalism and anti-European feeling before World War II is taken from

Manfred Jonas, *Isolationism in America 1935–1941* (Ithaca: Cornell University Press, 1966).

2. Cited in ibid., p. 101.

3. Robert W. Tucker, David C. Hendrickson, *Empire of Liberty: The Statecraft of Thomas Jefferson* (New York: Oxford University Press, 1990).

4. Arthur M. Schlesinger, Jr., *The Cycles of American History* (Boston: Houghton Mifflin, 1986), pp. 3-5,6,9,10,12-13.

5. See George F. Kennan, *The Fateful Alliance: France, Russia, and the Coming of the First World War* (New York: Pantheon Books, 1984), pp. 163–164, 253–257. As Kennan also notes, it was not just technology that made a difference, but also the rise of popular nationalism. Wars fought by dynasties were constrained by limits—dynasties knew that they shared some common interests. Wars fought by nations were likely to be fiercer.

6. A 1944 public-opinion survey "indicated that of the one-third of the public dissatisfied with the extent of Big Three cooperation, 54 percent blamed Britain while only 18 percent blamed Russia." John Lewis Gaddis, *The United States and the Origins of the Cold War, 1941–1947* (New York: Columbia University Press, 1972), p. 155, footnote 39.

7. Edward R. Stettinius, Jr., *Roosevelt and the Russians: The Yalta Conference* (Garden City, N.Y.: Doubleday & Co., 1949), p. 237.

8. Sir Frank Roberts, "A Witness to Yalta and Its Myths," *International Herald Tribune,* February 5, 1990, p. 2.

9. Dean Acheson, *Present at the Creation: My Years in the State Department* (New York: W. W. Norton & Co., 1987), pp. 9–10, 27–34; Wm. Roger Louis, *Imperialism at Bay: The United States and the Decolonization of the British Empire, 1941–1945* (New York: Oxford University Press, 1978), pp. 24, 30–33.

10. U.S. policy was to control the lend-lease spigot to keep British reserves between $600 million and $1 billion. In March 1944, Churchill sent the following cable to Roosevelt:

> Will you allow me to say that the suggestion of reducing our dollar balances, which constitute our sole liquid reserve, to one billion dollars really would not be consistent with the equal treatment of allies or with any conception of equal sacrifice or pooling of resources? We have not shirked our duty or indulged in an easy way of living. We have already spent practically all our convertible foreign investments in the struggle. We alone of the Allies will emerge from the war with great overseas war debts. I do not know what would happen if we were now asked to disperse our last liquid reserves required to meet pressing needs, or how I could put my case to Parliament without it affecting public sentiment

in the most painful manner, and that at a time when British and American blood will be flowing in broad and equal streams and when the shortening of the war by even a month would far exceed the sums under consideration.

Churchill to Roosevelt, March 9, 1944, in *Churchill and Roosevelt: The Complete Correspondence,* Vol. III, ed. Warren F. Kimball (Princeton, N.J.: Princeton University Press, 1984), p. 35. The American insistence on free movement of capital and sterling convertibility was to have dire consequences in 1947 when Britain fulfilled its promise to make the pound convertible, sparking a stampede away from sterling and devouring the bulk of the $3.75 billion emergency American loan negotiated by John Maynard Keynes at the war's end.

11. In some of his correspondence with Churchill, Roosevelt implied that American politics and traditions required him to adopt more explicitly moralistic postures than he might otherwise have found useful. See, for example, Roosevelt's cable to Churchill, explaining that he could not publicly support the British intervention in Greece because of "limitations imposed in part by the traditional policies of the United States and in part by the mounting adverse reaction of public opinion in this country." Roosevelt to Churchill, (R-673) December 13, 1944, in ibid., pp. 455–457.

12. Louis, *Imperialism at Bay,* op. cit., pp. 20–22.

13. Gaddis, *The United States and the Origins of the Cold War,* op. cit., chapter 4.

14. *The Complete War Memoirs of Charles de Gaulle* (New York: Simon & Schuster, 1964), p. 269; Roosevelt to Churchill, June 12, 1944, in *Roosevelt and Churchill: Their Secret Wartime Correspondence,* ed. Francis L. Loewenheim, Harold D. Langley, and Manfred Jonas (New York: Saturday Review Press, 1975), pp. 530–531.

15. John Lewis Gaddis, *Strategies of Containment: A Critical Appraisal of Postwar American National Security Policy* (New York: Oxford University Press, 1982), p. 10.

16. Ibid., p. 11.

17. *Roosevelt and Churchill: Their Secret Wartime Correspondence,* op. cit., p. 563. Stalin, according to an historian of the Soviet campaigns, did "all he could to play down the scope and significance of the Warsaw rising." John Erickson, *The Road to Berlin* (Boulder, Colo.: Westview Press, 1983), p. 281.

18. The U.S. ambassador to Moscow, W. Averell Harriman, was, by George Kennan's account, "shattered" by Stalin's refusal to aid the uprising or to allow U.S. planes to use Ukrainian bases to do so. Kennan would later argue that "this was the moment when, if ever, there should have been a full-fledged and realistic political showdown with the Soviet leaders," George F. Kennan, *Memoirs: 1925–1950*

(New York: Pantheon Books, 1967), pp. 210–211. Churchill was also enraged and wanted to send Stalin a message, over both his and Roosevelt's signatures, asking permission for British and American planes to land on Soviet bases after dropping supplies to the underground. Roosevelt would not sign the cable claiming that he counted on the use of Soviet airfields for some more militarily critical operations and thus did not want to jeopardize that option. A few days later, a truly desperate Churchill wired Roosevelt, practically begging him to send American planes to drop supplies and land, if need be, on Soviet airfields. (Presumably he thought that the Russians would not shoot down the American planes). Roosevelt replied on September 5 that it was too late—the Germans had crushed the uprising and regained control. *Roosevelt and Churchill: Their Secret Wartime Correspondence,* op. cit., pp. 563–573.

19. As argued by Paul Johnson, *Modern Times: The World from the Twenties to the Eighties* (New York: Harper & Row, 1983), p. 435.

20. *Churchill and Roosevelt: The Complete Correspondence,* Vol. III, op. cit., pp. 547–630.

21. Actually, the turn may have been less conscious for some than for others. John Lewis Gaddis suggests that when Harry Truman became president, he sought advice from Roosevelt's experts. They had become increasingly disenchanted with Roosevelt's policies toward the Soviets and saw their chance to educate an impressionable student. The result was to convince the Russians that American policy had changed, which was ironic, since Truman had intended continuity. Gaddis, *Strategies of Containment,* op. cit., pp. 15–16.

22. Daniel Yergin, *Shattered Peace: The Origins of the Cold War and the National Security State* (Boston: Houghton Mifflin Co., 1978), chapter 2.

23. Kennan, *Memoirs: 1925–1950,* op. cit., p. 67.

24. The account of Kennan's views in this chapter benefits especially from David P. Calleo, *Beyond American Hegemony: The Future of the Western Alliance* (New York: Basic Books, 1987), chapter 3; Gaddis, *Strategies of Containment,* op. cit., chapters 2 and 3; and from Kennan's own memoirs, *Memoirs: 1925–1950,* op. cit.; *Memoirs: 1950–1963* (New York: Pantheon Books, 1972).

25. See Kennan's dispatch from Moscow to Washington of September 30, 1945, reprinted in *Memoirs, 1925–1950,* op. cit., pp. 296–297.

26. Ibid., pp. 219–220, 257–260.

27. Memo from Kennan to Ambassador Harriman, December 3, 1945, excerpted in ibid., p. 268.

28. Ibid., p. 293.

29. Telegram, the Chargé in the Soviet Union to the Secretary of State, Moscow, February 22, 1946, in *Foreign Relations of the United States 1946,* Vol. VI (Washington, D.C.: U.S. Government Printing Office, 1969), p. 706.

30. Ibid., p. 699.

31. Ibid., pp. 706–707.

32. Kennan, *Memoirs: 1925–1950,* op. cit., p. 294.

33. Telegram, the Chargé in the Soviet Union to the Secretary of State, Moscow, February 22, 1946, op. cit., p. 707.

34. Kennan, *Memoirs: 1925–1950,* op. cit., p. 295; Gaddis, *Strategies of Containment,* op. cit., p. 21; Yergin, *Shattered Peace,* op. cit., p. 171.

35. "X" (Kennan), "The Sources of Soviet Conduct," *Foreign Affairs* 25, no. 4 (July 1947), p. 575.

36. Yergin, *Shattered Peace,* op. cit., pp. 306–307; Acheson, *Present at the Creation,* op. cit., p. 212.

37. Richard J. Barnet, *The Alliance—America, Europe, Japan: Makers of the Postwar World* (New York: Simon & Schuster, 1983), p. 21.

38. Adam B. Ulam, *Dangerous Relations: The Soviet Union in World Politics, 1970–1982* (New York: Oxford University Press, 1984), pp. 9–10. For detailed comparisons of the immediate postwar productive capacities of the United States and the Soviet Union, see Paul Kennedy, *The Rise and Fall of the Great Powers: Economic Change and Military Conflict from 1500 to 2000* (New York: Random House, 1987), pp. 357–365.

39. Yergin, *Shattered Peace,* op. cit., p. 359.

40. Kennan, *Memoirs: 1950–1963,* op. cit., pp. 90–91.

41. Kennan, *Memoirs: 1925–1950,* op. cit., pp. 397–414, 446–463 (quote from p. 410).

42. Calleo, *Beyond American Hegemony,* op. cit., p. 28. For Kennan's rejection of the Hitler analogy, see *Memoirs: 1950–1963,* op. cit., pp. 91–92, and note 43, below.

43. "Soviet power, unlike that of Hitlerite Germany, is neither schematic nor adventurous. It does not work by fixed plans. It does not take unnecessary risks. Impervious to logic of reason, it is highly sensitive to the logic of force. For this reason it can easily withdraw—and usually does—when strong resistance is encountered at any point. Thus, if the adversary has sufficient force and makes clear his readiness to use it, he rarely has to. If situations are properly handled there need be no prestige-engaging showdowns." Telegram, the Chargé in the Soviet Union [Kennan] to the Secretary of State, Moscow, February 22, 1946, op. cit., p. 707.

44. George F. Kennan, lecture at Joint Orientation Conference, Pentagon, November 8, 1948, quoted in Gaddis, *Strategies of Containment,* op. cit., p. 45.

45. He articulated these possibilities in relation to Germany, notably in his Policy Planning Staff's "Program A" of 1948 and nine years later in his controversial BBC Reith lectures. Program A envisioned the withdrawal of U.S., British,

Russian and French occupation forces to "specified garrison areas," the suspension of military government, and the administration of most of Germany
by a new provisional government. See Paper Prepared by the Policy Planning
Staff, November 12, 1948, A Program for Germany (Program A), in *Foreign
Relations of the United States 1948*, Vol. II (Washington, D.C.: U.S. Government Printing Office, 1972), pp. 1324–1338. In the Reith Lectures Kennan
"urged . . . that we drop our insistence that an eventual all-German government
should be free to join NATO, and declare ourselves the partisans of a
neutralized and largely disarmed unified Germany." *Memoirs, 1950–1963*, op.
cit., p. 243.

46. It will be recalled that Kennan had scorned the notion that Stalinist hostility
derived from a real fear that Russian security was threatened. But that did not
mean that the Soviet Union had *no* legitimate security interests. On the
contrary, watching the Cold War develop from his post as ambassador to
Moscow, Kennan had viewed with alarm many of NATO's military preparations, deeming them provocative to a degree the United States would never
have tolerated. "Surely as one moves one's bases and military facilities toward
the Soviet frontiers there comes a point where they tend to create the very
thing they were designed to avoid. It is not for us to assume that there are no
limits to Soviet patience in the face of encirclement by American bases. Quite
aside from political considerations, no great country, peaceful or aggressive,
rational or irrational, could sit by and witness with indifference the progressive
studding of its own frontiers with the military installations of a great-power
competitor." Dispatch from Ambassador Kennan (Moscow) to Department
of State (Washington), September 8, 1952, reprinted in *Memoirs, 1950–1963*,
op. cit., p. 354.

47. Note from the Soviet Ministry for Foreign Affairs to the Embassy of the United
States, Moscow, March 10, 1952, in *Foreign Relations of the United States
1952–1954*, Vol. VII, Part I (Washington, D.C.: U.S. Government Printing
Office, 1986), pp. 169–172.

48. Winston Churchill's speech in the House of Commons on May 11, 1953, is
cited in Coral Bell, *Negotiation from Strength: A Study in the Politics of Power*
(New York: Alfred A. Knopf, 1963), pp. 106–107.

49. "Text of Acheson's Reply to Kennan," *New York Times*, January 12, 1958,
p. 25.

50. Dean Acheson, "The Illusion of Disengagement," *Foreign Affairs* 36, no. 3
(April 1958), p. 371.

51. Ibid., p. 375.

52. Ibid., p. 376.

53. Ibid., p. 377.

54. Kennan himself later admitted that the prophecy was mistaken. See *Memoirs: 1925–1950,* op. cit., p. 447. Another mistake was his view that the position of Berlin was untenable, although, in Kennan's defense, we must speculate on the stabilizing role of the Berlin Wall, a solution too monstrous for anyone to predict.

55. Kennan, *Memoirs: 1925–1950,* op. cit., p. 367.

56. Michael Howard, "Reassurance and Deterrence: Western Defense in the 1980s," *Foreign Affairs* 61, no. 2 (Winter 1982/83).

57. There was, for example, a U.S. Air Force campaign to promote strategic bombing as the first priority of a future war, despite the fact that the "Strategic Bombing Survey" showed that allied "terror bombing" in World War II did not have the intended effect on enemy morale. (The fact that "strategic bombing" would be carried out by the air force was an incidentally useful point to raise in interservice rivalry with the army and navy.) Yergin, *Shattered Peace,* op. cit., pp. 336–343.

58. John Foster Dulles, "Policy for Security and Peace," *Foreign Affairs* 32, no. 3 (April 1954), cited in Lawrence Freedman, *The Evolution of Nuclear Strategy* (London, Macmillan, 1982), p. 86.

59. Gaddis, *Strategies of Containment,* op. cit., pp. 134, 185–186. On symmetrical versus asymmetrical containment see ibid., p. 151.

60. See the chapter titled "NATO's Nuclear Addiction," in David N. Schwartz, *NATO's Nuclear Dilemmas* (Washington, D.C.: The Brookings Institution, 1983). For a criticism from the right, see Irving Kristol, "NATO at a Dead End," *Wall Street Journal,* July 15, 1981.

61. In his memoirs, for example, Dean Acheson recalled that "for some time in 1951 it had been dawning on us that we were trying to move our allies and ourselves faster toward the rearmament for defense than economic realities would permit. The gap between goals and performance, both on the part of the separate nations and of the group, was daily more apparent and more painful. In Britain Mr. Churchill, of all people, was criticizing Mr. Attlee for overstressing the military program; and in April, Aneurin Bevin resigned as Minister of Health in the Labour Government, protesting against cuts in his programs to find funds for rearmament. In France the press and elections of June 17 reflected similar sentiments." A few days after these elections, Acheson and U.S. defense secretary George Marshall chaired a meeting in Washington that proposed stretching out to "mid-1954 what we had hoped to accomplish by mid-1952." Acheson, *Present at the Creation,* op. cit., p. 559.

Nonetheless, NATO governments meeting one year later in Lisbon were still determined to match Soviet conventional forces and agreed to raise NATO strength from 25 to 96 divisions in two years. They never got close to these Lisbon goals, however, and the European governments, largely for fiscal reasons, enthusiastically embraced the Eisenhower administration's shift to an emphasis on cheaper nuclear defense, as Lawrence Freedman recounts: "As the war-scare subsided and the build-up turned out to be inflationary in its economic consequences, the New Look of the Eisenhower Administration was embraced because it offered a robust deterrence at a manageable cost." Freedman, *The Evolution of Nuclear Strategy,* op. cit., p. 288.

62. See chapter 5.

63. Kennedy was the first American president to adopt unreservedly the Keynesian assumptions that had provided the economic justification for NSC-68 and for other blueprints of American activism but that always had been viewed warily by presidential practitioners. Gaddis, *Strategies of Containment,* op. cit., pp. 204–206.

64. John F. Kennedy, *The Strategy of Peace* (New York: Harper & Row, 1960), pp. 37–38.

65. Richard Reeves, *President Kennedy: Profile of Power* (New York: Simon & Schuster, 1993), pp. 77, 78, 136, 137.

66. More than 30 years later, Zbigniew Brzezinski argued that the Berlin and (then-current) INF crises, taken together, demonstrated the continuity of Soviet aims in Western Europe. "The Future of Yalta," *Foreign Affairs* 63, no. 1 (Winter 1984/85), pp. 279–301.

67. The Berlin Wall was "where cowardice began," wrote a leading French neoconservative three decades later. NATO's August 1961 acquiescence in the Communist seizure of East Berlin, according to his interpretation, set the later pattern of détente: congratulating oneself for avoiding war after surrendering what the enemy demanded. Jean-François Révél, *How Democracies Perish,* translated by William Byron (London: Weidenfeld and Nicolson, 1985), pp. 230–240.

68. Alfred Grosser, *The Western Alliance: European-American Relations Since 1945* (New York: Vintage Books, 1982), pp. 190–199; Bell, *Negotiation from Strength,* op. cit., passim.

69. Grosser, *The Western Alliance,* op. cit., pp. 190–199.

70. Willy Brandt, *People and Politics: The Years 1960–1975* (London: Collins, 1978), p. 25.

71. Paul H. Nitze, "The World Situation: Strengthening of the United States Armed Forces," speech delivered at the annual meeting of the Association of the United States Army, Washington, D.C., September 7, 1961, p. 27., quoted in Schwartz, *NATO's Nuclear Dilemmas,* op. cit., p. 154.

72. "Remarks by Secretary McNamara, NATO Ministerial Meeting, 5 May 1962, Restricted Session," declassified August 17, 1979. These quotes are taken from

David N. Schwartz, who reprinted a large portion of the McNamara speech in *NATO's Nuclear Dilemmas,* op. cit., pp. 161–165.

73. Robert S. McNamara, "Defense Arrangements of the North Atlantic Community," speech at University of Michigan commencement, June 16, 1962, *Department of State Bulletin* 47, no. 1202 (July 9, 1962), p. 67.

74. Ibid., pp. 67–68.

75. Michael Harrison, *The Reluctant Ally* (Baltimore: Johns Hopkins University Press, 1981), pp. 134–153. Subsequently, French doctrine frankly imagined sabotaging flexible response. French strategists adopted the idea that independent nuclear forces represent "multiple centers of deterrence" that might, in a crisis, trigger a general nuclear war despite American efforts to prevent escalation. Ibid., p. 126.

76. Schwartz, *NATO's Nuclear Dilemmas,* op. cit., pp. 176–179, 187.

77. John Mearsheimer, "Back to the Future," *International Security* 15, no. 1 (Summer 1990), pp. 26–27.

78. Freedman, *The Evolution of Nuclear Strategy,* op. cit., p. 231.

79. "Flexible response" was a notable product of this rationalism. It was more than a strategy for defending Europe; indeed, it went well beyond military science. It was a philosophy of international relations—an overarching doctrine for applying and fine-tuning the whole range of American power symmetrically to the level of any threat. As John Gaddis shows, its assumptions formed the basis for America's war in Vietnam. And Vietnam was the spectacular failure that discredited many of those assumptions. See Gaddis, *Strategies of Containment,* op. cit., chapters 7, 8.

80. See the McNamara interview by Michael Charlton in *From Deterrence to Defense: The Inside Story of Strategic Policy* (Cambridge, Mass.: Harvard University Press, 1987), pp. 22–23. However Dean Rusk, another participant, argues that whatever modest view the Americans had of their nuclear options, the Soviets likely held another view. "We had some reason to believe, afterwards, that the Soviets thought we had counted missiles at the time of the Cuban missile crisis. In fact we had not. Apparently they thought so, because shortly after that crisis a high Russian official [Deputy Foreign Minister Kuznetsov] said to Mr. John J. McCloy in New York, 'Well, Mr. McCloy, you got away with it this time. You'll never get away with it again.' Ibid., p. 24. See also Robert W. Tucker's comment in *The Nuclear Debate: Deterrence and the Lapse of Faith* (New York: Holmes & Meier, 1985), pp. 74–75.

81. McNamara interview by Charlton, *From Deterrence to Defense,* op. cit., pp. 7–11.

82. Freedman, *The Evolution of Nuclear Strategy,* op. cit., p. 247. Freedman notes that the "levels chosen by McNamara were more influenced by an awareness of diminishing marginal returns than any notion of what was acceptable to

the Russians. After a certain point extra weapons produce few additional effects, because of the concentration of Soviet society into a finite number of large targets." Ibid.

83. See McNamara's account of the Glassboro, New Jersey, summit between President Johnson and Soviet premier Alexei Kosygin in Charlton, *From Deterrence to Defense*, op. cit., p. 27.

84. Ibid., p. 5.

Chapter 2

1. Barbara Tuchman, *The March of Folly: From Troy to Vietnam* (New York: Ballantine Books, 1984), p. 221.

2. Theodore Draper, *Present History: On Nuclear War, Détente, and Other Controversies* (New York: Vintage Books, 1984), p. 103.

3. Dwight D. Eisenhower, News Conference of February 10, 1954, in *Public Papers of the Presidents 1954* (Washington, D.C.: U.S. Government Printing Office, 1960), p. 253.

4. Eisenhower news conference of April 7, 1954 in ibid., p. 73. On the U.S. refusal to back the Geneva conference declaration, see Eisenhower news conference of July 21, 1954, in ibid., pp. 641–642.

5. Paul Johnson, *Modern Times: The World from the Twenties to the Eighties* (New York: Harper & Row, 1983), p. 633.

6. Arthur M. Schlesinger Jr., *A Thousand Days: John F. Kennedy in the White House* (Boston: Houghton Mifflin, 1965), p. 547.

7. "Mr. Brinkley: 'Mr. President, have you had any reason to doubt this so-called "domino theory," that if South Viet-Nam falls the rest of southeast Asia will go behind it?'

The President: 'No, I believe it. I believe it. I think the struggle is close enough. China is so large, looms so high just beyond the frontiers, that if South Viet-Nam went, it would not only give them an improved geographic position for a guerrilla assault on Malaya, but would also give the impression that the wave of the future in southeast Asia was China and the Communists. So I believe it.'" Transcript of broadcast of NBC's "Huntley-Brinkley Report," September 9, 1963, in *Public Papers of the Presidents 1963* (Washington, D.C.: U.S. Government Printing Office, 1964), p. 659. The Rostow draft statement of "Basic National Security Policy" is cited in John Lewis Gaddis, *Strategies of Containment: A Critical Appraisal of Postwar American Security Policy* (New York: Oxford University Press, 1982), p. 203.

8. Doris Kearns, *Lyndon Johnson and the American Dream* (New York: Harper & Row, 1976), p. 251.

9. Lyndon Baines Johnson, "Peace Without Conquest," Address at Johns Hopkins University, April 7, 1965, in *Public Papers of the Presidents 1965,* Book I (Washington, D.C.: U.S. Government Printing Office, 1966), p. 395. On Johnson's fear of a right-wing reaction, see Kearns, *Lyndon Johnson and the American Dream,* op. cit., pp. 251–254.

10. Richard M. Nixon, *U.S. Foreign Policy for the 1970s: A New Strategy for Peace,* Report to Congress, February 18, 1970 (Washington, D.C.: U.S. Government Printing Office, 1970), p. 7.

11. "Henry understands my views better than anyone at State ever has," Kennan told John L. Gaddis in 1974. Gaddis, *Strategies of Containment,* op. cit., p. 283.

12. Ibid., p. 32.

13. Henry Kissinger, *Years of Upheaval* (Little, Brown & Co., 1982), p. 145.

14. Ibid, p. 136.

15. Henry Kissinger, *White House Years* (Little, Brown & Co., 1979), p. 110.

16. Henry Kissinger, "Central Issues of American Foreign Policy," in Kermit Gordon, ed. *Agenda for the Nation* (Washington, D.C.: The Brookings Institution, 1968), p. 595.

17. Henry Kissinger, *The Troubled Partnership: A Re-appraisal of the Atlantic Alliance* (New York: McGraw-Hill, 1965), p. 40.

18. Kissinger, *White House Years,* op. cit., pp. 104–111.

19. Paul Johnson, *Modern Times,* op. cit., p. 593.

20. De Gaulle, cited in David P. Calleo, *Europe's Future: The Grand Alternatives* (New York: Horizon Press, 1965), p. 117.

21. De Gaulle press conference, January 14, 1963, in *Major Addresses, Statements and Press Conferences of General Charles de Gaulle, May 19, 1958–January 31, 1964* (New York: French Embassy Press and Information Division, 1964), p. 216.

22. Charles de Gaulle, *The Complete War Memoirs of Charles de Gaulle,* Vol. I: *The Call to Honor 1940–1942* (New York: Simon & Schuster, 1964), chapters 1, 2.

23. On this continuity, see Philip H. Gordon, *A Certain Idea of France: French Security Policy and the Gaullist Legacy* (Princeton, N.J.: Princeton University Press, 1993).

24. Brian Crozier, *De Gaulle* (New York: Scribners, 1973), pp. 419–427.

25. Richard J. Barnet, *The Alliance—America, Europe, Japan: Makers of the Postwar World* (New York: Simon & Schuster, 1983), p. 121.

26. De Gaulle press conference of January 14, 1963, *Major Addresses* (1964), op. cit., p. 217.

27. Charles de Gaulle, *Memoirs of Hope* (London: Weidenfeld & Nicolson, 1971), pp. 200–201.

28. Ibid., p. 201.

29. Ibid., pp. 255–256.

30. The effort was comical even in de Gaulle's own account; *The Complete War Memoirs,* op. cit., pp. 735–757.

31. De Gaulle's successor, Georges Pompidou, continued to hold these hopes, as expressed in conversation with Nixon. See Kissinger, *White House Years,* op. cit., p. 423.

32. See note 23, this chapter.

33. Willy Brandt, *People and Politics: The Years 1960–1975* (London: Collins, 1978), p. 168.

34. Coral Bell, *Negotiation from Strength: A Study in the Politics of Power* (New York: Alfred A. Knopf, 1963).

35. Brandt, *People and Politics,* op. cit., p. 29.

36. Ibid., p. 399.

37. Egon Bahr, interview with author, September 29, 1994 in Bonn.

38. Barnet, *The Alliance,* op. cit., p. 286.

39. Ibid., p. 294.

40. Kissinger, *Years of Upheaval,* op. cit., pp. 145–146.

41. Bahr, interview with author, op. cit.

42. Kissinger, *Years of Upheaval,* op. cit., p. 148.

43. Timothy Garton Ash, *In Europe's Name: Germany and the Divided Continent* (London: Jonathan Cape, 1993).

44. Kissinger, *White House Years,* op. cit., p. 409.

45. Pompidou said so explicitly in conversations with Nixon; ibid., p. 422.

46. De Gaulle, following the views of his close economic adviser, Jacques Rueff, elaborated on this critique in a press conference of February 4, 1965; *Major Addresses, Statements and Press Conferences of General Charles de Gaulle* (New York: French Embassy and Information Division, 1967), pp. 179–181. For a general analysis, see David P. Calleo, *The Imperious Economy* (Cambridge, Mass.: Harvard University Press, 1982), pp. 47–51.

47. Kissinger, *White House Years,* op. cit., pp. 955–956, 960.

48. Kissinger, *Years of Upheaval,* op. cit., p. 137.

49. Ibid., p. 165.

50. A phrase Kissinger repeats bitterly in various forms throughout his account; see ibid., p. 711.

51. Conor Cruise O'Brien, *The Siege* (London: Paladin Grafton Books, 1988), pp. 400–404.

52. William B. Quandt, *Decade of Decisions: American Policy Toward the Arab-Israeli Conflict, 1967–1976* (Berkeley, CA: University of California Press, 1977), pp. 72–104.

53. O'Brien, *The Siege,* op. cit., p. 490.

54. William Rogers, "A Lasting Peace in the Middle East" (a speech of December 9, 1969, unveiling the so-called Rogers Peace Plan), in *Department of State Bulletin 62, no. 1958* (January 5, 1970), pp. 7–11; and Nadav Safran, *Israel: The Embattled Ally* (Cambridge, Mass.: Harvard University Press, 1981), p. 418.

55. Ariel Sharon's conduct of the later Lebanon War was, in many respects, deplorable, but Israel's reasons for going to war in the first place were understandable, as argued eloquently by O'Brien, *The Siege,* op. cit., pp. 632–637.

56. "The issue today is not the Gulf of Aqaba or the Strait of Tiran or U.N.E.F. The issue is the rights of the people of Palestine, the aggression against Palestine that took place in 1948, with the help of Britain and the United States. . . . They want to confine it to the Straits of Tiran, U.N.E.F. and the rights of passage. We want the rights of the people of Palestine—complete." Nassar speech to Egyptian National Assembly, May 29, 1967, cited in O'Brien, *The Siege,* op. cit., p. 413.

57. Ibid.

58. Ibid., p. 416.

59. In any assessment of what the Israelis were prepared to offer in the way of a peace settlement after the Six-Day War, one must concede that the Jewish state often appeared too divided internally to formulate a coherent negotiating strategy and act on it. On this point, see Safran, *Israel: The Embattled Ally,* op. cit., pp. 414–447.

60. O'Brien, *The Siege,* op. cit., p. 496.

61. Ibid., pp. 489–521.

62. Kissinger, *Years of Upheaval,* op. cit., pp. 492–493.

63. Ibid., pp. 539, 561, 573.

64. Ibid., pp. 589–591.

65. Ibid., p. 587.

66. Ibid., p. 460.

67. Alfred Grosser, *The Western Alliance: European-American Relations Since 1945* (New York: Vintage Books, 1982), p. 274.

68. Kissinger, *Years of Upheaval,* op. cit., pp. 707–722.

69. Grosser, *The Western Alliance,* op. cit., pp. 277–278.

70. Kissinger, *Years of Upheaval,* op. cit., pp. 897–898.

71. Ibid., p. 708. Kissinger says that based on this principle, he had "bitterly opposed" Eisenhower administration policy in the Suez Crisis of 1956, even though he was "dubious" about the Anglo-French operation.

72. The European view, it should be noted, was shared by important officials in the Nixon administration. At a White House meeting called to consider

Israel's urgent appeal for emergency resupply, Defense Secretary James Schlesinger expressed misgivings about an American airlift because he saw a difference between defending Israel's recognized borders and helping it to hold on to 1967 conquests. Other administration officials, according to Kissinger, agreed. Ibid., p. 493.
73. Ibid., p. 934.

Chapter 3

1. John B. Judis, "The Great Awakening," *The New Republic* 208, no. 5 (February 1, 1993), p. 46.
2. Norman Podhoretz, *The Present Danger* (New York: Simon & Schuster, 1980), p. 69. The "offensive" against the CIA to which Podhoretz refers consisted of some fairly explosive revelations about CIA abuses that came out of Senator Frank Church's "Select Committee to Study Governmental Operations With Respect to Intelligence Activities" in the fall of 1975. These revelations are contained in a 16-volume "Hearings" transcript and a 6-volume "Final Report" (Washington, D.C: U.S. Government Printing Office, 1976).
3. Henry Kissinger, *Years of Upheaval* (Boston: Little, Brown & Co., 1982), pp. 303–304.
4. Kissinger interview by Michael Charlton, cited in his collection of interviews, *From Deterrence to Defense: The Inside Story of Strategic Policy* (Cambridge, Mass.: Harvard University Press, 1987), p. 40.
5. Ibid., p. 49.
6. Sidney Blumenthal, *The Rise of the Counter-Establishment* (New York: Harper & Row, 1988), pp. 122–165.
7. Blumenthal, *The Rise of the Counter-Establishment,* op. cit., p. 131.
8. Podhoretz, *The Present Danger,* op. cit., esp. pp. 79–86.
9. Coral Bell, *The Reagan Paradox: American Foreign Policy in the 1980s* (New Brunswick, N.J.: Rutgers University Press, 1989), pp. 11–13.
10. Kissinger, *Years of Upheaval,* op. cit., p. 983.
11. Adam B. Ulam, *Dangerous Relations: The Soviet Union in World Politics, 1970–1982* (New York: Oxford University Press, 1983), p. 91.
12. Ibid., p. 88.
13. Peter G. Peterson, *U.S.-Soviet Commercial Relations in a New Era* (Washington, D.C.: U.S. Government Printing Office, 1972), p. 3.
14. Kissinger, *Years of Upheaval,* op. cit., p. 986. It should be noted, however, that there were less nuanced views emanating from Kissinger's direct subordinates in the State Department. In December 1975, for example, Deputy Secretary

of State Robert S. Ingersoll went so far as to imagine trade affecting the basic political economy of the East: "Over time, increased trade can erode the autarkic tendencies of the Communist countries and tie them more closely into the world economic system. . . . Increased acceptance by these countries of the responsibilities inherent in more normal trade relations would reduce their capacity for, and their interest in, disrupting the trade and economic system created by the Western countries for the past 30 years." Statement before the Senate Committee on Commerce, December 12, 1975, reprinted in *Department of State Bulletin* 74, no. 1908 (January 19, 1976), p. 91.

15. Henry Kissinger, *White House Years* (Little, Brown & Co., 1979), p. 155.

16. Kissinger, *Years of Upheaval*, op. cit., p. 986.

17. The Jackson-Vanik amendment, which passed Congress at the end of 1974, did not, in the short run at least, help the cause of Jewish emigration from the Soviet Union. Emigration fell to 13,200 in 1975 from its 1973 peak of 20,000. Ibid., pp. 986–998. During 1979, however, the year of the U.S. SALT debate, over 50,000 Jews were allowed to leave. Ulam, *Dangerous Relations,* op. cit., p. 250.

18. Lawrence Freedman, *The Evolution of Nuclear Strategy* (London: Macmillan, 1982), pp. 355–358.

19. Kissinger, *Years of Upheaval,* op. cit., pp. 260, 1011, 1018–1019.

20. Ibid., p. 1155.

21. Strobe Talbott, *The Master of the Game: Paul Nitze and the Nuclear Peace* (New York: Alfred A. Knopf, 1988), pp. 136–141.

22. Paul Nitze interview with author, May 23, 1989; and Talbott, *The Master of the Game,* op. cit., pp. 141–161.

23. Press conference of July 3, 1974, published in *Survival* 16, no. 5 (September/October 1974), p. 245.

24. Richard Pipes, "Why the Soviet Union Thinks It Could Fight and Win a Nuclear War," *Commentary* 64, no. 1 (July 1977), p. 24.

25. Ibid., pp. 24–25. Pipes painted a questionable picture in several respects. Among these: (1) He equated the "strategic bombing" of World War II with mutual assured destruction (MAD), calling both a product of U.S. antiwar ethos. But strategic bombing was initiated by the British, based on British interwar writings; (2) McNamara is presented as a fanatical cost-cutter, which hardly squares with stress on conventional forces, flexible response, and whole approach in Vietnam; and (3) He also distorts the position of McNamara's "economist" aides, who were as much advocates for counterforce as for MAD. On all three points, see Freedman, *The Evolution of Nuclear Strategy,* op. cit., chapters 1, 15; on World War II terror bombing by the British and Americans, see also Paul Johnson, *Modern Times: The World From the Twenties to the Eighties* (New York: Harper & Row, 1983), pp. 369–371; 402–405.

26. Richard Pipes, "How to Cope With the Soviet Threat: A Long-term Strategy for the West," *Commentary* 78, no. 2 (August 1984), pp. 17,19.

27. Fred Charles Iklé, "Can Nuclear Deterrence Last Out the Century?" *Foreign Affairs* 51, no. 2 (January 1973); and "Nuclear Strategy: Can There Be a Happy Ending?" *Foreign Affairs* 63, no. 4 (Spring 1985).

28. Richard Pipes, "Team B: The Reality Behind the Myth," *Commentary* 82, no. 4 (October 1986), p. 29.

29. Ibid., p. 33.

30. Between November 1976 and April 1984 the committee published 20 statements or studies, all of which are collected in *Alerting America: The Papers of the Committee on the Present Danger,* ed. Charles Tyroler II (Washington, D.C.: Pergamon-Brassey's, 1984). The committee was named after a similar group of the early 1950s on which Nitze also served.

31. Eugene Rostow "Peace with Freedom," discussion by the Committee on the Present Danger before the Foreign Policy Association, New York, March 14, 1978, in Committee on the Present Danger, *Alerting America,* op. cit., p. 33.

32. Paul Nitze, "Peace with Freedom," discussion by the Committee on the Present Danger before the Foreign Policy Association, New York, March 14, 1978, in Committee on the Present Danger, *Alerting America,* op. cit., p. 28.

33. Committee on the Present Danger, "Is America Becoming Number 2? Current Trends in the US-Soviet Military Balance" (October 5, 1978), reprinted in Committee on the Present Danger, *Alerting America,* op. cit., pp. 39–93.

34. Ibid., p. 48.

35. Paul Nitze, "Is SALT II a Fair Deal for the United States?" (May 1979), in Committee on the Present Danger, *Alerting America,* op. cit., p. 161.

36. " . . . there are some 12,000 missile air launchers and 2,700 interceptor aircraft deployed in the Soviet Union. These air defenses are constantly being modernized." The committee was particularly critical of President Carter's cancellation of the B-1 bomber and was unimpressed by the prospect for B-52–launched cruise missiles to penetrate the air defenses. Committee on the Present Danger, "Is America Becoming Number 2?" op. cit., pp. 56–57.

37. A policy of launch on warning was generally considered a bad idea since, as Henry Kissinger noted, it could "be accomplished only by delegating the authority to the proverbially 'insane colonel' about whom so many movies have been made." "The Future of NATO," in *NATO—The Next Thirty Years: The Changing Political, Economic, and Military Setting,* ed. by Kenneth A. Myers (Boulder, Colo.: Westview Press, 1980), p. 6. Yet even if it was a bad idea that U.S. policy officially proscribed, it was an American option that the Soviets would have had to take into account.

38. Freedman, *The Evolution of Nuclear Strategy,* op. cit., p. 390.

39. ". . . conflict situations by definition are dynamic and extremely volatile. If deterrence were to fail, the stability of the relationship—and of the world—would be sensitive to the opportunities open to the antagonists quickly to alter the balance. With its growing MIRV capabilities and increasing hard-target kill potential, the Soviet Union could greatly change the initial strategic balance . . . in its own favor." Committee on the Present Danger, "Is America Becoming Number 2?" op. cit., p. 63. Concern that Soviet force structure worsened crisis instability was not confined to counterforce advocates. See, for example, Albert Gore, "A Noncounterforce Alternative to President Reagan's START Proposal," excerpts in *Survival* 25, no. 4 (July/August 1983), p. 187.

40. Committee on the Present Danger, "Is America Becoming Number 2?" op. cit., p. 89.

41. Ibid., p. 63. Later in the same pamphlet, the committee argued that "U.S. accommodation to the Soviet drive for strategic superiority would confer on the Soviet Union the ability to intimidate and coerce the West into accepting unfavorable bargains." Ibid., p. 89.

42. The move away from MAD, it should be noted, had already started when Schlesinger was appointed; see Freedman, *The Evolution of Nuclear Strategy,* op. cit., p. 378.

43. Albert Wohlstetter, "The Delicate Balance of Terror," *Foreign Affairs* 37, no. 2 (January 1959). Wohlstetter's later series of *Foreign Policy* articles became a central part of the neoconservative critique. See "Is There a Strategic Arms Race?" *Foreign Policy* 15 (Summer 1974); "Rivals but no 'Race,'" *Foreign Policy* 16 (Autumn 1974), and "Optimal Ways to Confuse Ourselves," *Foreign Policy* 20 (Autumn 1975).

44. Herman Kahn, *On Thermonuclear War* (Princeton, N.J.: Princeton University Press, 1961), pp. 559–560.

45. Herman Kahn, *On Escalation: Metaphors and Scenarios* (New York: Praeger, 1965), p. 290.

46. Robert S. McNamara, "The Military Role of Nuclear Weapons: Perceptions and Misperceptions," *Foreign Affairs* 62, no. 1 (Fall 1983), p. 79.

47. Nitze, "Is SALT II a Fair Deal for the United States?" op. cit., p. 160.

48. Ibid.

49. For example, Ronald Steel, "Afghanistan Doesn't Matter," *The New Republic* 182, no. 7 (February 16, 1980), pp. 14–15; Arthur Schlesinger, Jr., "Is This Journey Necessary?" *The Wall Street Journal,* January 18, 1980.

50. Rostow, "Peace With Freedom," op. cit., p. 33.

51. Pipes, in ibid., p. 26.

52. Paul Nitze, "Strategy in the Decade of the 1980s," *Foreign Affairs* 59, no. 1 (Fall 1980), pp. 82–91. See also *Alerting America,* op. cit., p. 160.

53. Nitze, "Strategy in the Decade of the 1980s," op. cit., pp. 84–89.

54. Zbigniew Brzezinski, *Power and Principle: Memoirs of the National Security Adviser, 1977–1981* (New York: Farrar Straus Giroux, 1983), p. 411.

55. Brzezinski casts a more positive light on the Chinese results: "From a military point of view, the Chinese operation was not as efficient or as effective as apparently the Chinese had anticipated. The Vietnamese proved more resilient, while Chinese command and control, as well as logistics, were more cumbersome than expected in conditions of modern warfare—but the political point was effectively made. The Vietnamese were forced to redeploy some of their forces from Cambodia, the conflict imposed very major costs on them, produced a great deal of devastation, and, above all, showed the limits of their reliance on the Soviets. Most importantly, thanks to Carter's steadfastness, the new American-Chinese relationship had successfully weathered its baptism by fire." Ibid., p. 414.

56. "Transcript of President's Interview on Soviet Reply," *New York Times,* January 1, 1980, p. A4.

57. "Let our position be absolutely clear: An attempt by any outside force to gain control of the Persian Gulf will be regarded as an assault on the vital interests of the United States of America, and such an assault will be repelled by any means necessary, including military force." Jimmy Carter, State of the Union Address, January 23, 1980, in *Public Papers of the Presidents 1980–81* (Washington, D.C: U.S. Government Printing Office, 1981), p. 197.

58. Henry Kissinger, *Nuclear Weapons and Foreign Policy* (New York: Harper, 1957).

59. Freedman, *The Evolution of Nuclear Strategy,* op. cit., p. 341.

60. Kissinger, "The Future of NATO," op. cit., p. 9.

61. Freedman, *The Evolution of Nuclear Strategy,* op. cit., p. 340.

62. See David N. Schwartz's survey of the European response in *NATO's Nuclear Dilemmas* (Washington, D.C.: The Brookings Institution, 1983), p. 236.

63. Kissinger, "The Future of NATO," op. cit., pp. 6–8.

64. Freedman, *The Evolution of Nuclear Strategy,* op. cit., p. 341.

65. Ibid., p. 383.

66. Ibid., p. 393.

67. For the articulation of the "countervailing" strategy, see Brown's speech of August 20, 1980, unveiling Presidential Directive (PD) 59, reprinted in *Survival* 22, no. 6 (November/December 1980), pp. 267–269.

68. Notwithstanding its ostensible alarm over the window of vulnerability, the Reagan administration proved equally unsettled by the opposition of Utah and Nevada voters to the idea of digging up large expanses of their states to implement the MX's "deceptive basing mode." Conveniently, Reagan's appointed commis-

sion to study the problem, headed by General Brent Scowcroft, reported back that the window of vulnerability was largely illusory anyway. Reagan accepted the commission's recommendation to deploy the MX in existing Minuteman silos (with deployment of a smaller, single-warhead missile in a less vulnerable mode put off until the early 1990s). See "MX Missile Basing System and Related Issues," Hearings before the Committee on Armed Services, United States Senate, April 18, 20, 21, 26; May 3, 1983, especially the testimony of Scowcroft, former defense secretary Harold Brown, and defense secretary Caspar Weinberger, pp. 3–9; 98–107. See also "Conclusion," chapter 4, below.

69. Robert W. Tucker, *The Nuclear Debate: Deterrence and the Lapse of Faith* (New York: Holmes & Meier, 1985), p. 99.

70. Carter interview by Charlton, *From Deterrence to Defense*, op. cit., pp. 88–89. Emphasis in original.

71. Richard Halloran, "Pentagon Draws Up First Strategy For Fighting a Long Nuclear War," *New York Times*, May 30, 1982, p. A1.

72. See, for example, the interesting exchange of letters between Weinberger and historian Theodore Draper in Draper's *Present History: On Nuclear War, Détente, and Other Controversies* (New York: Vintage Books, 1984), pp. 34–63.

73. See the March 23, 1983, "Address to the Nation by President Ronald Reagan: Peace and National Security," *Department of State Bulletin* 83, no. 2073 (Washington, D.C.: U.S. Government Printing Office, 1983), pp. 8–14. Skepticism was rampant. Paul Nitze, at the time a Reagan arms-control adviser, cautioned that Ballistic Missile Defense systems should not be deployed unless "cost effective at the margin . . . that is, they must be cheap enough to add additional defensive capability so that the other side has no incentive to add additional offensive capacity to overcome the defense." *New York Times*, February 21, 1985. This, as Henry Kissinger noted, amounted to "criteria that are in fact unfulfillable." Interview by Michael Charlton, in *From Deterrence to Defense*, op. cit., p. 55.

For a wide range of SDI assessments, see "Strategic Defense and Anti-Satellite Weapons," hearings before the Committee on Foreign Relations, U.S. Senate, 98th Cong., 2nd sess., April 25, 1984, pp. 94–175; Donald L. Hafner, "Assessing the President's Vision: The Fletcher, Miller, and Hoffman Panels," in *Weapons in Space*, vol. 1, "Concepts and Technologies," *Daedalus* 114, no. 3 (Summer 1985), pp. 219–237; George Rathjens and Jack Ruina, "BMD and Strategic Instability," in *Weapons in Space*, vol. 2, p. 255; and James R. Schlesinger, "Rhetoric and Reality in Star Wars," *International Security* 10, no. 1 (Summer 1985), p. 6.

74. "Brezhnev And Reagan on Atom War," *New York Times*, October 21, 1981, p. A5.

75. Draper, *Present History,* op. cit., p. 74.

76. Clay Clemens, "The CDU/CSU and Arms Control," in Barry M. Blechman and Cathleen Fisher, eds., *The Silent Partner: West Germany and Arms Control* (Cambridge, Mass.: Ballinger, 1988), pp. 61–128.

77. Sidney Blumenthal, *The Rise of the Counter-Establishment,* op. cit.

78. Coral Bell, *The Reagan Paradox,* op. cit., p. 22.

79. See Seymour M. Hersh, *The Target Is Destroyed: What Really Happened To Flight 007 And What America Knew About It* (New York: Random House, 1986), esp. pp. 33–179.

80. Bob Woodward, *Veil: The Secret Wars of the CIA, 1981–1987* (New York: Pocket Books, 1987).

81. See, for example, the interviews of Midge Decter, Irving Kristol, Michael Novak, Burton Hales Pines, Norman Podhoretz, and Richard A. Viguerie, *New York Times,* July 12, 1985.

82. Perle interview by Judy Swallow, broadcast in "The World's Policeman," BBC World Service, November 1993.

83. Cited in Draper, *Present History,* op. cit., pp. 97–98.

84. Barnard L. Collier, "McFarlane Says Hill Knew About Mining," *Washington Times,* April 13, 1984, p. 1.

85. Gates's assessments of the Soviet threat became a matter of particular controversy and scrutiny when President Bush nominated him in 1991 to be CIA director. At his confirmation hearings, a number of former CIA analysts came forward to charge that he had helped "politicize" the agency in his years as deputy director, creating a climate of fear in which independent analysis was subordinated to the Reagan administration's larger foreign-policy agenda. The charge of politicization was somewhat vague, and the Senate Intelligence Committee ultimately decided that the evidence for the charge was not sufficient to prevent his confirmation. But a more general point came out of the hearings: In the words of one of his CIA critics, Harold Ford, Gates was "wrong on the central analytic target of the past few years: the probable fortunes of the U.S.S.R and the Soviet European bloc." *Nomination of Robert M. Gates to be Director of Central Intelligence,* Report together with Additional Views [Exec. Rept. 102–19], 102nd Cong., 1st Sess., esp. pp. 100–178.

86. Ibid., p. 178.

87. See Theodore Draper, *A Very Thin Line: The Iran-Contra Affairs* (New York: Hill and Wang, 1991), esp. pp. 558–598.

88. Ibid., p. 590.

89. See Mark Danner, "The Truth of El Mozote," *The New Yorker* 69, no. 41 (December 6, 1993), pp. 50–133.

90. For the impact on world capital markets and the U.S. domestic economy, see David P. Calleo, *The Bankrupting of America: How the Federal Budget Is Impoverishing the Nation* (New York: Avon Books, 1992). Toward the end of the Bush administration, the impact on U.S. foreign policy was described, perhaps inadvertently, by Richard Nixon, who called the U.S. response to Russian needs "pathetically inadequate," part of "a new isolationism" in both political parties. "Nixon Scoffs at Level of Support for Russian Democracy by Bush," *The New York Times*, March 10, 1992; "Nixon Warns Bush to Aid Russia, Shun 'New Isolationism,'" *The Washington Post*, March 12, 1992.

91. Figures, in constant 1982 dollars, are for the fiscal years corresponding to the Reagan presidency, 1981–1988. In fact, the FY 1981 budget was prepared by the Carter administration, while Reagan was also responsible for FY 1989. Shifting the time-frame back one year would have no substantial effect on the numbers. A more important point is that the Reagan defense buildup was in reality a Carter-Reagan buildup: after declining from $254.8 billion to $155 billion during fiscal years 1968 to 1978, defense spending rebounded to $171.4 billion in the final Carter budget of 1981. Again, figures cited are constant 1982 dollars. *Historical Tables, Budget of the United States Government—Fiscal Year 1990* (Washington, D.C.: U.S. Government Printing Office, 1989), pp. 126–130.

Chapter 4

1. Eugene Rostow, "Peace with Freedom," discussion by the Committee on the Present Danger before the Foreign Policy Association, New York, March 14, 1978, in *Alerting America: The Papers of the Committee on the Present Danger*, ed. Charles Tyroler II (Washington, D.C.: Pergamon-Brassey's, 1984).

2. Data from *NATO and the Warsaw Pact: Force Comparisons* (Brussels: NATO Information Services, 1984).

3. In the period between one and two weeks after beginning its mobilization, the Warsaw Pact could have increased its numerical advantage on the central front to almost 2 to 1, according to an analysis prepared in the late 1970s. Robert Lucas Fischer, *Defending the Central Front: The Balance of Forces*, Adelphi Paper no. 127 (London: IISS, 1977), p. 23.

4. David P. Calleo, *Beyond American Hegemony: The Future of the Western Alliance* (New York: Basic Books, 1987), pp. 159–160.

5. Edward N. Luttwak, "How to Think About Nuclear War," *Commentary* (August 1982), p. 21.

6. Ibid., p. 24.

7. Ibid.

8. Ibid., p. 25.

9. Ibid.

10. Which is not to say that "decoupling" didn't refer as well to another, more explosive fear—that the waning credibility of American extended deterrence might inspire miscalculations leading to nuclear war.

11. Lawrence Freedman, *The Evolution of Nuclear Strategy* (London: Macmillan, 1982), p. 367. Emphasis in original.

12. The designation "SS-20" came from Western analysts.

13. Warheads of 150 kilotons have a soft-target lethal area about one-quarter that of a 1-megaton warhead, which was the assumed yield for earlier generation Soviet IRBMs. A 0.2 kilometers CEP meant that out of 350 SS-20 warheads, all should fall within 0.75 kilometers of the center of their targets—that is, within the boundaries of a target such as an air base with a 2 kilometer radius. Stephen M. Meyer, *Soviet Theatre Nuclear Forces, Part II: Capabilities and Implications,* Adelphi Papers 188 (London: International Institute for Strategic Studies, 1984), p. 27.

14. "Overview of Nuclear Arms Control and Defense Strategy in NATO," Hearings before the Subcommittees on International Security and Scientific Affairs and on Europe and the Middle East of the Committee on Foreign Affairs, House of Representatives, 97th Cong., 2nd Sess., February 28, 1982 (Washington, D.C.: U.S. Government Printing Office, 1982), p. 11.

15. President Reagan's Address to the American Legion Annual Conference, February 22, 1983; excerpts printed in *Survival* 25, no. 3 (May/June 1983), p. 128.

16. Richard Burt, testimony to Congress, February 23, 1982, in "Overview of Nuclear Arms Control and Defense Strategy in NATO," op. cit., p. 42.

17. McGeorge Bundy, "America in the 1980s: Reframing our Relations with our Friends and Among Our Allies," *Survival* 24, no. 1 (January/February 1982); George F. Kennan, "Zero Options," *New York Review of Books,* May 12, 1983.

18. Helmut Schmidt, "The 1977 Alastair Buchan Memorial Lecture," London, October 28, 1977, reprinted in *Survival* 20, no. 1 (January/February 1978), pp. 3–4.

19. Michel Tatu, *La bataille des euromissiles* (Paris: Editions du Seuil, 1983), p. 12.

20. David N. Schwartz, *NATO's Nuclear Dilemmas* (Washington, D.C.: The Brookings Institution, 1983), pp. 213–214.

21. See Zbigniew Brzezinski, *Power and Principle: Memoirs of the National Security Adviser, 1977–1981* (New York: Farrar Straus Giroux, 1983), pp. 301–307.

22. However, land-basing involved a difficult political trade-off, as Defense Secretary Harold Brown told a congressional committee after leaving office: The

fact that sea-based missiles "are offshore and invisible . . . make them very desirable from the point of view of moderating European public anti-nuclear pressures against European political leaders. They also make such forces seem less certain and less committed on the part of the U.S. in the eyes of European leaders." Brown testimony, "Overview of Nuclear Arms Control and Defense Strategy in NATO," hearings before the Subcommittees on International Security and Scientific Affairs and on Europe and the Middle East of the Committee on Foreign Affairs, House of Representatives, March 22, 1982 (Washington, D.C.: U.S. Government Printing Office, 1982), p. 194.

23. Brzezinski, *Power and Principle*, op. cit., pp. 307–309; David N. Schwartz, *NATO's Nuclear Dilemmas*, op. cit., p. 227.

24. See chapter 1.

25. Meyer, *Soviet Theatre Nuclear Forces*, op. cit., pp. 41–42.

26. See, for example, Paul Warnke, "The Illusion of NATO's Nuclear Defense," in Andrew J. Pierre, ed., *Nuclear Weapons in Europe* (New York: Council on Foreign Relations, 1984), p. 76.

27. Insofar as this was the rationale, it was, as Leon Sigal notes, "largely unstated." Leon V. Sigal, *Nuclear Forces in Europe: Enduring Dilemmas, Present Prospects* (Washington, D.C.: The Brookings Institution, 1984), pp. 46–48.

28. Sigal, *Nuclear Forces in Europe*, op. cit., pp. 61–62.

29. Henry A. Kissinger, "Strategy and the Atlantic Alliance," *Survival* 24, no. 5 (September/October 1982), p. 194.

30. *The New York Times*, August 12, 1983, p. 8.

31. Harold Brown, testimony to Congress, "Overview of Nuclear Arms Control and Defense Strategy in NATO," op. cit., p. 197.

32. McGeorge Bundy, George F. Kennan, Robert S. McNamara and Gerard Smith, "Nuclear Weapons and the Atlantic Alliance," *Foreign Affairs* 60, no. 4 (Spring 1982), pp. 753–768.

33. Robert S. McNamara, "The Military Role of Nuclear Weapons: Perceptions and Misperceptions," *Foreign Affairs* 62, no. 1 (Fall 1983), p. 79.

34. See George F. Kennan, *Memoirs: 1925–1950* (New York: Pantheon Books, 1967), p. 473.

35. Bundy et al., "Nuclear Weapons and the Atlantic Alliance," op. cit., pp. 765–766.

36. McGeorge Bundy, George F. Kennan, Robert S. McNamara, Gerard Smith, Madalene O'Donnell, Leon V. Sigal, Richard H. Ullman and Paul Warnke, "Back From the Brink: The Case For a New U.S. Nuclear Strategy," *The Atlantic Monthly* 258, no. 2 (August 1986), p. 39.

37. Bundy et al., "Nuclear Weapons and the Atlantic Alliance," op. cit., p. 765.

38. Ibid.

39. Bundy et al., "Nuclear Weapons and the Atlantic Alliance," op. cit., p. 765.

40. A judgment discussed further in the conclusion.

41. Richard Perle, testimony to Congress, February 28, 1982, "Overview of Nuclear Arms Control and Defense Strategy in NATO," Hearings before the Subcommittees on International Security and Scientific Affairs and on Europe and the Middle East of the Committee on Foreign Affairs, House of Representatives, 97th Cong., 2nd Sess., February 28, 1982 (Washington, D.C.: U.S. Government Printing Office, 1982), p. 54.

42. Ibid., pp. 56–57.

43. Ibid., pp. 54–55.

44. Strobe Talbott, *Deadly Gambits: The Reagan Administration and the Stalemate in Nuclear Arms Control* (New York: Alfred A. Knopf, 1984), pp. 43–51, 179.

45. See for example, Richard Pipes, "How to Cope With the Soviet Threat: A Long-term Strategy for the West," *Commentary* 78, no. 2 (August 1984), pp. 17–18.

46. Eugene Rostow, testimony to Congress, February 28, 1982, "Overview of Nuclear Arms Control and Defense Strategy in NATO," op. cit., p. 8.

47. Ibid., pp. 9–10.

48. See Brzezinski, *Power and Principle,* op. cit., pp. 287–311, 461–463. "Schmidt had let it be known to all and sundry what a low opinion he had of the U.S. President. In turn, Carter, who had tried to avoid public polemics, had concluded that Schmidt was unstable, egotistical, and unreliable." Ibid., p. 462.

49. Ibid., p. 307.

50. Talbott, *Deadly Gambits,* op. cit., pp. 40–41.

51. Brzezinski, *Power and Principle,* op. cit., p. 309.

52. Talbott, *Deadly Gambits,* op. cit., p. 41. There followed a deeply rancorous meeting between the president and the chancellor at the June 1980 Venice Summit in which, according to Brzezinski, Schmidt "repeatedly described the letter as an insult." See Brzezinski, *Power and Principle,* op. cit., pp. 309–310.

53. Talbott, *Deadly Gambits,* op. cit., pp. 135–136.

54. Richard Perle, "Don't Let Germany Run the Alliance," *The Washington Post* (May 28, 1989), p. B1.

55. Ibid.

56. As it turned out, events were to give lie to the nonnegotiability thesis, albeit under radically changed circumstances in the Soviet Union.

57. This account of the "walk-in-the-woods" compromise is taken from Talbott, *Deadly Gambits,* op. cit., pp. 122–168. Nitze has confirmed the accuracy of "all the parts" of Talbott's account "that deal directly with me and what I said." Paul Nitze, interview with author, May 1989.

58. Paul Nitze, interview with author, op. cit., and Talbott, *Deadly Gambits*, op. cit., pp. 135–144.

59. Nitze, interview with author, op. cit.; also Talbott, *Deadly Gambits*, op. cit., p. 137.

60. Talbott, *Deadly Gambits*, op. cit., p. 143.

61. Ibid., p. 131.

62. Ibid., p. 136.

63. Nitze, interview with author, op. cit.

64. "And the Soviets, you know, made the same mistake. They thought it was going to be easier" to derail the deployment than it was. Ibid.

65. The NATO commanding general Bernard Rogers retired at this time and came out publicly against the agreement; see this chapter, below. For other expressions of unease, see Richard M. Nixon and Henry A. Kissinger, "An Arms Agreement—on Two Conditions," *Washington Post*, April 16, 1987; Brent Scowcroft, "INF: Fewer Is Not Better," *Washington Post*, April 20, 1987; and John Deutsch, Brent Scowcroft and James R. Woolsey, "The Danger of the Zero Option," *Washington Post*, March 31, 1987.

66. Richard Perle interview in Newhouse documentary, "War and Peace in the Nuclear Age," op. cit.

67. See the collection of essays by Robert W. Tucker, George Liska, Robert E. Osgood and David P. Calleo, *SDI and U.S. Foreign Policy* (Boulder, Colo.: Westview Press, 1987).

68. See chapter 3.

69. For a comprehensive account, see Simon Head, "The Battle Inside NATO," *The New York Review of Books* (May 18, 1989), pp. 41–46.

70. And it was questionable whether they would reach beyond *West* German territory, given the suggestion that "current Army military doctrine calls for such tactical nuclear weapons to be moved out of harm's way toward the rear in the early stages of combat . . . making their detonation on foreign soil problematic." R. Jeffrey Smith, "Alliance Caught in Superpower Squeeze," *Washington Post*, May 14, 1989, pp. A1, A31.

71. The original formulation is attributed to CDU defense specialist Volker Rühe, whose actual words were less elegant: "The shorter the range of the weapons, the more Germans killed." Quoted by Head, "The Battle Inside NATO," op. cit., p. 45.

72. See, for example, Les Aspin, "Europe: Soviet Force Withdrawals May Void the Old Equation," *International Herald Tribune*, October 18, 1989, p. 10.

73. See Robert Gerald Livingston, "No New Nuclear Weapons For Bonn," *Washington Post*, February 15, 1989, p. A25.

74. David Marsh interview with Helmut Kohl, "A Chancellor for All Seasons," *Financial Times,* February 10, 1989, p. 1. Significantly, Kohl's announcement followed dismal CDU performances in West Berlin and Frankfurt elections.

75. Thomas L. Friedman, "U.S. Rejects Appeal by Bonn for Battlefield-Arms Talks," *New York Times,* April 25, 1989, p. 1.

76. In an interview with Head, as reported in "The Battle Inside NATO," op. cit., p. 43.

77. Ibid., pp. 41–42. See also the article by Rogers himself, "How the West Can Safeguard Its Deterrent Strength," *International Herald Tribune,* June 29, 1987; plus his interview in the *Financial Times,* February 5, 1987.

78. This is one more example of confusion about whether the Pershing IIs would have contributed to the credibility of deterrence because they invited retaliation against the United States or because they avoided such retaliation.

79. Paul H. Nitze, "What Bush Should Do To Solve the NATO Flap," *Washington Post,* May 14, 1989, p. C1.

80. "The relevant purpose" of short-range nuclear forces based in Europe, said U.S. Defense Secretary Richard B. Cheney, "isn't to counter Soviet short-range forces. U.S. nuclear forces, tactical forces, are in Europe to counter Soviet conventional capability." *Washington Post,* May 4, 1989, p. A30.

81. Including artillery, bombers and fighter-bombers equipped with nuclear weapons, ballistic missiles launched from submarines, and soon, especially, the accurate Trident II D-5 missile. See Head, "The Battle Inside NATO," op. cit., p. 42.

82. *Washington Post,* May 4, 1989, p. A30.

83. *Washington Post,* April 26, 1989, p. A22. The "third zero" is an expression stemming from Helmut Schmidt's "Null Lösung," adopted by Ronald Reagan as the "zero option." The first zero referred to INF with ranges over 1,000 kilometers—the SS-20, the Pershing II, and the GLCM. The second zero, added in the course of negotiations, barred short-range intermediate nuclear forces, defined as having a range between 500 and 1,000 kilometers. A third zero would presumably cover SNF—that is, missiles with a range of under 500 kilometers.

84. George F. Will, "Germany's Importance," *Washington Post,* May 4, 1989, p. A23.

85. Nitze resigned from the government in early May 1989, after being offered the post of "emeritus" adviser on arms-control issues. Nitze said that he had argued in the later days of the Reagan administration, as well as to Bush aides, that the policy of deploying without negotiating would not work. This summary of his views was taken from an interview with the author, op. cit.; from the *Washington Post,* May 4, 1989, p. A1; and from a written comment by Nitze himself, "What Bush Should Do To Solve the NATO Flap," op. cit.

86. Nitze, interview with author, op. cit.

87. Nitze, "What Bush Should Do To Solve the NATO Flap," op. cit.

88. "Now there's another question, that is whether the Russians will agree to that. But it is consistent with Gorbachev's doctrine: that is, where there are inequalities, the first thing you do is remove the inequalities, get to equal ceilings at lower levels." Nitze, interview with author, op. cit.

89. Nitze, "What Bush Should Do to Solve the NATO Flap," op. cit.

90. Nitze, interview with author, op. cit.

91. Nitze, "What Bush Should Do To Solve the NATO Flap," op. cit.

92. One must concede that the administration exited its quarrel with the West German government rather quickly. To meet the challenge of change in the East and Gorbachev initiatives toward the West, Bush proposed an impressive package of mutual force reductions in Europe. West German and other European leaders praised the proposals lavishly. This success helped defuse the SNF controversy, with the Americans conceding, in principle, that negotiations over the missiles might be appropriate once a substantial lessening of the Soviet conventional threat was assured. NATO deferred any decision on new deployments. Meanwhile, Bush aides and State Department officials put out the word that they hoped the West German and other European NATO governments would take de facto command of Western aid and response to political reform in Eastern Europe. Such policies seem dictated by circumstances: West German insistence on negotiations and American inability to reduce the federal budget deficit. Nonetheless, the policies clearly reflected a new found readiness to trust the Germans.

93. Jonathan Dean, *Watershed in Europe: Dismantling the East-West Military Confrontation* (Lexington, Mass.: Lexington Books, 1987), pp. 82–85.

94. Pipes, "How to Cope with the Soviet Threat: A Long-term Strategy for the West," op. cit., p. 24.

95. Luttwak, "How To Think About Nuclear War," op. cit., p. 25.

96. The Committee on the Present Danger, "Is America Becoming Number 2?" October 5, 1978, in Charles Tyroler II, ed., *Alerting America,* op. cit., p. 75.

97. Meyer, *Soviet Theatre Nuclear Forces,* op. cit., pp. 24–25.

98. Ibid., p. 25.

99. "The SS-20 did not and does not give the Soviet Union any nuclear capability against Europe alone that she did not have in overflowing measure before a single SS-20 was deployed." McGeorge Bundy, "America in the 1980s: Reframing our Relations with our Friends and Among Our Allies," op. cit., p. 25.

     In the early 1970s, 120 SS-11 ICBMs were believed targeted against Europe. Later, 60 SS-19 ICBMs were deployed on old SS-4 and SS-5 sites— these were also believed by Western analysts to have primary targets in Western

Europe. They were new-generation missiles, MIRVed with six high-yield warheads each, with impressive hard-target kill capacity.

The 50 or so hardened NATO targets were obviously and redundantly vulnerable to these 180 ICBMs. Another 110 soft targets that had to be destroyed quickly would have virtually no chance of survival if the Russians threw four SS-4s or SS-5s against each of them, notwithstanding the primitive design of these 1950s-vintage, liquid-fueled, intermediate-range rockets. Such saturation targeting would still have left 100 IRBMs that could be sent, along with almost 100 sea-based missiles and between 100 to 200 long-range bombers against the remaining 120 soft targets. But this exercise has already reached an almost absurd level of redundancy, since only 30 SS-19s could destroy confidently the hard targets and 120 SS-11s were enough for the remaining soft targets. The Soviet theater nuclear forces needn't come into play at all. Meyer, *Soviet Theatre Nuclear Forces,* op. cit., pp. 25–26.

100. Meyer, *Soviet Theatre Nuclear Forces,* op. cit., p. 28.

101. Tatu, *La bataille des euromissiles,* op. cit., p. 19.

102. Meyer, *Soviet Theatre Nuclear Forces,* op. cit., p. 26.

103. "In effect, a Soviet disarming strike against NATO TNF would also have disarmed the USSR," wrote Meyer. Ibid., p. 27.

104. Sigal, *Nuclear Forces in Europe,* op. cit., p. 38.

105. Paul Bracken, "Collateral Damage and Theater Warfare," *Survival* 22, no. 5 (September/October 1980), p. 204.

106. Ibid., p. 205.

107. "Dr. Kissinger's comments to the press after the Brussels Conference on NATO," September 3, 1979, published in *NATO—The Next Thirty Years: The Changing Political, Economic, and Military Setting,* ed. Kenneth A. Myers (Boulder, Colo.: Westview Press, 1980), p. 14.

108. Robert Jervis makes this argument in *The Illogic of American Nuclear Strategy* (Ithaca, N.Y.: Cornell University Press, 1984), pp. 86–95.

109. Committee on the Present Danger, "Has America Become Number 2?" June 29, 1979, reprinted in *Alerting America,* op. cit., p. 226. The statement by Brown, quoted by the Committee, was as follows: "We do not plan to match the Soviet program system by system or warhead by warhead . . . Instead, we seek to strengthen the linkage of U.S. strategic forces to the defense of Europe." Secretary of Defense, *Annual Report to Congress, FY 1981,* p. 7.

110. " . . . U.S. strategic force vulnerabilities and Soviet superiority at that level," said the Committee, "leads to the conclusion that the strategic level cannot make up for imbalances and deficiencies at the theater-tactical nuclear level. The strategic imbalance now magnifies inadequacies at the theater level." Committee on the Present Danger, "Has America Become Number 2?" op. cit., p. 226.

111. Robert W. Tucker, *The Nuclear Debate: Deterrence and the Lapse of Faith* (New York: Holmes & Meier, 1985), p. 120.

112. "In the period from 1980 to 1985 Soviet behavior was as cautious and circumspect as it has ever been." Ibid.

113. ". . . the different components of our strategic forces would force the Soviets, if they were to contemplate an all-out attack, to make choices which would lead them to reduce significantly their effectiveness against one component in order to attack another. For example, if Soviet war planners should decide to attack our bomber and submarine bases and our ICBM silos with simultaneous detonations—by delaying missile launches from close-in submarines so that such missiles would arrive at our bomber bases at the same time the Soviet ICBM warheads (with their longer time of flight) would arrive at our ICBM silos—then a very high proportion of our alert bombers would have escaped before their bases were struck. This is because we would have been able to, and would have, ordered our bombers to take off from their bases within moments after the launch of the first Soviet ICBMs. If the Soviets, on the other hand, chose rather to launch their ICBM and SLBM attacks at the same moment (hoping to destroy a higher proportion of our bombers with SLBMs having a short time of flight), there would be a period of over a quarter of an hour after nuclear detonations had occurred on US bomber bases but before our ICBMs had been struck. In such a case the Soviets should have no confidence that we would refrain from launching our ICBMs during that interval after we had been hit. It is important to appreciate that this would not be a 'launch-on-warning' or even a 'launch under attack,' but rather a launch *after* attack—after massive nuclear detonations had already occurred on US soil." "Report of the President's Commission on Strategic Forces," ("Scowcroft Commission," April 11, 1983), excerpted in *Survival* 25, no. 4 (July/August 1983), pp. 179–180.

114. Tucker, *The Nuclear Debate,* op. cit., p. 84.

115. As Robert Jervis argued: "In a crisis or to respond to a major Soviet provocation, the United States certainly needs alternatives to passivity or an all-out strike. But it has had them for at least twenty years. The missiles need not be fired all at once. The common claim that an American president might be left with only the choice between humiliation and holocaust is silly. If the C3 system survives, there are any number of actions that can be taken to increase the costs to the Soviets and risks to both sides." *The Illogic of American Nuclear Strategy,* op. cit., p. 167.

116. ". . . would Soviet leaders have such confidence in the NATO no-first-use policy that they would be encouraged to launch a conventional attack? We believe that the answer is no . . . we believe that no change in Western doctrine

could or should give the Soviets reliable assurance that NATO's nuclear weapons would not be used if the fighting got out of control.

"The Soviets have repeatedly stated their determination not to be the first to use nuclear weapons, but no NATO planner would take such public statements at face value. . . . With or without such a declaration, any Soviet leader would be hesitant to mass Warsaw Pact divisions for an offensive and thereby create valuable targets for NATO nuclear weapons." Bundy et al., "Back From the Brink," op. cit., pp. 39–40.

117. In Tucker's analysis, "when command systems that cannot be reliably controlled are joined to weapons systems that cannot be reliably protected, the stage is set for the breakdown of deterrence." The arms race worsened this instability insofar as it generated weapons that were ever more effective at destroying other weapons, but were themselves vulnerable to preemptive attack. "If we but once examine this view with any care, we find that it rests on a truism. For what it says is that when it seems better to strike than to hold back, deterrence will in all likelihood break down. . . . The critical condition must be the emerging conviction on one or both sides that nuclear war is inevitable but that something—perhaps even a great deal—can be gained by striking first. This conviction is quite compatible with the belief that a preemptive attack will result in far greater costs than gains. For the alternative to attacking may also appear to carry far greater costs than would be the case if one were to strike first rather than second." *The Nuclear Debate*, op. cit., pp. 64–65.

118. George Kennan, "Zero Options," op. cit., p. 3.

119. "Mutual deterrence was a condition before it was a policy." Tucker, *The Nuclear Debate*, op. cit., p. 97.

Chapter 5

1. "Secretary Kissinger Interviewed at the Annual Meeting of the American Society of Newspaper Editors in Washington, D.C. D.C., April 15, 1976," *Department of State Bulletin* 74, no. 1923 (May 3, 1976), p. 568.

2. Estimate by Joint Intelligence Committee of U.S. Joint Chiefs, cited in Daniel Yergin, *Shattered Peace: The Origins of the Cold War and the National Security State* (Boston: Houghton Mifflin Co., 1978), pp. 348–49.

3. Ibid., pp. 349–350.

4. For an early, rigorous assessment of the "ungovernability" thesis, see Michel Crozier, Samuel P. Huntington and Joji Wtanunki, *The Crisis of Democracy: Report on the Governability of Democracies to the Trilateral Commission* (New York: New York University Press, 1975).

5. Cited in Jean-François Révél, *How Democracies Perish*, translated by William Byron (London: Weidenfeld and Nicolson, 1985), p. 94.

6. Tad Szulc, "Lisbon and Washington: Behind the Portuguese Revolution," *Foreign Policy* no. 21 (Winter 1975–76), p. 3.

7. Richard J. Barnet, *The Alliance—America, Europe, Japan: Makers of the Postwar World* (New York: Simon & Schuster, 1983), p. 354.

8. Ibid., p. 352; John G. Stoessinger, *Henry Kissinger: The Anguish of Power* (New York: W. W. Norton & Co, 1976), pp. 145–149.

9. Editorial, "Impasse in Portugal," *New York Times*, August 5, 1975, p. A30; editorial, "Portugal on the Brink?" *New York Times*, August 9, 1975, p. A16; Henry Ginger, "Portugal: Now the Left Threatens a Dictatorship," *New York Times*, August 10, 1975, p. E4; editorial, "Support for Portugal," *New York Times*, August 17, 1975, p. E14; editorial, "Portugal Confrontation," *New York Times*, August 20, 1975, p. L36.

10. John G. Stoessinger, *Henry Kissinger: The Anguish of Power* (New York: W. W. Norton & Co, 1976), p. 147; also *New York Times* editorial, "Support for Portugal," op. cit.

11. Kissinger's August 14, 1975 speech in Birmingham, Alabama, *New York Times*, August 15, 1975, p. A2.

12. "Social Democrats of Germany Aiding Portuguese Socialists," *New York Times*, August 29, 1975, p. A3. See also Helmut Schmidt, *Die Deutschen und ihre Nachbarn: Menschen und Mächte II* (Berlin: Siedler, 1990), pp. 435–436.

13. After watching Communist revolutionaries fail in Portugal, argues Joan Barth Urban, "there is reason to believe that the USSR's decision of late summer 1975 to escalate dramatically its military support for the Movement for the Liberation of Angola (MPLA) reflected pressure from the revolutionary sectarians within the Soviet Communist Party" Joan Barth Urban, "The Soviets and the West European Communist Parties," in *Soviet Policy Toward Western Europe*, ed. Herbert J. Ellison (Seattle: University of Washington Press, 1983), p. 97. Russia was also under pressure from China, which after 1970 extended almost twice as much economic aid to African nations as did Russia, and which noisily charged the Soviets of having a "morbid fear of and hatred for any war of national liberation." George T. Yu, "China's Impact," *Problems of Communism* 27 (January/February 1978), pp. 42, 47.

14. Frederic Spotts and Theodor Wieser, *Italy: A Difficult Democracy* (Cambridge: Cambridge University Press, 1986), pp. 41–42.

15. H. Stuart Hughes, *Consciousness and Society: The Reorientation of European Social Thought, 1890–1930* (Brighton, U.K.: The Harvester Press, 1979), p. 99.

16. Ibid., pp. 99–104; Spotts and Wieser, *Italy: A Difficult Democracy*, op. cit., p. 56.

17. Gianfranco Pasquino, "From Togliatti to the Compromesso Storico: A Party with a Governmental Vocation," in Simon Serfaty and Lawrence Gray, eds., *The Italian Communist Party: Yesterday, Today, and Tomorrow* (Westport, Conn.: Greenwood Press, 1980).

18. See James E. Dougherty and Diane K. Pfaltzgraff, eds., *Eurocommunism and the Atlantic Alliance* (Cambridge, Mass.: Institute for Foreign Policy Analysis, 1977), p. 47.

19. Spotts and Wieser, *Italy: A Difficult Democracy,* op. cit., p. 51.

20. Ibid., pp. 42–51. The French Communists' brief flirtation with Eurocommunist independence appears to have been inspired mainly by irritation over what seemed like tacit Soviet support for Valery Giscard d'Estaing in the 1974 presidential election; Urban, "The Soviets and the West European Communist Parties," op. cit., p. 106.

21. Ibid., pp. 118–124.

22. Berlinguer's address to the 13th Italian Communist Party Congress, as reported by *Corriere della Sera,* March 14, 1972, p. 2.

23. Amendola added a standard PCI appeal for continued détente to accelerate "the gradual obsolescence of the present system of military alliances." Giorgio Amendola, "Italy and Europe," *L'Unita,* June 24, 1975, translated and cited in Dougherty and Pfaltzgraff, *Eurocommunism and the Atlantic Alliance,* op. cit., p. 40.

24. Berlinguer interview by Giampaolo Pansa, *Corriere della Sera,* June 15, 1976, p. 2.

25. Spotts and Wieser, *Italy: A Difficult Democracy,* op. cit., p. 50.

26. Robert J. Flanagan, David W. Soskice, Lloyd Ulman, *Unionism, Economic Stabilization, and Incomes Policy* (Washington, D.C: The Brookings Institution, 1983), p. 510.

27. Ibid., p. 528.

28. Ibid., p. 548.

29. Carlo Levi showed this reflexive antipathy most memorably when he described southern peasants' attitudes toward Rome at a time when the deification of national authority had reached its ostensible pinnacle; see *Christ Stopped at Eboli: The Story of a Year* (New York: Farrar, Straus, 1963).

30. Joseph LaPalombara, "Italian Elections as Hobson's Choice," in *Italy at the Polls: The Parliamentary Elections of 1976,* ed. Howard Penniman (Washington, D.C.: American Enterprise Institute, 1977), p. 5.

31. Ibid., p. 6.

32. Ibid., p. 7.

33. Sidney Tarrow, "Three Years of Italian Democracy," in *Italy at the Polls, 1979,* ed. Howard Penniman (Washington, D.C.: American Enterprise Institute, 1981), p. 24.

34. *Economist Intelligence Unit Quarterly Economic Survey of Italy*, no. 2 (1984), p. 11.
35. Spotts and Wieser, *Italy: A Difficult Democracy*, op. cit., p. 184.
36. Ibid., pp. 175–185.
37. Estimates of numbers of armed terrorists vary, but were generally large: Richard Drake cited the figure of 3,000, "roughly equivalent to the number of Italian partisans who fought from September 1943 to March 1944." His large estimate of "part-time members" (3,000 to 8,000) and "active sympathizers" (200,000 to 350,000) for terrorist groups appears even more significant. Richard Drake, "The Red Brigades and the Italian Political Tradition," in *Terrorism in Europe*, ed. Yonah Alexander and Kenneth A. Myers, p. 102.
38. In 1969 a bomb exploded in Milan's Piazza Fontana killing 16; an anarchist was arrested and died in custody (police claimed it was suicide). Later, however, two neofascists were arrested for the bombing. Similar bombings followed, including the August 4, 1974, explosion on the Rome - Munich train that killed 12. Lower-level incidents, such as beatings and nonfatal shootings, were especially reminiscent of the *squadristi* terror of the *dopoguerra* preceding Mussolini's March on Rome. The fascist violence appeared as a reaction to factory seizures, rural agitation and socialist advances in the *dopoguerra;* to leftist political gains, student agitation and the "*autunno caldo*" of strikes in 1968, 1969 and the early 1970s. Leonard Weinberg, "Patterns of Neo-Fascist Violence in Italian Politics," *Terrorism: An International Journal* 2, no. 3–4, 1979, pp. 231–259. See also Spotts and Wieser, *Italy: A Difficult Democracy*, op. cit., pp. 175–178, 183–184.
39. Although spectacular right-wing attacks, such as a 1980 Bologna train station bombing and the 1984 bombing of a train in the tunnel between Florence and Bologna, continued. Ibid.
40. The PCI was unable to adopt the demands of the student movement as its own. Italy's major student insurrection (1977) pitted students against the PCI administration of Bologna, Italy's communist "showplace." Something similar happened when economic downturn and northward/cityward migration swelled the ranks of urban unemployment and misery. By then the PCI had identified itself with government pleas for austerity. "A furious propaganda war broke out on the left, with extremist groups, such as the Red Brigades, picking up added support, or at least tolerance from Communists who expressed disenchantment with their party's moderation. Many Communists—mostly of the younger generation—were left ideologically homeless by the revisionist shifts within the PCI. Among such disillusioned leftists the Red Brigades would find both recruits and a sympathetic audience." Richard Drake, "The Red Brigades and the Italian Political Tradition," op. cit.

41. Gianfranco Pasquino, "From Togliatti to the Compromesso Storico: A Party with a Governmental Vocation," op. cit., pp. 75–106.

42. "He argued that the failures of the parties of the center and the severity of Italy's economic and social problems made PCI participation in the Government an 'ineluctable' fact of contemporary Italian history." Joseph LaPalombara, "Two Steps Forward, One Step Back: The PCI's Struggle for Legitimacy," in *Italy at the Polls, 1979,* ed. Howard Penniman, op. cit., p. 108.

43. Douglas A. Wertman, "The Christian Democrats: Masters of Survival," in *Italy at the Polls, 1979,* ed. Howard Penniman, op. cit., pp. 84–85.

44. The Socialists, Social Democrats, Republicans and Liberals.

45. Wertman, "The Christian Democrats: Masters of Survival," op. cit., pp. 86–90.

46. Flanagan et al., *Unionism, Economic Stabilization, and Incomes Policies,* European Experience, op. cit., p. 547.

47. LaPalombara, "Two Steps Forward, One Step Back: The PCI's Struggle for Legitimacy," op. cit., pp. 110–115.

48. Tarrow, "Three Years of Italian Democracy," op. cit., p. 15.

49. Flanagan et al., *Unionism, Economic Stabilization, and Incomes Policies,* op. cit., pp. 551–553.

50. Spotts and Wieser, *Italy: A Difficult Democracy,* op. cit., p. 198; Tarrow, "Three Years of Italian Democracy," op. cit., p. 15; LaPalombara, "Two Steps Forward, One Step Back: The PCI's Struggle for Legitimacy," op. cit., pp. 114–115.

51. Flanagan et al., *Unionism, Economic Stabilization, and Incomes Policy,* op. cit., pp. 551–553.

52. Ibid. p. 554.

53. Ibid.

54. Henry Kissinger, "Communist Parties in Western Europe: Challenge to the West," in *Eurocommunism: The Italian Case,* ed. Austin Ranney and Giovanni Sartori (Washington, D.C.: The American Enterprise Institute, 1978), pp. 187–188.

55. Henry Kissinger, Chicago speech, July 6, 1976, *Department of State Bulletin* 75, no. 1936 (August 2, 1976), p. 157. In a press conference a few days later, Kissinger observed: ". . . this is not the first time in history that there have been statements about 'different roads toward Communism.' And I would urge all of you to read statements that were made between 1945 and 1948 by the leaders of the Communist Parties of Eastern Europe, by Mr. Gottwald, by Mr. Gomulka, by Mr. Dimitrov—we have a compilation of those which we can make available next week—in which, in effect, at the time they set their different roads to communism: We have chosen in Eastern Europe the democratic road; the revolutionary means or the dictatorship of the proletariat is not the inevitable result." Press conference, July 10, 1976, in ibid., p. 167.

56. Kissinger, "Communist Parties in Western Europe," op. cit., p. 188.

57. Ibid., pp. 185–186.

58. Ibid., p. 188.

59. Ibid., p. 184.

60. Ibid., p. 185.

61. Kissinger, interviewed at the Annual Meeting of the American Society of Newspaper Editors, op. cit.

62. Kissinger, "Communist Parties in Western Europe," op. cit., p. 189.

63. Ibid., p. 188.

64. Kissinger, "The Permanent Challenge of Peace: U.S. Policy Toward the Soviet Union," speech in San Francisco, February 3, 1976, *Department of State Bulletin* 74, no. 1913 (February 23, 1976), p. 202.

65. Kissinger, "Communist Parties in Western Europe," op. cit., p. 190.

66. Ibid., p. 191.

67. Kissinger, interviewed at the Annual Meeting of the American Society of Newspaper Editors, op. cit., p. 569.

68. Kissinger, "Communist Parties in Western Europe," op. cit., p. 189.

69. Ibid., p. 191.

70. Kissinger, remarks before the foreign policy panel sponsored by the Blue Ribbon 400, Los Angeles, *Department of State Bulletin* 74, no. 1914 (March 1, 1976), p. 264. See also Kissinger, interviewed at the Annual Meeting of the American Society of Newspaper Editors, op. cit., p. 568; Kissinger, Press conference in San Francisco, February 3, 1976, *Department of State Bulletin* 74, no. 1913, p. 218; Kissinger, Speech before the Boston World Affairs Council, March 11, 1976, *Department of State Bulletin* 74, no. 1919, p. 430.

71. See correspondence between Roosevelt and Churchill in *Roosevelt and Churchill: Their Secret Wartime Correspondence,* ed. Francis L. Loewenheim, Harold D. Langley, and Manfred Jonas (New York: Saturday Review Press, 1975), pp. 425, 465–468, 470–473, 526, 529–530, 532, 535, 619–620, 624.

72. Simon Serfaty, "The United States and the PCI: The Year of Decision, 1947," in Serfaty and Gray, eds., *The Italian Communist Party: Yesterday, Today and Tomorrow,* op. cit., p. 60.

73. Barnet, *The Alliance,* op. cit., p. 355.

74. Alan A. Platt and Robert Leonardi, "American Foreign Policy and the Postwar Italian Left," *Political Science Quarterly* 93, no. 2 (Summer 1978), pp. 209–213; "U.S. Paid 800,000 to Italian General; CIA Fought Move," *New York Times,* January 30, 1976.

75. Leslie Gelb, "U.S. and Allies Bar Loans if Reds Join Italy Cabinet," *New York Times,* July 18, 1976; David Willey, "Italy Jolted by Disclosure of Secret Allied Pact," *Christian Science Monitor,* July 19, 1976; Alvin Shuster, "Tempest in

Italy over Allied Threat to Bar Aid if Reds Share Rule," *New York Times,* July 24, 1976.

76. Anthony Lewis, "Mr. Kissinger's Folly," *New York Times,* July 29, 1976.

77. "Excerpts From Carter's Speech and His Replies," *New York Times,* June 24, 1976, p. A22.

78. Carter, in an interview with C. L. Sulzberger, "Jingo: Not as It Sounds," *New York Times,* August 29, 1976, Section 4, p. 17.

79. Zbigniew Brzezinski, *Power and Principle: Memoirs of the National Security Adviser, 1977–1981* (New York: Farrar Straus Giroux, 1983), pp. 311–313. For full text of statement, see *New York Times,* January 13, 1978, p. A2.

80. Brzezinski, *Power and Principle,* op. cit.

81. Tarrow, "Three Years of Italian Democracy," op. cit., p. 16.

82. Italy's left-wing terrorism was effective. It is naturally impossible to say whether it was decisive in blocking the historic compromise, as some Communist leaders argued. But the damage to Italy's civil and political fabric was dire. The PCI had "stressed that, by kidnapping Moro, the Red Brigades had pushed the DC toward the right and blocked the Communist advance," wrote Patrick McCarthy after the 1979 parliamentary elections. "Certainly the Red Brigades have harmed the right less than they have harmed the left. But they have done damage to all parliamentary parties and to parliamentary government itself." McCarthy, "The Parliamentary and Nonparliamentary Parties of the Far Left," in *Italy at the Polls, 1979,* op. cit., p. 210. Yet Moro's murder damaged the Red Brigades as well: " . . . since 1976 the Red Brigades had pulled their militants out of protest movements and had set up a tighter, more centralized chain of command. This had brought greater efficiency, as the Moro kidnapping revealed, but it had isolated the terrorists from the masses and prevented them from making political gains. Certainly the brutal execution of Moro and his guards diminished the tolerance or comprehension which some New Left members felt for the Red Brigades." Ibid.

83. Recent allegations were laid out in a *Westdeutscher Rundfunk* (German television) broadcast of November 28, 1993, *Anatomie eines Verbrechens: Die Ermordung Aldo Moros und das italienische Drama,* by Michael Busse and Maria-Rosa Bobbi, edited by Rainer Hoffmann.

84. Wertman, "The Christian Democrats: Masters of Survival," op. cit., p. 92.

85. Howard R. Penniman's preface to *Italy at the Polls, 1979,* op. cit., p. xii; Joseph LaPalombara, "Two Steps Forward, One Step Back," op. cit., p. 134.

86. Philip H. Gordon, *A Certain Idea of France: French Security Policy and the Gaullist Legacy* (Princeton, N.J.: Princeton University Press, 1993), p. 120.

87. Richard Perle, testimony of November 12, 1981, "Proposed Trans-Siberian Natural Gas Pipeline," Hearing before the Committee on Banking, Hous-

ing, and Urban Affairs, U.S. Senate, 97th Cong., 1st Sess. (Washington, D.C.: U.S. Government Printing Office, 1982), p. 114. In another hearing a month later, Perle again faulted Socialist ideology, this time for European laxity in impeding the flow of militarily significant technology from West to East. "There is another dimension here that is terribly important, and that is the political dimension. The simple fact is that in many countries in Europe, in Germany in particular, there exists a significant body of political opinion that believes that trade between East and West has positive political consequences. This has been at the center of socialist politics in Germany for many years. The result of that is that they are not nearly as concerned as we about the transfer of sensitive technologies." Perle, testimony of November 12, 1981, "Export Controls on Oil and Gas Equipment," Hearings and Markup before the Committee on Foreign Affairs and its Subcommittees on Europe and the Middle East and on International Economic Policy and Trade, House of Representatives, 97th Cong., 1st Sess., on H.R. 6838, Proposed Repeal of Oil and Gas Equipment Export Controls, November 12, 1981 (Washington, D.C.: U.S. Government Printing Office, 1983), p. 38. See also Meyer Rashish, Under Secretary of State for Economic Affairs, testimony of September 16, 1981, "East/West Economic Relations," Hearing before the Subcommittee on International Economic Policy of the Committee on Foreign Relations, U.S. Senate, 97th Cong., 1st Sess., September 16, 1981 (Washington, D.C.: U.S. Government Printing Office, 1981), p. 27.

88. Irving Kristol, "Does NATO Exist?" in *NATO: The Next Thirty Years: The Changing Political, Economical, and Military Setting,* ed. Kenneth A. Myers (Boulder, Colo.: Westview Press, 1980), p. 367.

89. Ibid. See also Richard Pipes, "How to Cope With the Soviet Threat: A Long-term Strategy for the West," *Commentary* 78, no. 2 (August 1984), p. 24.

90. Irving Kristol, "NATO at a Dead End," *Wall Street Journal,* July 15, 1981.

91. Barnet, *The Alliance,* op. cit., p. 297.

92. Among the accused were the Socialist leader Bettino Craxi and Christian Democrat Giulio Andreotti, who had headed more Italian governments than any other postwar politician. Mafia informants accused Andreotti of being the Mafia's highest interlocutor.

93. Eduard Bernstein, *Die Voraussetzungen des Sozialismus und die Aufgaben der Sozialdemokratie* (Stuttgart, 1906), p. 10, cited in Carl E. Schorske, *German Social Democracy, 1905–1917: The Development of the Great Schism* (Cambridge, Mass.: Harvard University Press, 1955), p. 18.

94. Bernstein, *Voraussetzungen,* cited in ibid., p. 19.

95. Eduard Bernstein, *Evolutionary Socialism: A Criticism and Affirmation,* trans. Edith Harvey (New York: Schoeken Books, 1961), author's preface to English edition, p. xxii.

96. See Alan S. Milward, *The Reconstruction of Western Europe, 1945–1951* (Berkeley: University of California Press, 1984), pp. 18–21; 37–55; 462–477.

97. Barnet, *The Alliance,* op. cit., p. 288.

98. Schorske, *German Social Democracy, 1905–1917,* op. cit.

99. Yergin, *Shattered Peace,* op. cit., p. 117.

100. Willy Brandt, *People and Politics: The Years 1960–1975* (London: Collins, 1978), p. 318.

101. Jeane J. Kirkpatrick, *Dictatorships and Double Standards: Rationalism and Reason in Politics* (New York: Simon & Schuster, 1982), p. 49. Looking back, one can be genuinely exasperated by some Western liberals' infinite readiness to apologize for whatever the Russians might do or say. But Kirkpatrick and her ideological soulmates were equally guilty of minimizing state terror of the right.

Chapter 6

1. Paul H. Nitze, "Strategy in the Decade of the 1980s," *Foreign Affairs* 59, no. 1 (Fall 1980), p. 84.

2. Richard Perle, testimony of November 12, 1981, "Proposed Trans-Siberian Natural Gas Pipeline," Hearing before the Committee on Banking, Housing, and Urban Affairs, U.S. Senate, 97th Cong., 1st Sess. (Washington, D.C.: U.S. Government Printing Office, 1982), pp. 116–117.

3. Bruce W. Jentleson, *Pipeline Politics: The Complex Political Economy of East-West Trade* (Ithaca, N.Y.: Cornell University Press, 1986), pp. 51–75, 79, 89. From the start, West Germany's overwhelming interest was an export market for its steel industry. The Soviets were quite happy to take up some of the excess capacity from which West Germany and the rest of Europe were already suffering. During the 1950s West German steel exports to the Soviet Union increased from $13.9 million to $83.5 million. Ibid., pp. 89–90.

4. Angela E. Stent, *From Embargo to Ostpolitik: The Political Economy of West German–Soviet Relations, 1955–1980* (New York: Cambridge University Press, 1980), pp. 154–178.

5. Helmut Schmidt, "The 1977 Alastair Buchan Memorial Lecture," London, October 28, 1977, reprinted in *Survival* 20, no. 1 (January/February 1978), p. 9.

6. Angela E. Stent, *Soviet Energy and Western Europe* (New York: Praeger Publishers, 1982), pp. 20–21. As a share of total energy requirements, Soviet

sources accounted for 6.1 percent, 4.7 percent and 9.9 percent of West German, French and Italian needs. (Italy reexported some of its imported energy.)

7. Ibid., p. 2. In 1979 Soviet oil exports to the three countries totalled 22.6 mtoe (metric tons of oil, equivalent); gas exports were 15.3 mtoe. Ibid., pp. 20–21.

8. Jentleson, *Pipeline Politics,* op. cit., chapter 5.

9. W. Kenneth Davis (Deputy Secretary, Department of Energy), testimony of October 14, 1981, "Soviet Energy Exports and Western European Energy Security," Hearing before the Subcommittee on Energy, Nuclear Proliferation, and Government Processes of the Committee of Governmental Affairs, U.S. Senate, 97th Cong., 1st Sess. (Washington, D.C.: U.S. Government Printing Office, 1982), p. 6.

10. Jentleson, *Pipeline Politics,* op. cit., pp. 164, 169.

11. The gas source was later changed, for cost reasons, to the Urengoi fields, 150 miles to the south. Ibid., pp. 166–167, 172. Ironically, these controversial negotiations between the Soviets, European governments and a consortium of European companies had been preceded by an aborted effort between the Soviets and American companies to set up a similar pipeline. This "North Star" project was for development of the Urengoi gas reserves and construction of a 1,600-mile pipeline to Murmansk by an American consortium of Tenneco, Texas Transmission, and Brown & Root. From Murmansk gas would be shipped to the United States. A parallel project by American and Japanese companies envisioned a 2,400-mile pipeline from eastern Siberia's Yakutsk reserves to the Pacific port of Nakhodka. The Nixon administration, having explicitly considered and rejected arguments that energy dependence upon the Soviet Union threatened U.S. national security, had encouraged the deals. But they were killed by Jackson-Vanik, which withheld Export-Import financing and most-favored-nation tariff status, both of which were deemed necessary for the projects to be commercially viable. Ibid., pp. 137–143.

12. Cost estimates from Stent, *Soviet Energy and Western Europe,* op. cit., p. 79.

13. Belgium and the Netherlands later dropped out. Ibid., p. 86.

14. Financing agreements were complex and, in many aspects, confidential. Richard Perle spoke of interest rates "on the order of" 7.5 percent (Perle testimony of November 12, 1981, "Proposed Trans-Siberian Natural Gas Pipeline, op. cit., p. 117.) Jonathan Stern reported that the interest rates offered by the West Europeans averaged 7.8 percent. "Specters and Pipe Dreams," *Foreign Policy,* no. 48 (Fall 1982), p. 30. The Soviets were apparently able to capitalize on competition among various European participants, among whom the French were particularly aggressive. Bruce Jentleson reports that, in February 1982, "the French banking consortium that already had

agreed to provide $850 million in low-interest credits announced that it also would finance the $140 million originally scheduled to be made as a down payment. . . . The Deutsche Bank consortium had rejected a similar Soviet request for 100 percent financing and was reported to be furious that the French bankers had broken a gentleman's agreement to keep the concessionary terms at least within some limits." *Pipeline Politics,* op. cit., p. 192.

15. Stent, *Soviet Energy and Western Europe,* op. cit., p. 61.

16. Ibid., pp. 62–64.

17. Robert D. Hormats (Assistant Secretary for Economic and Business Affairs, Department of State), testimony of October 14, 1981, "Soviet Energy Exports and Western European Energy Security," Hearing before the Subcommittee on Energy, Nuclear Proliferation, and Government Processes of the Committee of Governmental Affairs, U.S. Senate, 97th Cong., 1st Sess. (Washington, D.C.: U.S. Government Printing Office, 1982), p. 12.

18. Jentleson, *Pipeline Politics,* op. cit., pp. 189–190.

19. As was admitted by administration spokesman Robert D. Hormats, "Soviet Energy Exports and Western European Energy Security," op. cit., pp. 11–12. Jonathan Stern noted that the French "obtained a price for Soviet gas around $1 per MMBtu less than the price agreed upon in their new contract with Algiers—a price difference roughly equivalent to $5.80 per barrel of crude oil." "Specters and Pipe Dreams," op. cit., p. 30.

20. Stern, "Specters and Pipe Dreams," op. cit., pp. 30–31.

21. Jentleson, *Pipeline Politics,* op. cit., p. 162.

22. For the Carter-Schmidt meeting in Venice, see chapter 4.

23. Robert D. Putnam and Nicholas Bayne, *Hanging Together: Cooperation and Conflict in the Seven-Power Summits* (Cambridge, Mass.: Harvard University Press, 1987), pp. 128–129.

24. Stern, "Specters and Pipe Dreams," op. cit., pp. 27–28.

25. Hormats, testimony of November 12, 1981, "Proposed Trans-Siberian Natural Gas Pipeline," Hearing before the Committee on Banking, Housing, and Urban Affairs, U.S. Senate, 97th Cong., 1st Sess. (Washington, D.C.: U.S. Government Printing Office, 1982), p. 130. Algeria was one of the most aggressive OPEC price hawks. Its aggressive bargaining and then reneging on recent contracts was one reason the French and Italians had turned to the Soviets.

26. Alexander M. Haig, Jr., *Caveat: Realism, Reagan and Foreign Policy* (London: Weidenfeld & Nicolson, 1984), pp. 254–255.

27. Putnam and Bayne, *Hanging Together,* op. cit., pp. 135–140.

28. Haig, *Caveat,* op. cit, pp. 303–309.

29. This happened for complicated reasons. In Haig's account, Treasury Secretary Donald Regan, in a meeting with reporters, disavowed any agreement to support the franc. A few days later "an angered President Mitterrand called a news conference in order to state that the European participants at the summit had made no agreement on credits, either." Ibid., p. 309.

30. Ibid., pp. 303–307, 312–313; Jentleson, *Pipeline Politics,* op. cit., pp. 193–196.

31. Putnam and Bayne, *Hanging Together,* op. cit., pp. 137–138.

32. Initially these countersanctions barred all exports from the United States; the new secretary of state, George Shultz and Commerce Secretary Malcolm Baldridge succeeded in limiting it to gas and oil equipment and services. Jentleson, *Pipeline Politics,* op. cit., p. 196.

33. Lawrence Brady (Assistant Secretary for Trade Administration, Department of Commerce), testimony of September 16, 1981, "East-West Economic Relations," Hearing before the Subcommittee on International Economic Policy of the Committee on Foreign Relations, U.S. Senate (Washington, D.C.: U.S. Government Printing Office, 1981), p. 13; see also Brady's testimony of November 12, 1981, "Export Controls on Oil and Gas Equipment," Hearings before the Committee on Foreign Affairs, House of Representatives (Washington, D.C.: U.S. Government Printing Office, 1983), p. 40.

34. Statement by Thierry de Montbrial, testimony of September 22, 1982, "Soviet Pipeline Sanctions: The European Perspective," Hearing before the Joint Economic Committee, U.S. Congress (Washington, D.C.: U.S. Government Printing Office, 1983), p. 23. In fact, a number of experts on the Soviet economy have made the plausible claim that overreliance on Western trade generally hindered Soviet economic progress. However, for administration spokesmen who opposed East-West trade in general to apply the argument selectively to American grain sales was obviously less convincing.

35. "Europe's outrage," George Ball told congressmen, "should not be underestimated. I have been following the affairs of Europe closely for 35 or 40 years, and I assure you the anger and bitterness I detect there today I have not seen in the postwar period. The Europeans detect hypocrisy—and in my view they are right—when the administration tries to impose economic hardships on America's Western allies at the very moment it is making a new wheat deal with Moscow." George Ball, former undersecretary of state, testimony of August 25, 1982, "Export Controls on Oil and Gas Equipment," Hearings and markup before the Committee on Foreign Affairs, House of Representatives (Washington, D.C.: U.S. Government Printing Office, 1983), p. 121. In a book published a few months later, Robert Tucker warned, "The alliance is visibly unravelling today, and the rising tempo of its disintegration can fail

to impress only the most determined of optimists." *The Atlantic Alliance and Its Critics* (New York: Praeger, 1983), p. 188.

36. There were, however, a number of other reasons for Haig's and the administration's mutual disenchantment. Haig, *Caveat,* op. cit., pp. 303–320.

37. Jentleson, *Pipeline Politics,* op. cit., p. 197.

38. Richard Perle, testimony of November 12, 1981, "Proposed Trans-Siberian Natural Gas Pipeline," op. cit., p. 115. See also Assistant Commerce Secretary Lawrence Brady's testimony, "Proposed Trans-Siberian Natural Gas Pipeline," op. cit., p. 121, and his statement of September 16, 1981, in "East-West Economic Relations," op. cit., pp. 2–4.

39. Brady testimony, "Proposed Trans-Siberian Natural Gas Pipeline," op. cit., p. 122.

40. Brady testimony, "East-West Economic Relations," op. cit., p. 8.

41. Perle testimony, "Proposed Trans-Siberian Natural Gas Pipeline," op. cit., p. 116.

42. Brady testimony, "Proposed Trans-Siberian Natural Gas Pipeline," op. cit., p. 119.

43. Hormats testimony, "Proposed Trans-Siberian Natural Gas Pipeline," op. cit., p. 107.

44. Perle testimony, "Proposed Trans-Siberian Natural Gas Pipeline," op. cit., p. 16.

45. Hormats testimony, "Soviet Energy Exports and Western European Energy Security," op. cit., p. 13.

46. Hormats testimony, "Proposed Trans-Siberian Natural Gas Pipeline," op. cit., p. 107.

47. Perle testimony, "Proposed Trans-Siberian Natural Gas Pipeline," op. cit., p. 117.

48. Hormats testimony, "Soviet Energy Exports and Western European Energy Security," op. cit., p. 13.

49. Perle testimony, "Proposed Trans-Siberian Natural Gas Pipeline," op. cit., p. 116. Emphasis added.

50. Perle testimony, "East-West Economic Relations," op. cit., pp. 7–8.

51. Perle testimony, "Proposed Trans-Siberian Natural Gas Pipeline," op. cit., p. 117.

52. Hormats testimony, "Proposed Trans-Siberian Natural Gas Pipeline," op. cit., p. 108.

53. Fred C. Iklé (Undersecretary of Defense) testimony, "East-West Economic Relations," Hearing before the Subcommittee on International Economic Policy of the Committee on Foreign Relations, U.S. Senate (Washington, D.C.: U.S. Government Printing Office, 1981), p. 49.

54. Brady testimony, "Proposed Trans-Siberian Natural Gas Pipeline," op. cit., p. 120.

55. W. Kenneth Davis (deputy secretary, Department of Energy) testimony, "Soviet Energy Exports and Western European Energy Security," op. cit., p. 6.

56. Iklé testimony, "East-West Economic Relations," op. cit., p. 48. Iklé's scenario was somewhat at odds with the picture presented by another administration official, Department of Energy deputy secretary W. Kenneth Davis, who testified before another Senate committee one month later. Davis argued that Soviet oil production was likely to decline precipitously in the 1980s, and the Russians therefore desperately needed to increase their gas exports, "for without energy-generated hard-currency earnings, it would be virtually impossible for the Soviet Union to maintain current levels of purchases from the West." Davis testimony, "Soviet Energy Exports and Western European Energy Security," op. cit., p. 6.

57. Brady testimony, "Proposed Trans-Siberian Natural Gas Pipeline," op. cit., p. 121. He did not really explain what he meant.

58. Ibid., p. 120.

59. They were, according to Brady, on the COCOM list. Ibid., pp. 119–120.

60. Brady testimony, "East-West Economic Relations," op. cit., p. 7.

61. Iklé in "East-West Economic Relations," p. 37.

62. Brady testimony, "East-West Economic Relations," p. 7.

63. Theodore Draper, "The Western Misalliance," *Washington Quarterly* (Winter 1981), reprinted in *Present History: On Nuclear War, Détente, and Other Controversies* (New York: Vintage Books, 1984), p. 161.

64. Ibid, p. 162.

65. Ibid., p. 164.

66. Ibid., pp. 164–165.

67. " . . . most Europeans recognized the need to develop a safety net, so that there were sufficient alternative supplies to deter the U.S.S.R. from any gas black-mail. The safety net involved the following arrangements: interchangeable gas networks, developing more gas from the North Sea and other sources, increasing interruptible contracts with industry, increasing the number of dual-fired burners, and enlarging underground storage." Angela E. Stent, "East-West Economic Relations and the Western Alliance," *Trade, Technology and Soviet-American Relations,* ed. Bruce Parrott (Bloomington, Ind.: Indiana University Press, 1985), p. 308.

68. "No one can tell me that the Strait of Hormuz is a safer energy channel than a gas pipeline from Russia," a West German official is quoted as saying in August 1981; Jentleson, *Pipeline Politics,* op. cit., p. 169.

69. Don Hedly, *World Energy: The Facts and the Future* (London: Euromonitor Publications Ltd., 1986), pp. 1–5.

70. Estimates from Bruce Jentleson, who notes that "the actual gas prices nego-
    tiated in these deals never have been made public." *Pipeline Politics,* op. cit.,
    pp. 199–200.

71. The high point of $3.8 billion was reached in 1985. Earnings then fell each
    year, to $2.6 billion in 1988. Total hard-currency earnings for all energy
    exports that year were $13 billion. Overall, according to the CIA, Soviet energy
    industries were running into a quagmire of difficulty: declining oil production;
    a levelling off in gas output; higher costs of production; declining energy
    efficiency at a time when the West was becoming more efficient; and the fact
    that untapped reserves, although vast, were located in northern regions where
    backward Russian technology was hard-put to extract them profitably. *Soviet
    Energy Data Resource Handbook: A Reference Aid* (Washington, D.C.: Central
    Intelligence Agency, 1990), pp. 1, 6–7, 11–13, 15–16, 23–25.

72. Joseph Berliner and Franklyn Holzman, "The Soviet Economy: Domestic and
    International Issues," in *The Soviet Empire: Expansion and Détente,* ed. William
    E. Griffith (Lexington, Mass.: Lexington Books, 1976), pp. 105–113.

73. Ibid., p. 85.

74. Abram Bergson, "Soviet Economic Perspectives: Toward a New Growth
    Model," *Problems of Communism* 22, no. 2 (March/April 1973), pp. 3–4.

75. Ibid.

76. Robert Campbell, "The Economy," in *After Brezhnev: Sources of Soviet Conduct
    in the 1980s,* ed. Robert F. Byrnes (Bloomington, Ind.: Indiana University Press,
    1983), p. 69; Timothy J. Colton, *The Dilemma of Reform in the Soviet Union*
    (New York: Council on Foreign Relations, 1984), p. 15; and Alec Nove, "The
    Twelfth Five-Year Plan and Soviet Statistics," in *The Soviet Economy under
    Gorbachev,* Colloquium of March 20–22, 1991 (Brussels: NATO, 1991), p. 17.

77. Campbell, "The Economy," op. cit., pp. 75–76.

78. Berliner and Holzman, "The Soviet Economy: Domestic and International
    Issues," op. cit., p. 80.

79. Campbell, "The Economy," op. cit., pp. 75–76.

80. Bergson, "Soviet Economic Perspectives: Toward a New Growth Model," op.
    cit., p. 8.

81. Ibid.

82. Alec Nove, *The Soviet Economic System* (Boston: Allen & Unwin, 1986), pp.
    124–153.

83. Colton, *The Dilemma of Reform in the Soviet Union,* op. cit., pp. 15–17.

84. Gertrude Schroeder, "The Soviet Economy on a Treadmill of 'Reforms'," in
    The Soviet Economy in a Time of Change: A Compendium of Papers, submitted
    to the Joint Economic Committee, Congress of the United States (Washing-
    ton, D.C.: U.S. Government Printing Office, 1979), Vol. I, pp. 312–340.

85. Pricing methods of the 1970s discouraged innovation by favoring producers of established products. See Berliner and Holzman, "The Soviet Economy: Domestic and International Issues," op. cit., pp. 95–100.

86. Ibid.

87. Berliner and Holzman, Ibid., pp. 115–118.

88. See Robert B. Reich, *The Work of Nations: Preparing Ourselves for 21st-Century Capitalism* (New York: Vintage Books, 1992), esp. pp. 171–240.

Chapter 7

1. Conversation with Maciej Kozlowski, reporter for *Tygodnik Powszechny,* July 12, 1985, in Kraków.

2. Jeane J. Kirkpatrick, *Dictatorships and Double Standards: Rationalism and Reason in Politics* (New York: Simon & Schuster, 1982), pp. 23–52. For a perceptive critique, see Theodore Draper, *Present History: On Nuclear War, Détente, and Other Controversies* (New York: Vintage Books, 1984), pp. 313–319.

3. Henry Kissinger has offered a similar analysis: ". . . modern totalitarianism is a caricature, a reductio ad absurdum, of democracy: modern authoritarianism is a vestige of traditional personal rule. This is why some authoritarian governments have been able to evolve into democracies and why no totalitarian state has ever done so. Personal rule has inherent limits; government that claims to reflect the general will countenances no such restraint." *Years of Upheaval* (Boston: Little, Brown & Co., 1982), pp. 312–313.

4. Draper, *Present History,* op. cit., p. 318.

5. Timothy Garton Ash, *The Uses of Adversity: Essays on the Fate of Central Europe* (Cambridge: Granta Books, 1989), p. 172.

6. Cited in ibid., p. 172.

7. Ibid., p. 173.

8. The calculation is based on East European censuses taken from 1970 to 1975; see Paul S. Shoup, *The East European and Soviet Data Handbook* (New York: Columbia University Press, 1981), pp. 41–45.

9. Bernard Gwertzman, "Ford Denies Moscow Dominates East Europe; Carter Rebuts Him," *New York Times,* October 7, 1976, p. A1.

10. Author interview with Jerzy Turowcz, Kraków, July 1985.

11. Conversation with Tomasz Goban-Klas, Press Research Institute in Kraków, July 1985.

12. Conversation with Maciej Kozlowski, op. cit.

13. Timothy Garton Ash's 1983 essay is reprinted in *The Uses of Adversity,* op. cit., p. 54.

14. Lawrence Weschler, "Poland: Three Years After," *Harper's,* December 1985, pp. 19–20.
15. Under the Gdansk accords, censorship was regulated by a new censorship law. Papers were allowed to print four dashes to mark a deleted article or passage—a small concession, one might argue, but in Soviet-bloc terms, an extraordinary symbolic limit on the power of the regime. After martial law, the censorship law survived (albeit with some tightening; where originally it was forbidden to advocate changing the constitution, now the law more vaguely proscribed attacks on the "security of the state").
16. Weschler, "Poland: Three Years After," op. cit., p. 18.
17. Roundtable discussion with Leszek Zapotowski, Polish prime minister's office, Kraków, July 1985.
18. He was speaking to Western scholars, but Poles we met confirmed they were hearing a similar message from the government.
19. Interview with author, May 1989.
20. Edward N. Luttwak, "After Afghanistan, What?" *Commentary* (April 1980), pp. 40–49.
21. Ibid., p. 49.
22. Richard Pipes, "Can the Soviet Union Reform?" *Foreign Affairs* (Fall 1984), pp. 47–61.
23. Richard Ned Lebow and Janice Gross Stein, "Reagan and the Russians," *The Atlantic Monthly,* February 1994, p. 37.
24. Robert G. Kaiser, *Why Gorbachev Happened: His Triumphs and His Failure* (New York: Simon & Schuster, 1991), pp. 86–92.
25. Timothy J. Colton, *The Dilemma of Reform in the Soviet Union* (New York: Council on Foreign Relations, 1984) pp. 4, 7. See also Joseph Berliner and Franklyn Holzman, "The Soviet Economy: Domestic and International Issues," in *The Soviet Empire: Expansion and Détente,* ed. William E. Griffith (Lexington, Mass.: Lexington Books, 1976), pp. 105–113.
26. Colton, *The Dilemma of Reform in the Soviet Union,* op. cit., pp. 20–31.
27. Zbigniew Brzezinski, "The Soviet System: Transformation or Degeneration?" *Problems of Communism* (January–February 1966), pp. 5, 14.
28. Murray Feshbach and Alfred Friendly, Jr., *Ecocide in the USSR: Health and Nature Under Siege* (New York: Basic Books, 1992), esp. pp. 2–11; 181–197.
29. Colton, *The Dilemma of Reform in the Soviet Union,* op. cit., pp. 18, 23.
30. Kaiser, *Why Gorbachev Happened,* op. cit., p. 66.
31. Ibid, p. 57.
32. Ibid.
33. Cited in Adam B. Ulam, *Dangerous Relations: The Soviet Union in World Politics, 1970–1982* (New York: Oxford University Press, 1984), p. 295.

34. Cited in Robert Campbell, "The Economy," in *After Brezhnev: Sources of Soviet Conduct in the 1980s,* ed. Robert F. Byrnes (Bloomington, Ind.: Indiana University Press, 1983), p. 74.

35. Colton, *The Dilemma of Reform in the Soviet Union,* op. cit., p.28.

36. Paul Berman, "The Vanities of Patriotism," *The New Republic* 205, no. 1 (July 1, 1991), p. 33.

37. Hendrik Hertzberg, "The Child Monarch," *The New Republic* 205, no. 11 (September 9, 1991), p. 34.

38. Patrick Glynn, a former special assistant to the director of the U.S. Arms Control and Disarmament Agency during the Reagan administration, plays on the antidétente theme in a recent Cold War history, *Closing Pandora's Box: Arms Races, Arms Control, and the History of the Cold War* (New York: Basic Books, 1992). Pre-Reagan administrations, according to Glynn, suffered from a détente and especially an arms-control mania that was easily manipulated by Moscow. This is an elaboration of the argument made by many neoconservatives in the 1970s. Reagan's breakthrough, according to Glynn, was to stop making arms control a priority of Washington's Soviet policy. Yet Glynn's reading of the Reagan record is highly selective. Reagan not only discussed with Gorbachev the idea of eventually eliminating *all* nuclear weapons. He also signed a 1987 INF agreement that many members of the U.S. and West European defense establishment opposed because they thought NATO was giving up more than the Soviets. Moreover, even if one accepts the view that Reagan broke a previous pattern, the larger Glynn thesis depends on the view that the arms-control agreements of the 1970s put the United States at a significant disadvantage. My conclusion to chapter 4 is a lengthy refutation of this proposition.

39. Timothy Garton Ash, *In Europe's Name: Germany and the Divided Continent* (London: Jonathan Cape, 1993), pp. 257–258.

40. Ibid., pp. 369–370.

41. Jeane J. Kirkpatrick, "Doctrine of Moral Equivalence," speech in London, April 9, 1984, reprinted in *Department of State Bulletin* 84, no. 2085 (August 1984), p. 58.

42. Jean-François Révél, *How Democracies Perish,* translated by William Byron (London: Weidenfeld and Nicolson, 1985), p. 37.

Chapter 8

1. Included in this estimate are lives lost through fighting in the former Soviet Union—Georgia, Azerbaijan, Tajikistan and so on—as well as wars, such as

those in Yugoslavia and the Persian Gulf, that really became possible only with the end of Soviet power and the breakdown of Cold War divisions. In the former Yugoslavia alone, it is estimated that up to 200,000 have perished. In pointing to these destructive effects of the collapse of Soviet power, I am *not* suggesting a preference for the Cold War's stability. First of all, the Soviet Union was rotten as well as tyrannical: It was headed for a fall; and while Moscow might have held it together with force, that repression also would have meant the vast loss of lives. Second, it is hardly the case that the Cold War was a time of universal tranquility, as can be seen in just one example, the other Persian Gulf war that raged for most of the 1980s between Iraq and Iran.

2. In Russia's December 1993 parliamentary elections, Zhirinovsky's Liberal-Democratic party won 23 percent of the popular vote, along with a lesser share of seats in the new parliament—66 out of 450, or 14.7 percent. In Germany's 1930 Reichstag elections, the Nazis won a popular vote of 18.3 percent and a comparable share of seats, 107 of 595. See Heinrick Pleticha, *Deutsche Geschichte,* Vol. 11 (Gütersloh: Bertelsmann Verlagsgruppe, 1984), p. 99; "Weimar on the Volga," *The Economist,* December 18, 1993, p.25.

3. Daniel Vernet, "France in a New Europe," *The National Interest* 29 (Fall 1992), p. 32.

4. German officials protested that they were only trying to catch up with events, the pace of which was being set by the thousands of East Germans crossing daily to the West. The subsequently published account of Kohl adviser Horst Teltschik makes clear, however, that whatever the pressures of westward emigration, the Bonn chancellery was strongly motivated by its own enthusiasm for German reunification. Teltschik, *329 Tage: Innenansichten der Einigung* (Berlin: Siedler Verlag, 1991), passim.

5. Julius Friend, *The Linchpin: French-German Relations 1950-1990,* The Washington Papers, 155 (New York: Praeger, 1991), p.82; John Newhouse, "Sweeping Change," *The New Yorker,* August 27, 1990, pp. 78–79.

6. Gorbachev probably realized that Bonn had far more to offer him, in desperately needed economic assistance, than did Paris.

7. Teltschik, *329 Tage,* op. cit., p. 61 (author's translation).

8. George Soros, "Prospect for European Disintegration," delivered as the Aspen Institute Berlin's Wallenberg Lecture, September 29, 1993.

9. Charles Krauthammer, "The Lonely Superpower," *The New Republic,* July 29, 1991, p. 23. The notion that the war against Iraq was fought by an international coalition is "pious nonsense," Krauthammer goes on to assert. The Gulf war was an example of "pseudo-multilateralism," a politically convenient cloak for American hegemony. Ibid.

10. David P. Calleo, *Beyond American Hegemony: The Future of the Western Alliance* (New York: Basic Books, 1987), and Paul Kennedy, *The Rise and Fall of the Great Powers: Economic Change and Military Conflict from 1500 to 2000* (New York: Random House, 1987), esp. pp. 347–540.

11. "Lone Superpower Plan: Ammunition for Critics," *New York Times,* March 10, 1992; "Keeping the U.S. First: Pentagon Would Preclude a Rival Superpower," *Washington Post,* March 11, 1992.

12. William Pfaff, "Who Would Have Thought Europe So Fragile?" *International Herald Tribune,* November 26, 1992.

13. Francis Fukuyama, "The End of History?" *The National Interest* (Summer 1989), pp. 3–17.

14. *Crisis Management in Eastern Europe: Yugoslavia, a Case Study,* Aspen Institute Berlin Conference Report (Berlin, 1992), pp. 6–8.

15. The number of exterminated remains the subject of some dispute. The official claim of the Tito regime was that 600,000 were murdered in the Jasenovac extermination camp. In the early 1980s Franjo Tudjman, the current Croatian president, was prosecuted for his claims that "only" 60,000 were killed. See Wolfgang Libal, *Das Ende Jugoslawiens* (Vienna: Europaverlag, 1993), pp. 57–58.

16. "Genscher will einheitliche EG-Politik: Die Frage der Anerkennung Sloveniens und Kroatiens," *Frankfurter Allgemeine Zeitung,* July 5, 1991. On the German ultimatum, *Le Monde,* July 30, 1992.

17. John Newhouse, "The Diplomatic Round: Dodging the Problem," *The New Yorker,* August 24, 1992, p. 65.

18. The court decided that German participation in the flights was politically necessary to avoid damaging Germany's "Bündnisfähigkeit," that is its standing in NATO.

19. "Das Urteil des Bundesverfassungsgerichts vom 12. Juli 1994," in *Europa Archiv,* no. 15 (October 8, 1994).

20. *Perspektiven einer neuen Außen- und Sicherheitspolitik,* Resolution passed by the SPD convention in Wiesbaden, November 16–19, 1993 (Bonn: Vorstand der SPD, Referat Öffentlichkeitsarbeit, 1993), pp. 13–15.

21. William Pfaff, "Is Liberal Internationalism Dead?" *World Policy Journal* 10, no. 3 (Fall 1993), p. 5.

22. George Ball testimony, "Export Controls on Oil and Gas Equipment," Hearings and markup before the Committee on Foreign Affairs, House of Representatives, August 25, 1982 (Washington, D.C.: U.S. Government Printing Office, 1983), p. 119.

23. Calleo, *Beyond American Hegemony,* op. cit., p. 135.

24. As Charles Krauthammer once argued, "It is hard to imagine any foreign event that can threaten the freedom of a continental power protected by two oceans

and possessing 10,000 nuclear warheads. . . . Even if all the dominoes fell right up to the Rio Grande, no adversary in his right mind would dare cross it." "Isolationism, Left and Right," *The New Republic,* March 4, 1985.

25. Ibid.
26. William Pfaff, "Is Liberal Internationalism Dead?" op. cit., p. 5.

SELECTED BIBLIOGRAPHY

Acheson, Dean, "The Illusion of Disengagement," *Foreign Affairs* 36, no. 3 (April 1958).

———, *Present at the Creation: My Years in the State Department* (New York: W. W. Norton & Co., 1987).

———, "Text of Acheson's Reply to Kennan," *New York Times,* January 12, 1958.

Ash, Timothy Garton, *In Europe's Name: Germany and the Divided Continent* (London: Jonathan Cape, 1993).

———, *The Uses of Adversity: Essays on the Fate of Central Europe* (Cambridge: Granta Books, 1989).

Aspen Institute Berlin, *Crisis Management in Eastern Europe: Yugoslavia, a Case Study* (Berlin: 1992).

Aspin, Les, "Europe: Soviet Force Withdrawals May Void the Old Equation," *International Herald Tribune,* October 18, 1989.

Ball, George, Testimony of August 25, 1982, "Export Controls on Oil and Gas Equipment," Hearings and markup before the Committee on Foreign Affairs, House of Representatives (Washington, D.C.: U.S. Government Printing Office, 1983).

Barnet, Richard J., *The Alliance—America, Europe, Japan: Makers of the Postwar World* (New York: Simon & Schuster, 1983).

Bell, Coral, *Negotiation from Strength: A Study in the Politics of Power* (New York: Alfred A. Knopf, 1963).

———, *The Reagan Paradox: American Foreign Policy in the 1980s* (New Brunswick, N.J.: Rutgers University Press, 1989).

Bergson, Abram, "Soviet Economic Perspectives: Toward a New Growth Model," *Problems of Communism* 22, no. 2 (March/April 1973).

Berliner, Joseph, and Franklyn Holzman, "The Soviet Economy: Domestic and International Issues," in *The Soviet Empire: Expansion and Détente,* ed. William E. Griffith (Lexington, Mass.: Lexington Books, 1976).

Berlinguer, Enrico, address to the 13th Italian Communist Party Congress, as reported by *Corriere della Sera,* March 14, 1972.

———, interviewed by Giampaolo Pansa, *Corriere della Sera,* June 15, 1976.

Berman, Paul, "The Vanities of Patriotism," *The New Republic,* July 1, 1991.

Bernstein, Eduard, *Die Voraussetzungen des Sozialismus und die Aufgaben der Sozialdemokratie* (Stuttgart, 1906).

Blumenthal, Sidney, *The Rise of the Counter-Establishment* (New York: Harper & Row, 1988).

Bracken, Paul, "Collateral Damage and Theater Warfare," *Survival* 22, no. 5 (September/October 1980).

Brady, Lawrence, Testimony of September 16, 1981, "East-West Economic Relations," Hearing before the Subcommittee on International Economic Policy of the Committee on Foreign Relations, U.S. Senate (Washington, D.C.: U.S. Government Printing Office, 1981).

———, Testimony of November 12, 1981, "Export Controls on Oil and Gas Equipment," Hearings before the Committee on Foreign Affairs, House of Representatives (Washington, D.C.: U.S. Government Printing Office, 1983).

Brandt, Willy, *People and Politics: The Years 1960–1975* (London: Collins, 1978).

Brown, Harold, Testimony of March 22, 1982, "Overview of Nuclear Arms Control and Defense Strategy in NATO," hearings before the Subcommittees on International Security and Scientific Affairs and on Europe and the Middle East of the Committee on Foreign Affairs, House of Representatives (Washington, D.C.: U.S. Government Printing Office, 1982).

Brzezinski, Zbigniew, "The Future of Yalta," *Foreign Affairs* 63, no. 1 (Winter 1984/85).

———, *Power and Principle: Memoirs of the National Security Adviser, 1977–1981* (New York: Farrar Straus Giroux, 1983).

———, "The Soviet System: Transformation or Degeneration?" *Problems of Communism* (January–February 1966).

Bundy, McGeorge, "America in the 1980s: Reframing our Relations with our Friends and Among Our Allies," *Survival* 24, no. 1 (January/February 1982).

———, George F. Kennan, Robert S. McNamara, Gerard Smith, Madalene O'Donnell, Leon V. Sigal, Richard H. Ullman and Paul Warnke, "Back From the Brink: The Case For a New U.S. Nuclear Strategy," *The Atlantic Monthly* 258, no. 2 (August 1986).

———, George F. Kennan, Robert S. McNamara and Gerard Smith, "Nuclear Weapons and the Atlantic Alliance," *Foreign Affairs* 60, no. 4 (Spring 1982).

Burt, Richard, *New Weapons and Technologies: Debate and Directions* (London: International Institute for Strategic Studies, 1976).

———, Testimony of February 23, 1982, "Overview of Nuclear Arms Control and Defense Strategy in NATO," Hearings before the Subcommittees on International Security and Scientific Affairs and on Europe and the Middle East of the Committee on Foreign Affairs, House of Representatives, 97th Cong., 2nd Sess., February 28, 1982 (Washington, D.C.: U.S. Government Printing Office, 1982).

Busse, Michael, and Maria-Rosa Bobbi, *Anatomie eines Verbrechens: Die Ermordung Aldo Moros und das italienische Drama* , Westdeutscher Rundfunk (German television) broadcast of November 28, 1993, ed. Rainer Hoffmann.

Calleo, David P., *The Bankrupting of America: How the Federal Budget Is Impoverishing the Nation* (New York: Avon Books, 1992).

————, *Beyond American Hegemony: The Future of the Western Alliance* (New York: Basic Books, 1987).

————, *Europe's Future: The Grand Alternatives* (New York: Horizon Press, 1965).

————, *The Imperious Economy* (Cambridge, Mass.: Harvard University Press, 1982).

Campbell, Robert, "The Economy," in *After Brezhnev: Sources of Soviet Conduct in the 1980s,* ed. Robert F. Byrnes (Bloomington, Ind.: Indiana University Press, 1983).

Carter, Jimmy, "Excerpts From Carter's Speech and His Replies," *New York Times,* June 24, 1976.

Central Intelligence Agency, *Soviet Energy Data Resource Handbook: A Reference Aid* (Washington, D.C.: Central Intelligence Agency, 1990).

Charlton, Michael, *From Deterrence to Defense: The Inside Story of Strategic Policy* (Cambridge, Mass.: Harvard University Press, 1987).

Churchill, W. S., and F. D. Roosevelt, *Churchill and Roosevelt: The Complete Correspondence,* Vol. III, ed. Warren F. Kimball (Princeton, N.J.: Princeton University Press, 1984).

————, *Roosevelt and Churchill: Their Secret Wartime Correspondence,* ed. Francis L. Loewenheim, Harold D. Langley, and Manfred Jonas (New York: Saturday Review Press, 1975).

Colton, Timothy J., *The Dilemma of Reform in the Soviet Union* (New York: Council on Foreign Relations, 1984).

Committee on the Present Danger, *Alerting America: The Papers of the Committee on the Present Danger,* ed. Charles Tyroler II (Washington, D.C.: Pergamon-Brassey's, 1984).

————, "Is America Becoming Number 2? Current Trends in the US-Soviet Military Balance" (October 5, 1978), reprinted in *Alerting America: The Papers of the Committee on the Present Danger,* ed. Charles Tyroler II (Washington, D.C.: Pergamon-Brassey's, 1984).

————, "Has America Become Number 2?" (June 29, 1979), reprinted in *Alerting America: The Papers of the Committee on the Present Danger,* ed. Charles Tyroler II (Washington, D.C.: Pergamon-Brassey's, 1984).

Crozier, Brian, *De Gaulle* (New York: Scribners, 1973).

Crozier, Michel, Samuel P. Huntington and Joji Wtanunki, *The Crisis of Democracy: Report on the Governability of Democracies to the Trilateral Commission* (New York: New York University Press, 1975).

Davis, W. Kenneth, Testimony of October 14, 1981, "Soviet Energy Exports and Western European Energy Security," Hearing before the Subcommittee on Energy, Nuclear Proliferation, and Government Processes of the Committee of Governmental Affairs, U.S. Senate (Washington, D.C.: U.S. Government Printing Office, 1982).

Dean, Jonathan, *Watershed in Europe: Dismantling the East-West Military Confrontation* (Lexington, Mass.: Lexington Books, 1987).

De Gaulle, Charles, *The Complete War Memoirs of Charles de Gaulle* (New York: Simon & Schuster, 1964).

———, *Major Addresses, Statements and Press Conferences of General Charles de Gaulle* (New York: French Embassy and Information Division, 1967).

———, *Memoirs of Hope* (London: Weidenfeld and Nicolson, 1971).

———, Press conference of January 14, 1963, in *Major Addresses, Statements and Press Conferences of General Charles de Gaulle, May 19, 1958–January 31, 1964* (New York: French Embassy Press and Information Division, 1964).

De Montbrial, Thierry, Testimony of September 22, 1982, "Soviet Pipeline Sanctions: The European Perspective," Hearing before the Joint Economic Committee, U.S. Congress (Washington, D.C.: U.S. Government Printing Office, 1983).

Deutsch, John, Brent Scowcroft, and James R. Woolsey, "The Danger of the Zero Option," *Washington Post,* March 31, 1987.

Dougherty, James E., and Diane K. Pfaltzgraff, *Eurocommunism and the Atlantic Alliance* (Cambridge, Mass.: Institute for Foreign Policy Analysis, 1977).

Drake, Richard, "The Red Brigades and the Italian Political Tradition," in *Terrorism in Europe,* ed. Yonah Alexander and Kenneth A. Myers (New York: St. Martin's Press, 1982).

Draper, Theodore, *Present History: On Nuclear War, Détente, and Other Controversies* (New York: Vintage Books, 1984).

Economist Intelligence Unit Quarterly Economic Survey of Italy, no. 2 (1984).

Eisenhower, Dwight D., News Conference of February 10, 1954, in *Public Papers of the Presidents 1954* (Washington, D.C.: U.S. Government Printing Office, 1960).

Erickson, John, *The Road to Berlin* (Boulder, Colo.: Westview Press, 1983).

Evans, Roland, and Robert Novak, "Missile Misery," *Washington Post,* April 28, 1989.

Feshbach, Murray, and Alfred Friendly, Jr., *Ecocide in the USSR: Health and Nature Under Siege* (New York: Basic Books, 1992).

Financial Times, February 10, 1989.

Fischer, Robert Lucas, *Defending the Central Front: The Balance of Forces,* Adelphi Paper no. 127 (London: IISS, 1977).

Flanagan, Robert J., David W. Soskice, Lloyd Ulman, *Unionism, Economic Stabilization, and Incomes Policy* (Washington, D.C: The Brookings Institution, 1983).

Freedman, Lawrence, *The Evolution of Nuclear Strategy* (London: Macmillan, 1982).

Friend, Julius, *The Linchpin: French-German Relations, 1950–1990,* The Washington Papers, 155 (New York: Praeger, 1991).

Fukuyama, Francis, "The End of History?" *The National Interest,* Summer 1989.

Gaddis, John Lewis, *Strategies of Containment: A Critical Appraisal of Postwar American National Security Policy* (New York: Oxford University Press, 1982).

————, *The United States and the Origins of the Cold War, 1941–1947* (New York: Columbia University Press, 1972).

Garfinkle, Adam M., *"Finlandization": A Map to a Metaphor* (Philadelphia: Foreign Policy Research Institute, 1978).

Gelb, Leslie, "U.S. and Allies Bar Loans if Reds Join Italy Cabinet," *New York Times,* July 18, 1976.

"Genscher will einheitliche EG-Politik: Die Frage der Anerkennung Sloveniens und Kroatiens," *Frankfurter Allgemeine Zeitung,* July 5, 1991.

Ginger, Henry, "Portugal: Now the Left Threatens a Dictatorship," *New York Times,* August 10, 1975.

Glynn, Patrick, *Closing Pandora's Box: Arms Races, Arms Control and the History of the Cold War* (New York: Basic Books, 1992).

Gordon, Philip H., *A Certain Idea of France: French Security Policy and the Gaullist Legacy* (Princeton, N.J.: Princeton University Press, 1993).

Gore, Albert, "A Noncounterforce Alternative to President Reagan's START Proposal," excerpts in *Survival* 25, no. 4 (July/August 1983).

Grosser, Alfred, *The Western Alliance: European-American Relations Since 1945* (New York: Vintage Books, 1982).

Gwertzman, Bernard, "Ford Denies Moscow Dominates East Europe; Carter Rebuts Him," *New York Times,* October 7, 1976.

Haig, Alexander M., Jr., *Caveat: Realism, Reagan and Foreign Policy* (London: Weidenfeld and Nicolson, 1984).

Harrison, Michael, *The Reluctant Ally* (Baltimore: Johns Hopkins University Press, 1981).

Head, Simon, "The Battle Inside NATO," *The New York Review of Books,* May 18, 1989.

Hedly, Don, *World Energy: The Facts and the Future* (London: Euromonitor Publications Ltd., 1986).

Hertzberg, Hendrik, "The Child Monarch," *The New Republic* 205, no. 11 (September 9, 1991).

Hormats, Robert D., Testimony of November 12, 1981, "Proposed Trans-Siberian Natural Gas Pipeline," Hearing before the Committee on Banking, Housing, and Urban Affairs, U.S. Senate, 97th Cong., 1st Sess. (Washington, D.C.: U.S. Government Printing Office, 1982).

————, Testimony of October 14, 1981, "Soviet Energy Exports and Western European Energy Security," Hearings Before the Subcommittee on Energy, Nuclear Proliferation and Government Processes of the Committee on Governmental Affairs, U.S. Senate, 97th Cong., 1st Sess. (Washington, D.C.: U.S. Government Printing Office, 1982).

Howard, Michael, "Reassurance and Deterrence: Western Defense in the 1980s," *Foreign Affairs* 61, no. 2 (Winter 1982/83).

Hughes, H. Stuart, *Consciousness and Society: The Reorientation of European Social Thought, 1890–1930,* (Brighton, U.K.: The Harvester Press, 1979).

Iklé, Fred Charles, "Can Nuclear Deterrence Last Out the Century?" *Foreign Affairs* 51, no. 2 (January 1973).

————, "Nuclear Strategy: Can There Be a Happy Ending?" *Foreign Affairs* 63, no. 4 (Spring 1985).

————, Testimony of December 16, 1981, "East-West Economic Relations," Hearing before the Subcommittee on International Economic Policy of the Committee on Foreign Relations, U.S. Senate (Washington, D.C.: U.S. Government Printing Office, 1981).

Ingersoll, Robert S., statement before the Senate Committee on Commerce, December 12, 1975, reprinted in *Department of State Bulletin* 74, no. 1908 (January 19, 1976).

Jentleson, Bruce W., *Pipeline Politics: The Complex Political Economy of East-West Trade* (Ithaca, N.Y.: Cornell University Press, 1986).

Jervis, Robert, *The Illogic of American Nuclear Strategy* (Ithaca, N.Y.: Cornell University Press, 1984).

Johnson, Lyndon Baines, "Peace Without Conquest," Address at Johns Hopkins University, April 7, 1965, in *Public Papers of the Presidents 1965,* Book I (Washington, D.C.: U.S. Government Printing Office, 1966).

Johnson, Paul, *Modern Times: The World from the Twenties to the Eighties* (New York: Harper & Row, 1983).

Jonas, Manfred, *Isolationism in America 1935–1941* (Ithaca, N.Y.: Cornell University Press, 1966).

Judis, John B., "The Great Awakening," *The New Republic* 208, no. 5 (February 1, 1993).

Kahn, Herman, *On Escalation: Metaphors and Scenarios* (New York: Praeger, 1965).

————, *On Thermonuclear War* (Princeton, N.J.: Princeton University Press, 1961).

Kaiser, Robert G., *Why Gorbachev Happened: His Triumphs and His Failure* (New York: Simon & Schuster, 1991).

Kearns, Doris, *Lyndon Johnson and the American Dream* (New York: Harper & Row, 1976).

Kennan, George F. "Europe's Problems, Europe's Choices," *Foreign Policy,* no. 14 (Spring 1974).

———, *The Fateful Alliance: France, Russia, and the Coming of the First World War* (New York: Pantheon Books, 1984).

———, *Memoirs: 1925–1950* (New York: Pantheon Books, 1967).

———, *Memoirs: 1950–1963* (New York: Pantheon Books, 1972).

———, Paper Prepared by the Policy Planning Staff, November 12, 1948, A Program for Germany (Program A), in *Foreign Relations of the United States 1948*, Vol. II (Washington, D.C.: U.S. Government Printing Office, 1972).

——— (as "X"), "The Sources of Soviet Conduct," *Foreign Affairs* 25, no.4 (July 1947).

———, Telegram, the Chargé in the Soviet Union to the Secretary of State, Moscow, February 22, 1946, in *Foreign Relations of the United States 1946*, Vol. VI (Washington, D.C.: U.S. Government Printing Office, 1969).

———, "Zero Options," *New York Review of Books*, May 12, 1983.

Kennedy, John F., *The Strategy of Peace* (New York: Harper & Row, 1960).

———, Transcript of broadcast of NBC's "Huntley-Brinkley Report," September 9, 1963, in *Public Papers of the Presidents 1963* (Washington, D.C.: U.S. Government Printing Office, 1964).

Kennedy, Paul, *The Rise and Fall of the Great Powers: Economic Change and Military Conflict from 1500 to 2000* (New York: Random House, 1987).

Kirkpatrick, Jeane J., *Dictatorships and Double Standards: Rationalism and Reason in Politics* (New York: Simon & Schuster, 1982).

———, "Doctrine of Moral Equivalence," speech in London, April 9, 1984, reprinted in *Department of State Bulletin* 84, no. 2085 (August 1984).

Kissinger, Henry A, "Central Issues of American Foreign Policy," in Kermit Gordon, ed., *Agenda for the Nation* (Washington, D.C.: The Brookings Institution, 1968).

———, "Communist Parties in Western Europe: Challenge to the West," in *Eurocommunism: The Italian Case*, ed. Austin Ranney and Giovanni Sartori (Washington, D.C.: The American Enterprise Institute, 1978).

———, "The Future of NATO," in *NATO—The Next Thirty Years: The Changing Political, Economic, and Military Setting*, ed. Kenneth A. Myers (Boulder, Colo.: Westview Press, 1980).

———, "The Permanent Challenge of Peace: U.S. Policy Toward the Soviet Union," speech in San Francisco, February 3, 1976, *Department of State Bulletin* 74, no. 1913 (February 23, 1976).

———, Press conference of July 3, 1974, published in *Survival* 16, no. 5 (September/October 1974).

———, Press conference of February 3, 1976, *Department of State Bulletin* 74, no. 1913.

———, Press conference of July 10, 1976, *Department of State Bulletin* 75, no. 1936 (August 2, 1976).

————, Remarks before the foreign policy panel sponsored by the Blue Ribbon 400, Los Angeles, *Department of State Bulletin* 74, no. 1914 (March 1, 1976).

————, "Secretary Kissinger Interviewed at the Annual Meeting of the American Society of Newspaper Editors in Washington D.C., April 15, 1976," *Department of State Bulletin* 74, no. 1923 (May 3, 1976).

————, Speech before the Boston World Affairs Council, March 11, 1976, *Department of State Bulletin* 74, no. 1919.

————, Speech in Birmingham, Alabama, August 14, 1975, excerpted in *New York Times,* August 15, 1975.

————, Speech in Chicago, July 6, 1976, *Department of State Bulletin* 75, no. 1936 (August 2, 1976).

————, "Strategy and the Atlantic Alliance," *Survival* 24, no. 5 (September/October 1982).

————, *The Troubled Partnership: A Re-appraisal of the Atlantic Alliance* (New York: McGraw-Hill, 1965).

————, *White House Years* (Boston: Little, Brown & Co., 1979).

————, *Years of Upheaval* (Boston: Little, Brown & Co., 1982).

Krauthammer, Charles, "Isolationism, Left and Right," *The New Republic,* March 4, 1985.

————, "The Lonely Superpower," *The New Republic,* July 29, 1991.

Kristol, Irving, "Does NATO Exist?" in *NATO: The Next Thirty Years: The Changing Political, Economic, and Military Setting,* ed. Kenneth A. Myers (Boulder, Colo.: Westview Press, 1980).

————, "NATO at a Dead End," *Wall Street Journal,* July 15, 1981.

LaPalombara, Joseph, "Italian Elections as Hobson's Choice," in *Italy at the Polls: The Parliamentary Elections of 1976,* ed. Howard Penniman (Washington, D.C.: American Enterprise Institute, 1977).

————, "Two Steps Forward, One Step Back: The PCI's Struggle for Legitimacy," in *Italy at the Polls, 1979* ed. Howard Penniman (Washington, D.C.: American Enterprise Institute, 1981).

Levi, Carlo, *Christ Stopped at Eboli: The Story of a Year* (New York: Farrar, Straus, 1963).

Lewis, Anthony, "Mr. Kissinger's Folly," *New York Times,* July 29, 1976.

Libal, Wolfgang, *Das Ende Jugoslawiens* (Vienna: Europaverlag, 1993).

Livingston, Robert Gerald, "No New Nuclear Weapons For Bonn," *Washington Post,* February 15, 1989.

Louis, Wm. Roger, *Imperialism at Bay: The United States and the Decolonization of the British Empire, 1941–1945* (New York: Oxford University Press, 1978).

Luttwak, Edward N., "After Afghanistan, What?" *Commentary* (April 1980).

————, "How to Think About Nuclear War," *Commentary* (August 1982).

McCarthy, Patrick, "The Parliamentary and Nonparliamentary Parties of the Far Left," in *Italy at the Polls, 1979,* ed. Howard Penniman (Washington, D.C.: American Enterprise Institute, 1981).

McNamara, Robert S., "Defense Arrangements of the North Atlantic Community," speech at University of Michigan commencement, June 16, 1962, *Department of State Bulletin* 47, no. 1202 (July 9, 1962).

———, "The Military Role of Nuclear Weapons: Perceptions and Misperceptions," *Foreign Affairs* 62, no. 1 (Fall 1983).

Mearsheimer, John, "Back to the Future," *International Security* 15, no. 1 (Summer 1990).

Meyer, Stephen M., *Soviet Theatre Nuclear Forces, Part II: Capabilities and Implications,* Adelphi Papers 188 (London: International Institute for Strategic Studies, 1984).

Milward, Alan S., *The Reconstruction of Western Europe, 1945–1951* (Berkeley: University of California Press, 1984).

NATO and the Warsaw Pact: Force Comparisons (Brussels: NATO Information Services, 1984).

Newhouse, John, "The Diplomatic Round: Dodging the Problem," *The New Yorker,* August 24, 1992.

———, "Sweeping Change," *The New Yorker,* August 27, 1990.

New York Times articles: April 25, 1989; "Social Democrats of Germany Aiding Portuguese Socialists," August 29, 1975; "U.S. Paid 800,000 to Italian General; CIA Fought Move," January 30, 1976; "Lone Superpower Plan: Ammunition for Critics," March 10, 1992.

New York Times editorials: "Impasse in Portugal," August 5, 1975; "Portugal on the Brink?" August 9, 1975; "Support for Portugal," August 17, 1975; "Portugal Confrontation," August 20, 1975.

Nitze, Paul H., "Is SALT II a Fair Deal for the United States?" May 1979, in *Alerting America: The Papers of the Committee on the Present Danger,* ed. Charles Tyroler II (Washington, D.C.: Pergamon-Brassey's, 1984).

———, "Strategy in the Decade of the 1980s," *Foreign Affairs* 59, no. 1 (Fall 1980).

———, "What Bush Should Do To Solve the NATO Flap," *Washington Post,* May 14, 1989.

Nixon, Richard M., and Henry A. Kissinger, "An Arms Agreement—on Two Conditions," *Washington Post,* April 16, 1987.

———, *U.S. Foreign Policy for the 1970s: A New Strategy for Peace,* Report to Congress, February 18, 1970 (Washington, D.C.: U.S. Government Printing Office, 1970).

Nove, Alec, *The Soviet Economic System* (Boston: Allen & Unwin, 1986).

———, "The Twelfth Five-Year Plan and Soviet Statistics," in *The Soviet Economy under Gorbachev,* Colloquium of March 20–22, 1991 (Brussels: NATO, 1991).

O'Brien, Conor Cruise, *The Siege* (London: Paladin Grafton Books, 1988).

Pasquino, Gianfranco, "From Togliatti to the Compromesso Storico: A Party with a Governmental Vocation," in Simon Serfaty and Lawrence Gray, eds., *The Italian Communist Party: Yesterday, Today, and Tomorrow* (Westport, Conn.: Greenwood Press, 1980).

Penniman, Howard R., "Preface" to *Italy at the Polls, 1979,* op. cit.

Perle, Richard, "Don't Let Germany Run the Alliance," *Washington Post* (May 28, 1989).

———, Testimony of November 12, 1981, "Export Controls on Oil and Gas Equipment," Hearings and Markup before the Committee on Foreign Affairs and its Subcommittees on Europe and the Middle East and on International Economic Policy and Trade, House of Representatives, 97th Cong., 1st Sess., on H.R. 6838, Proposed Repeal of Oil and Gas Equipment Export Controls, November 12, 1981 (Washington, D.C.: U.S. Government Printing Office, 1983).

———, Testimony of November 12, 1981, "Proposed Trans-Siberian Natural Gas Pipeline," Hearing before the Committee on Banking, Housing, and Urban Affairs, U.S. Senate, 97th Cong., 1st Sess. (Washington, D.C.: U.S. Government Printing Office, 1982).

———, Testimony of February 28, 1982, "Overview of Nuclear Arms Control and Defense Strategy in NATO," Hearings before the Subcommittees on International Security and Scientific Affairs and on Europe and the Middle East of the Committee on Foreign Affairs, House of Representatives, 97th Cong., 2nd Sess. (Washington, D.C.: U.S. Government Printing Office, 1982).

Peterson, Peter G., *U.S.-Soviet Commercial Relations in a New Era* (Washington, D.C.: U.S. Government Printing Office, 1972).

Pfaff, William, "Is Liberal Internationalism Dead?" *World Policy Journal* 10, no. 3 (Fall 1993).

———, "Who Would Have Thought Europe So Fragile?" *International Herald Tribune,* November 26, 1992.

Pipes, Richard, "Can the Soviet Union Reform?" *Foreign Affairs* (Fall 1984).

———, "How to Cope With the Soviet Threat: A Long-term Strategy for the West," *Commentary* 78, no. 2 (August 1984).

———, "Team B: The Reality Behind the Myth," *Commentary* 82, no. 4 (October 1986).

———, "Why the Soviet Union Thinks It Could Fight and Win a Nuclear War," *Commentary* 64, no. 1 (July 1977).

Platt, Alan A., and Robert Leonardi, "American Foreign Policy and the Postwar Italian Left," *Political Science Quarterly* 93, no. 2 (Summer 1978).

Podhoretz, Norman, *The Present Danger* (New York: Simon & Schuster, 1980).

Putnam, Robert D., and Nicholas Bayne, *Hanging Together: Cooperation and Conflict in the Seven-Power Summits* (Cambridge, Mass.: Harvard University Press, 1987).

Quandt, William B., *Decade of Decisions: American Policy Toward the Arab-Israeli Conflict, 1967–1976* (Berkeley: University of California Press, 1977).

Rashish, Meyer, Testimony of September 16, 1981, "East/West Economic Relations," Hearing before the Subcommittee on International Economic Policy of the Committee on Foreign Relations, U.S. Senate, 97th Cong., 1st Sess., (Washington, D.C.: U.S. Government Printing Office, 1981).

Reagan, Ronald, address to the American Legion Annual Conference, February 22, 1983; excerpts printed in *Survival* 25, no. 3 (May/June 1983).

Reich, Robert B., *The Work of Nations: Preparing Ourselves for 21st-Century Capitalism* (New York: Vintage Books, 1992).

Révél, Jean-François, *How Democracies Perish,* translated by William Byron (London: Weidenfeld and Nicolson, 1985).

Rizopoulos, Nicholas X., "Pride, Prejudice, and Myopia: Greek Foreign Policy in a Time Warp," *World Policy Journal* 10, no. 3 (Fall 1993).

Roberts, Sir Frank, "A Witness to Yalta and Its Myths," *International Herald Tribune,* February 5, 1990.

Rogers, Bernard, "How the West Can Safeguard Its Deterrent Strength," *International Herald Tribune,* June 29, 1987.

———, interview published in the *Financial Times,* February 5, 1987.

Rogers, William, "A Lasting Peace in the Middle East," in *Department of State Bulletin* 62, no. 1958 (January 5, 1970).

Rostow, Eugene, "Peace with Freedom," discussion by the Committee on the Present Danger before the Foreign Policy Association, New York, March 14, 1978, in *Alerting America: The Papers of the Committee on the Present Danger,* ed. Charles Tyroler II (Washington, D.C.: Pergamon-Brassey's, 1984).

———, testimony of February 28, 1982: "Overview of Nuclear Arms Control and Defense Strategy in NATO," hearings before the Subcommittees on International Security and Scientific Affairs and on Europe and the Middle East of the Committee on Foreign Affairs, House of Representatives, 97th Cong., 2nd Sess., February 28, 1982 (Washington, D.C.: U.S. Government Printing Office, 1982).

Rush, Kenneth, "The Nixon Administration's Foreign Policy Objectives," remarks before the national foreign policy conference for editors and broadcasters at the Department of State, March 29, 1973, Department of State Bulletin 68, no. 1765 (April 23, 1973).

Schlesinger, Arthur M., Jr., *The Cycles of American History* (Boston: Houghton Mifflin, 1986).

————, *A Thousand Days: John F. Kennedy in the White House* (Boston: Houghton Mifflin, 1965).

Schmidt, Helmut, *Die Deutschen und ihre Nachbarn: Menschen und Mächte II* (Berlin: Siedler, 1990).

————, "The 1977 Alastair Buchan Memorial Lecture," London, October 28, 1977, reprinted in *Survival* 20, no. 1 (January/February 1978).

Schorske, Carl E., *German Social Democracy, 1905–1917: The Development of the Great Schism* (Cambridge, Mass.: Harvard University Press, 1955).

Schroeder, Gertrude, "The Soviet Economy on a Treadmill of 'Reforms,'" in *The Soviet Economy in a Time of Change: A Compendium of Papers*, submitted to the Joint Economic Committee, Congress of the United States (Washington, D.C.: U.S. Government Printing Office, 1979), Vol. I.

Schwartz, David N., *NATO's Nuclear Dilemmas* (Washington, D.C.: The Brookings Institution, 1983).

Scowcroft, Brent, "INF: Fewer Is Not Better," *Washington Post*, April 20, 1987.

————, "Report of the President's Commission on Strategic Forces," April 11, 1983, excerpted in *Survival* 25, no. 4 (July/August 1983).

Senate Select Committee to Study Governmental Operations With Respect to Intelligence Activities, Hearings and Final Report (Washington, D.C: U.S. Government Printing Office, 1976).

Serfaty, Simon, "The United States and the PCI: The Year of Decision, 1947," in Simon Serfaty and Lawrence Gray, eds., *The Italian Communist Party: Yesterday, Today, and Tomorrow* (Westport, Conn.: Greenwood Press, 1980).

Shoup, Paul S., *The East European and Soviet Data Handbook* (New York: Columbia University Press, 1981).

Shuster, Alvin, "Tempest in Italy over Allied Threat to Bar Aid if Reds Share Rule," *New York Times*, July 24, 1976.

Sigal, Leon V., *Nuclear Forces in Europe: Enduring Dilemmas, Present Prospects* (Washington, D.C.: The Brookings Institution, 1984).

Smith, Jeffrey R., "Alliance Caught in Superpower Squeeze," *Washington Post*, May 14, 1989.

Soros, George, "Prospect for European Disintegration," Aspen Institute Berlin Wallenberg Lecture, September 29, 1993.

Soviet Ministry for Foreign Affairs, Note to the Embassy of the United States, Moscow, March 10, 1952, in *Foreign Relations of the United States 1952–1954*, Vol. VII, Part I (Washington, D.C.: U.S. Government Printing Office, 1986).

Sozialdemokratische Partei Deutschlands, *Perspektiven einer neuen Außen- und Sicherheitspolitik*, Resolution passed by the SPD convention in Wiesbaden, November 16–19, 1993 (Bonn: Vorstand der SPD, Referat Öffentlichkeitsarbeit, 1993).

Spotts, Frederic, and Theodor Wieser, *Italy: A Difficult Democracy* (Cambridge: Cambridge University Press, 1986).

Steel, Ronald, "Afghanistan Doesn't Matter," *The New Republic* 182, no. 7, February 16, 1980.

Stent, Angela E., "East-West Economic Relations and the Western Alliance," in *Trade, Technology and Soviet-American Relations,* ed. Bruce Parrott. (Bloomington, Ind.: Indiana University Press, 1985).

———, *From Embargo to Ostpolitik: The Political Economy of West German-Soviet Relations, 1955–1980* (New York: Cambridge University Press, 1980).

———, *Soviet Energy and Western Europe* (New York: Praeger Publishers, 1982).

Stern, Jonathan, "Specters and Pipe Dreams," *Foreign Policy,* no. 48 (Fall 1982).

Stettinius, Edward R., Jr., *Roosevelt and the Russians: The Yalta Conference* (Garden City, N.Y.: Doubleday & Co., 1949).

Stoessinger, John G., *Henry Kissinger: The Anguish of Power* (New York: W. W. Norton & Co, 1976).

Sulzberger, C. L. "Jingo: Not as It Sounds," *New York Times,* August 29, 1976.

Szulc, Tad, "Lisbon and Washington: Behind the Portuguese Revolution," *Foreign Policy* no. 21 (Winter 1975–76).

Talbott, Strobe, *Deadly Gambits: The Reagan Administration and the Stalemate in Nuclear Arms Control* (New York: Alfred A. Knopf, 1984).

———, *The Master of the Game: Paul Nitze and the Nuclear Peace* (New York: Alfred A. Knopf, 1988).

Tarrow, Sidney, "Three Years of Italian Democracy," in *Italy at the Polls, 1979,* ed. Howard Penniman (Washington, D.C.: American Enterprise Institute, 1981).

Tatu, Michel, *La bataille des euromissiles* (Paris: Editions du Seuil, 1983).

Teltschik, Horst, *329 Tage: Innenansichten der Einigung* (Berlin: Siedler Verlag, 1991).

Tuchman, Barbara, *The March of Folly: From Troy to Vietnam* (New York: Ballantine Books, 1984).

Tucker, Robert W., *The Atlantic Alliance and Its Critics* (New York: Praeger, 1983).

———, *The Nuclear Debate: Deterrence and the Lapse of Faith* (New York: Holmes & Meier, 1985).

Tucker, Robert W., George Liska, Robert E. Osgood, and David P. Calleo, *SDI and U.S. Foreign Policy* (Boulder, Colo.: Westview Press, 1987).

Ulam, Adam B., *Dangerous Relations: The Soviet Union in World Politics, 1970–1982* (New York: Oxford University Press, 1984).

Urban, Joan Barth, "The Soviets and the West European Communist Parties," in *Soviet Policy Toward Western Europe,* ed. Herbert J. Ellison (Seattle: University of Washington Press, 1983).

Vernet, Daniel, *The National Interest* 29 (Fall 1992).

Vloyantes, John P., *Silk Glove Hegemony: Finnish-Soviet Relations, 1944–1974; A Case Study of the Theory of the Soft-Sphere of Influence* (Kent, Ohio: Kent State University Press, 1975).

Warnke, Paul, "The Illusion of NATO's Nuclear Defense," in Andrew J. Pierre, ed., *Nuclear Weapons in Europe* (New York: Council on Foreign Relations, 1984).

Washington Post articles: April 26, 1989; May 4, 1989; "Keeping the U.S. First: Pentagon Would Preclude a Rival Superpower," March 11, 1992.

Weinberg, Leonard, "Patterns of Neo-Fascist Violence in Italian Politics," *Terrorism: An International Journal* 2, no. 3–4.

Wertman, Douglas A., "The Christian Democrats: Masters of Survival," in *Italy at the Polls, 1979,* ed. Howard Penniman (Washington, D.C.: American Enterprise Institute, 1981).

Weschler, Lawrence, "Poland: Three Years After," *Harper's* (December 1985).

Will, George F., "Germany's Importance," *Washington Post,* May 4, 1989.

Willey, David, "Italy Jolted by Disclosure of Secret Allied Pact," *Christian Science Monitor,* July 19, 1976.

Wohlstetter, Albert, "The Delicate Balance of Terror," *Foreign Affairs* 37, no. 2 (January 1959).

———, "Is There a Strategic Arms Race?" *Foreign Policy* 15 (Summer 1974).

———, "Optimal Ways to Confuse Ourselves," *Foreign Policy* 20 (Autumn 1975).

———, "Rivals but no 'Race'" *Foreign Policy* 16 (Autumn 1974).

Yergin, Daniel, *Shattered Peace: The Origins of the Cold War and the National Security State* (Boston: Houghton Mifflin Co., 1978).

Yu, George T., "China's Impact," *Problems of Communism* 27 (January/February 1978).

INDEX